High Praise for
Transforming America's Schools

DENIS P. DOYLE, Senior Fellow, Hudson Institute, and co-author of *Winning the Brain Race*:

"A must read! *Transforming America's Schools* is by two of the most knowledgeable and savvy educators in the country. Murphy is the nation's most successful—and wisest—superintendent, Schiller an authority on applied research. Together they take the reader beyond reform platitudes to the rough and tumble world of implementation."

CHESTER E. FINN, JR., Professor of Education and Public Policy, and Director, Education Excellence Network:

"Amid the welter of books about education reform, it has been nearly impossible to find practical advice for administrators contending with the tough issues—and trying to overhaul the vehicle while they drive it. Fortunately, American public education has no leader with a surer blend of vision and pragmatism than John Murphy, who worked near-magic in Maryland and may be about to achieve a miracle in North Carolina. The book he and Jeffry Schiller have written is a major service to all who would act and not just talk."

DR. LAWRENCE W. LEZOTTE, Senior Vice President, Effective Schools:

"Must reading for anyone who cares about our children, their education, and the future of our country! Successful transformation of our schools requires three ingredients: first, a sense of urgency that change is needed; second, a clear vision of the new destination; and third, leadership that guides us towards it. In their 'letters from the front lines', Murphy and Schiller clearly articulate all three."

H. WILLIAM LURTON, Chairman of the Board, Chamber of Commerce of the United States of America:

"*Transforming America's Schools* should certainly revolutionize education. John Murphy and Jeffry Schiller have laid out a model for managing

K–12 schools to world class excellence. Their outstanding book should be the bible for school districts throughout the country."

DONALD J. MCCARTY, Professor of Educational Administration, University of Wisconsin-Madison:

"Murphy and Schiller offer a program of action that has a real chance to work in today's turbulent school environment. The beauty of this book is the ability of the authors to provide a specific plan of action buttressed by research findings without being boring and repetitive.... *Transforming America's Schools* does not dodge difficult issues. The authors have labored successfully in the schools; they know that good teaching is hard work and that school improvement requires intense effort and commitment on the parts of many. They offer valuable suggestions to individuals of every educational persuasion. You cannot read this book and not feel you have a better grasp of what educators need to do right now to meet society's high expectations for good education."

SAM REDDING, Executive Director, Academic Development Institute:

"This book is different. It is written by educators who can write. It is neither stilted jargon nor patronizing cute-talk. *Transforming America's Schools* is straightforward, and logically structured, and written in plain language. It answers the questions every educator, every parent, and every citizen might ask about the problems in our schools, and more importantly, it lays out practical remedies.

"Murphy and Schiller make the case that the old ways no longer work for a large segment of schoolchildren. But new ways (some of them older ways!) will work—like expecting children to master a demanding set of core subjects, encouraging children to work and learn together, and putting a well-prepared and enthusiastic teacher in front of a classroom to engage in nose-to-nose, direct and interactive teaching."

HERBERT J. WALBERG, Research Professor of Education, University of Illinois at Chicago:

"In *Transforming America's Schools,* Murphy and Schiller show how citizens and educators can build world-class schools where children achieve standards necessary for better lives in the information age of economic competition. Even though their goals are idealistic, their practical approach is based on research and demonstrably better than other current efforts."

TRANSFORMING
AMERICA'S SCHOOLS

TRANSFORMING AMERICA'S SCHOOLS

AN ADMINISTRATORS' CALL TO ACTION

John Murphy
Jeffry Schiller

La Salle, Illinois

OPEN COURT and the above logo are registered in the U.S. Patent and Trademark Office.

© 1992 by Open Court Publishing Company

First printing 1992

All rights reserved. No part of this publication may be reproduced, stored in a retrieval system, or transmitted, in any form or by any means, electronic, mechanical, photocopying, recording, or otherwise, without the prior written permission of the publisher, Open Court Publishing Company, La Salle, Illinois 61301.

Printed and bound in the United States of America.

Library of Congress Cataloging-in-Publication Data

Murphy, John, 1935–
    Transforming America's schools : an administrators' call to action /John Murphy, Jeffry Schiller.
      p.   cm.
    Includes bibliographical references and index.
    ISBN 0-8126-9203-9
    1. Educational change—United States. 2. School manangement and organization—United States. 3. Education—Social aspects—United States. I. Schiller, Jeffry. II. Title.
LA217.2.M86 1992
371'.00973—dc20   92-21020
                                                                                   CIP

This book is dedicated to those visionaries who 'dare to make it happen'; whether they labor as superintendents, school board members, political leaders, principals, teachers, or members of the general public who have a true commitment to the future of America. They understand that the transformation of our schools is critical to the survival of our nation. While they now represent a minority, hopefully their numbers will multiply.

Leaders are the custodians of a nation's ideals, of the beliefs it cherishes, of its permanent hopes, of the faith which makes a nation out of a mere aggregation of individuals.
                                    Walter Lippmann

Contents

Foreword by James Comer   xi
Acknowledgments   xiii

INTRODUCTION
Nothing Less than Transformation Will Do   1

CHAPTER 1   Changing Roles in the Transformation Process   19

CHAPTER 2   Setting the Stage with Effective Polices and Practices   51

CHAPTER 3   Pieces of the Puzzle: The Elements of School Improvement   81

CHAPTER 4   Transforming the Content and Delivery of Curriculum   113

CHAPTER 5   Tools for Diagnosis, Prescription, and Accountability   187

CHAPTER 6   Rewarding Excellence: Evaluating Staff and Recognizing Exemplary Performance   225

EPILOGUE   Reviewing the Steps toward Transformation   257

APPENDIX A   Grouping Strategies for Reading Instruction   263

APPENDIX B   Maintaining a Reality Check: Data Collection Forms for Auditing Progress and Identifying Problems   269

APPENDIX C   Examples of Information that Could be Included as Part of School Level Report Cards   295

Index   303

Foreword

I

We do not have time to wait. The past several years have been marked by one study after another documenting the relatively poor performance of American students in the classroom. Every year that passes, tens of thousands of students fall farther and farther behind in their learning. They are dropping out of school in large numbers. Many do graduate but are neither prepared to support themselves nor contribute to the common good. Although there are differences of opinion on the exact status of American schools, there is agreement that our schools are not working for many of our students.

There are three prevailing explanations for our unsatisfactory performance:

1. First, the quality of education in the schools is poor. Many of the advocates of this position argue that the quality of teaching is inadequate, that curriculum standards are low, that classes are too large, and that the instructional materials are inadequate for effective teaching and learning.

2. Second, many students are coming to school as victims of intergenerational poverty and consequently, are not able to benefit from what schools have to offer.

3. Third, many schools are reluctant to modify traditional delivery systems, which work with middle class students, to suit the needs of the disadvantaged, while maintaining standards.

Each of these explanations has merit, and much will undoubtedly be done in the coming years to improve our understanding of our shortcomings. However, the question that now faces those in school systems and schools that have to address these problems is: What can we *do* about it? *Transforming America's Schools* provides a framework that educational leaders can use *now* to improve their schools. The suggestions for improvement made in the book are not contingent on the need for further research. They are based on the most recent research and, perhaps even more importantly, on practices that have already proven to be successful in public school systems. Major sections are devoted to relating what has been learned from research in effective schools, school restructuring, school-based management, and accountability, to effect specific and significant changes in educational practices and student outcomes. The latest research in disciplines such as reading and mathematics, and the use of technology for delivering quality instruction are also addressed in very practical and useful ways. The book contains sample data collection forms that can be used to design and monitor school improvement efforts. Examples of various ways to analyze data are also provided to help identify the precise causes of problems.

Transforming America's Schools carefully weaves what is known to work in schools and classrooms together with specific methods that education leaders can use to ensure success. The book is practical but not overly prescriptive. The case studies and anecdotes are designed to stimulate the development of a wide variety of solutions in the reader's 'mind's eye'. Though it pulls no punches, the book is by no means dogmatic. The authors understand that greater flexibility, greater participation, more autonomy, and more experimentation are concomitants of greater accountability. They are not looking for 'quick fixes', but for soundly-based, long-term improvement. They make the point that school system success will not be achieved unless educational leaders are willing to be courageous and take unpopular positions.

In my opinion, this book ought to be read by anyone who is in a position to influence what happens in a school building, especially members of boards of education, superintendents, senior staff members, staff development specialists, school principals, and those aspiring to the principalship. It represents an ideal text for school administration courses in colleges and education. The successful application of research findings and organizational behavior principles to school system problem-solving situations is urgently required if we are to create a generation of effective school leaders. The book will also be useful for parents and other concerned citizens who want to judge the effectiveness of their local school systems.

The greatest contribution of *Transforming America's Schools* lies in its inspiring optimism and its ability to move beyond mere rhetoric to a set of principles and practices that will result in improved teaching and learning.

James Comer

Acknowledgments

This book could never have been written without the dedication, hard work, and creative thinking of many professional educators in school systems thoughout the nation. Particular thanks are given to John Brown, Daniel Saltrick, and Louise Waynant. Their commitment to educating the youth of America, combined with their willingness to take risks in trying new effective instructional stategies, generated much of the knowledge that served as the basis of this book. Their keen sense of insight and ability to convert theoretical concepts into concrete educational interventions were a key to developing this book.

More generally, Bruce Katz, Scott Schiller, and Susan Henry were helpful in reviewing earlier manuscripts of the book, suggesting ways of making it more relevant to the readers.

INTRODUCTION

NOTHING LESS THAN TRANSFORMATION WILL DO

It must be remembered that there is nothing more difficult to plan, more doubtful of success, nor more dangerous to manage than the creation of a new system.

For the initiator has the enmity of all who would profit by the preservation of the old institution, and merely lukewarm defenders in those who would gain by the new one.

Machiavelli, The Prince *(1513)*

ISSUES

The need for change   High standards for all
The underclass   The need for resources
The need to adjust   Prerequisites for improvement

I. Confronting the Need for Change

The poor performance of American schools is now so well-known that it makes the front page of the daily newspaper and is a source of public humiliation. Yet many educators persist with an outlook of complacency and even self-congratulation. The solution to this seeming paradox lies in the fact that these educators, while aware of reports about the sorry state of American education in general, all believe that their *own* schools are exceptional!

This protective self-delusion cannot last much longer. America is now paying the price for its past failure to place the needs of its children—all its children—at the top of its priority list. The U.S. is no longer in a position to keep its pre-eminent international status in the next century, because we have not produced enough citizens with the skills, or in many cases even the moral values, necessary for improving our quality of life.

Well-documented evidence for the failure of our schools comes in two categories. First, there are international comparisons, which invariably place American students at or near the bottom. For example, the 1988 International Assessment of Mathematics and Science compared U.S. students with students in four other nations and in four Canadian provinces. It found that:

- American students placed last in math. Americans not only performed more poorly than students from industrial nations, but also more poorly than those from less-developed countries. More than 75 percent of Korean 13-year-olds were able to use intermediate mathematical skills to solve problems, compared to only 40 percent of American 13-year-olds;
- American students tied for last in science. Korean students were first. Nearly three-quarters of Korean and British Columbian students could use scientific procedures and analyze scientific data, while only about a third of American students could do so.

The evidence from international comparisons is consistent and alarming. There simply is no evidence suggesting that American schools even approach the standards of the rest of the developed world, or much of the less-developed world. It is still possible to encounter some educators who maintain that the performance of American schools has not worsened, or has not worsened much, over the decades. But even if that were true, it would merely suggest that the rest of the world has made giant strides while we have stood still. Whatever the details of the historical background, there is no disputing the fact that American schools *now* are well below 'world class'.

The other type of evidence comes from studies of our students' level of competence, measured by objective standards unrelated to compara-

INTRODUCTION Nothing Less than Transformation Will Do   3

tive performance. For example, a study conducted by the Educational Testing Service found that:

- American students did not have the skills to read beyond a rudimentary level, and could not read complex materials or read analytically;
- American students did not possess basic competence in addition, subtraction, multiplication, division, or elementary problem-solving;
- American students did not have the basic knowledge required for solving science problems;
- American students were ignorant of the significance or relevance of events that have influenced American history;
- American students did not possess the communication skills needed to compete favorably in today's society.

It is our responsibility to graduate students who are equipped to read, write, compute, think, and solve problems. These graduates must also possess those ethical values imperative for any civilized society. All of our children are entitled to the highest quality education—not an education that we believe fits their supposed capacity to learn.

Our schools have fallen tragically short of meeting these obligations, and we are paying a high price for that failure. If we take our charge seriously, then we must be willing to create a new paradigm for schooling: one which redefines what we do and how we do it.

Recently a panel of U.S. education experts convened in Charlotte, North Carolina, and concluded that a 'world class' school system must be willing to:

1. Set genuinely high standards for all students, and expect students of all backgrounds to meet those standards;
2. Develop a curriculum that teaches intellectual, civic, and personal competence;
3. Define new units of learning that students must acquire before graduation. Abandon definitions of achievement that don't measure real 'mastery' of a subject;
4. Require all students to take a demanding set of core subjects;
5. Emphasize in the early grades an explicit concentration on reading, writing, and computation skills. Nothing should detract from the mastery of these subjects which, in turn, enable students in the early grades to learn higher-order material and apply knowledge to practical and theoretical problem-solving;

6. Set high expectations at each school for the number and percentage of students who will meet the highest world-class standards of achievement;
7. Abandon organizing the school system around the average student and the concept of 'minimum requirements'. Substitute an assumption of achievement for all;
8. Undertake a revolutionary agenda for change that will acknowledge the need for community involvement, hard work, and a longer school day or year.

Although this book is primarily designed to familiarize educators with the nuts and bolts of school improvement, this Introduction first reviews some of the big issues that educators must resolve in their own minds before they can undertake serious reform.

The rhetoric of the 1980s, which characterized our schools as being 'at risk', has been replaced with the certainty that if our schools cannot be reformed, our nation will not be able to maintain its leadership position in the world, or be a place where the majority of citizens can be productive and self-fulfilled.

We must find a way to re-invigorate our educational system—to re-institute it as an agency that transmits American values and gives all students an equal opportunity to succeed in life. As Professor Chester E. Finn, Jr. has observed:

> All Americans . . . would benefit from an education system that produced informed citizens. . . . Education isn't just a service we obtain for our own daughters and sons and grandchildren. It is a public good, after defense perhaps our most important form of common provision and, in a sense, itself a defense against the ills that plague us at home. It has incalculable influence on the quality of our social relationships, the vitality of our culture, the strength of our economy, the comfort we feel in our communities, and the wisdom of our government decisions. The better our education system, the better our public and private lives become.

II. The Issue of the Underclass

The fact that there are now societal problems that make educators' jobs more difficult is just that—a 'fact'. Some day all of our social ills may be things of the past and all of our students may come to school ready to learn. But that day has not yet arrived, and schools must find ways to teach students as they are.

> **KEY POINT:** *Many students no longer come to our public schools equipped with the middle-class values of the 1940s and 1950s, and do not have the advantages that we may romantically associate with lifestyles of the past.*

From delinquency to homelessness, from poverty to violence, from alcohol abuse to 'crack' and 'ice', problem after problem bedevils many of today's students. Our schools serve children victimized and debilitated by appalling conditions, not the least of which is their poverty of moral values. Many students come to school believing ethics to be passé, convinced that manliness is measured by egocentric thinking, and that violence is the proper way to obtain any desired object. According to the Children's Defense Fund:

> Being a teenager today is far riskier than it ever has been. Many teens are poor and unhealthy, unsafe in their homes, their neighborhoods, and their schools. Many are at risk of drug or alcohol dependency, or become pregnant long before they are ready to become parents.

The most frightening aspect of this predicament is its cumulative quality. If vile conditions make it difficult for many students to benefit from schooling, they can do little more than perpetuate these conditions as they enter adulthood. Schools become mere warehouses for many students, accepting them with their various handicaps and deficiencies, and causing no major changes in attitudes or learning before the students graduate or drop out.

Many students no longer come to our public schools equipped with the middle-class values of the 1940s and 1950s, and do not have the advantages that we may romantically associate with lifestyles of the past.

Yet educational research and a few local models clearly indicate that there is a way to break the vicious circle. There is an educational approach that will largely compensate for deficiencies of background and home life, and enable disadvantaged students to make genuine progress.

In other words, although today's schools do face unprecedented problems, many of them associated with large numbers of students from deprived backgrounds, the available evidence refutes the notion that such problems can be offered as excuses for poor performance by the schools. Research evidence clearly indicates that, although the social problems are gigantic and menacing (and, of course, urgently require to be tackled outside the educational arena), the strategies and techniques do exist to make up for the students' deficiencies—at least as far as scholastic performance and passably decent behavior go. But experience suggests that to implement these effective strategies and techniques demands a momentous shake-up of the schools: a real transformation which cannot be painless or comfortable for all concerned.

III. The Need to Adjust

A newcomer to educational issues might infer that, since the schools are now performing badly, and less effectively than they performed in the past, the solution lies in strengthening traditional methods, or even returning to past methods now abandoned or modified. Nothing could be further from the truth.

Many of the strategies which were reasonably effective with the predominantly middle- or working-class students of the past do not work with many of today's children. Students of the past came to school with a set of values, including a work ethic, which could be taken for granted. The governing educational strategy grouped students into high, middle, and low ability groups, and then gave all students substantial amounts of non-direct-instructional time—time in which they were expected to do much work on their own (completing worksheets, reading silently, or copying from the chalk board). This strategy worked tolerably well for many children, but it no longer works for a very high proportion of today's students, who don't come to school equipped with the attitudes and values that would enable them to work reliably on their own.

As the Educational Testing Service noted:

> Across the past twenty years, little seems to have changed in how students are taught. Despite much research suggesting better alternatives, classrooms still appear to be dominated by textbooks, teacher lectures, and short-answer activity sheets.

As a direct result of maintaining the status quo, our schools are sending two dramatically different groups into the world: one that has benefited from schooling and is relatively well-prepared to compete successfully for society's rewards; the other for whom schooling has been a failure, and for whom permanent underclass status is a likelihood. The long-term problems associated with a large, growing, and frustrated underclass threaten the very integrity of the political order and the nation-state.

> **KEY POINT**: *The governing educational strategy grouped students into high, middle, and low ability groups, and then gave all students substantial amounts of non-direct-instructional time. This strategy no longer works for a very high proportion of today's students, who don't come to school equipped with the attitudes and values that would enable them to work reliably on their own.*

The bad news, then, is that educational practice has not changed. The good news is that research shows that the educational disadvantages of poor and deprived students can be largely compensated for by appropriate teaching methods—notably more emphasis on, and more time allocated for, direct instruction. It would be wonderful if all parents would instill appropriate values in their children and give them abundant encouragement and support for scholastic achievement. But we don't have to wait for this desirable state of affairs to come about to make dramatic improvements in student attainment.

IV. Facing Up to High Standards for All

The first step to improving the effectiveness of our schools is to hold all students to the highest academic standards. For instance, we must stop feeling satisfied with A's on a report card, if in fact the grades were earned in a mediocre or unchallenging course of study.

> **KEY POINT**: *The fact that some students come from deprived backgrounds does not mean that less should be*

> *expected of them. Rather, educators have to individualize services to reach children where they are, and deliver a program of services to compensate for deficiencies arising from life circumstances.*

As we have seen, American students perform badly, yet many educators are quite satisfied with the performance of *their own* schools. Surveys show that most of our principals, teachers, and even parents are satisfied with the output of their schools. They believe that the educational system is doing badly, but that their own schools and their own children are among the outstanding exceptions! They have lost touch with meaningful academic standards; they live in a dream world where they are most gratified to find that their children are not doing too badly—as measured by lax or abysmal standards.

We educators and parents *have low expectations for our children and our schools.* As long as we fail to understand that our expectations are low, and believe that students are fulfilling our expectations, we will not be properly motivated to bring about revolutionary change in the way our schools are run.

Naturally, most educators indignantly deny that they have low expectations. They claim to have high expectations, because they define their low expectations as high. They demonstrate their low expectations in the following ways:

- They favor invidious grouping practices, lower-level courses, and lower standards for children from socio-economically deprived backgrounds;
- They permit instructional practices that worked in the past but are now inappropriate for many students;
- They refuse to accept that educational expectations should be equally high for students from all socio-economic groups, and that it is the schools' responsibility to find the best mix of organizational and instructional strategies to maximize the chances that children from all backgrounds will meet those expectations.

These educators must be required to discard their ineffective methods of organizing and delivering instruction. If they refuse, they must be replaced.

The fact that some students come from deprived backgrounds

INTRODUCTION Nothing Less than Transformation Will Do

does not mean that less should be expected of them. Rather, educators have to individualize services to reach children where they are, and deliver a program of services to compensate for deficiencies arising from life circumstances.

It is terribly ironic that we, as a nation, fought aggressively for integrated public schools, so that American children of all backgrounds would have access to quality learning experiences, only to re-segregate our children through our grouping and leveling practices. It is outrageous that many minority students are now condescendingly exposed to lower expectations in supposedly integrated schools than similar children were in formerly all-segregated schools.

This 'killing by condescension' approach has recently taken the form of classifying schools as high, middle, or low income, and then establishing separate expectations for the performance of each group. Supporters of this practice argue that since students from low-income families begin school with more deficits, and enjoy fewer support structures at home, it's only natural that they cannot be expected to learn as fast or as much as more advantaged students. Making allowances for these factors is supposed to "create a level playing field." But in truth, it creates several separate and unequal playing fields. Children from low-income families who succeed are still not adequately prepared to compete with their peers from higher-income families.

Some educators welcome such an approach, because it lets them off the hook. If they believe that disadvantaged students can only attain low levels, the schools will be declared 'successful' as long as those low levels are reached. But this comfortable conclusion flies in the face of recent research and experience, which tell us that disadvantaged students will benefit from the same higher level of instruction that is provided to more advantaged children.

Relegating disadvantaged children to lower-level instruction merely perpetuates their disadvantage. A system which embodies low expectations cannot give educators the right incentives to change. Equal educational outcomes for students of all backgrounds cannot become a reality until all students are held to the same standards.

KEY POINT: *It is terribly ironic that we, as a nation, fought aggressively for integrated public schools, so that American children of all backgrounds would have access to quality learning experiences, only to re-segregate our children through our grouping and leveling practices. It is outrageous*

> *that many minority students are now condescendingly exposed to lower expectations in supposedly integrated schools than similar children were in formerly all-segregated schools.*

In many cases, the failure of some students reflects the fact that schools do nothing to compensate for students' special needs. Instead of using differences in family background as an excuse for poor performance, educators must determine what specific instructional or other services are required to improve the performance of those not currently benefiting. Leaders of school systems must take concrete measures to signal to all staff that expectations for all students are high, and that by varying instructional and other strategies, positive results can be achieved with all students.

When system leaders do begin to address the problems associated with the poor performance of minority and disadvantaged students, they encounter difficult public relations problems. Parents of the more middle-class or advantaged students can easily jump to the conclusion that programs tailored to the disadvantaged can only be implemented at the expense of advantaged students. Administrators had better be sensitive to this fact, and should launch an aggressive public relations campaign to inform parents that their children's interests are best served if all students are effectively served. In fact, most school systems which have raised the academic performance of minority students have also raised the academic performance of majority students. It is the responsibility of the educational leader to tackle this issue head on by explaining that improved education for lower-achieving students is like a rising tide which lifts all boats.

Since nothing is easier than for legislators and educators to pay lip service to 'high expectations' in a completely vacuous manner, we want to make this point crystal clear. By 'high expectations', we mean *never* adjusting down the standards by which schools or school districts are judged, and for which their managers and instructors are held accountable, to the actual performance or observed output of the schools, but *always* setting standards unrelated to the past record of the schools, imposing these standards on the schools and compelling the schools to do whatever it takes to meet these standards. At the same time, we believe in giving the schools a great deal of freedom to select the specific *methods* by which they meet these standards—and hence, our approach leads to empowering the individual schools and reducing interference by the bureaucracy.

V. Schools Do Need More Money!

As evidence of school failure mounted, the first and loudest cry from educators was 'We need more resources!' This refrain continues today, and turns many politicians and citizens away from supporting their public schools.

Two polar views have emerged on the issue of 'more resources'. First, there are those who broadly take the view that educators know how to improve the schools, and merely lack sufficient resources to put things right. If the schools received large additional transfusions from the taxpayers, most of the key problems could substantially be solved. At the other extreme, there are those who repeat that problems cannot be solved 'by throwing money at them', who point out that the schools have failed to use their existing resources effectively, and who believe that additional funds for the schools would only be wasted, until the schools first shape up.

Neither of these positions is adequate. It's true that, as expenditures on education have risen, educational outcomes have declined. Courses have proliferated and performance has deteriorated. Equally true, however, is that new burdens and new opportunities indicate a need for more resources.

Our position is that the public schools should indeed get more dollars from the taxpayers—but these should be dollars with strings attached. "Strings" means accountability and willingness to change. In effect, the taxpayers, through their elected representatives, must demand accountability from their schools: more money for schooling, contingent upon school staff adopting tested educational practices and achieving measurable improvements in student performance. Leading educators must be *personally* accountable to the taxpayers: unless results measurably and dramatically improve, these individuals must be willing to step aside.

With that quid pro quo understood, here are some of the urgent uses for new funds:

- *New services.* Many students require different and additional services, including Saturday or after-school classes, counseling, or special remedial sessions. Teaching staffs need to be retrained, and time must

be found for staff development. New and different instructional materials had better be purchased. Smaller classes are desirable and specialists (psychologists, guidance counselors, social workers) need to be hired;
- *Extended learning time.* Of all industrialized nations, the U.S. requires the least time in school for both students and teachers. Learning time can be increased by extending the school year or the school day, for students or teachers;
- *New technology.* Computers and other new technologies involve high purchase and training costs. Research shows that, infused directly into the classroom, they can be effective in improving student performance;
- *Basic infrastructure.* Many school buildings are in or near disrepair, and defy the most heroic efforts to maintain them in acceptable or safe condition.

> **KEY POINT**: *The taxpayers, through their elected representatives, must demand accountability from their schools: more money for schooling, contingent upon school staff adopting tested educational practices and achieving measurable improvements in student performance. Leading educators must be personally accountable to the taxpayers: unless results measurably and dramatically improve, these individuals must be willing to step aside.*

VI. Prerequisites for School Improvement

Before we can begin the process of transforming the schools, we must develop a vision, a philosophy, or belief-system that will be a motor for change. The central commitment of this belief-system is the conviction that all students can learn, and students from all backgrounds can achieve academic excellence.

Various excuses, which have so often been trotted out, must be cut down to size and put in their proper perspective. We often hear that children would learn more IF:

- We only had more money;
- Students were as well-behaved and well-motivated as they used to be;

INTRODUCTION   Nothing Less than Transformation Will Do   13

- Administrative red tape were eliminated;
- Fewer students came from poor families;
- Parents cared more about their children;
- More mothers would stay at home;
- We didn't have to instill values in children who have none;
- Class sizes were smaller.

Though all these factors are relevant, they are not valid excuses. We no longer want to hear excuses: we want to see results.

Once the excuses are put aside, some brutally serious fact-finding and soul-searching are required to determine the extent to which there has been any effective school improvement lately.

> **KEY POINT:** *Before we can begin the process of transforming the schools, we must develop a vision, a philosophy, or belief-system that will be a motor for change. The central commitment of this belief-system is the conviction that all students can learn, and students from all backgrounds can achieve academic excellence.*

If we surveyed educators and asked them whether or not they have engaged in meaningful improvement programs, the overwhelming reply would be a resounding 'Yes!' But many of these educators would be deceiving themselves. They would cite such strategies as:

- Developing new curriculum;
- Raising standards;
- Recognizing exemplary schools;
- Restructuring the roles of teachers;
- Creating incentives for effective teaching;
- Decentralizing decisions;
- Hiring more staff;
- Purchasing computers.

And yet, in spite of all these efforts, progress often remains pitifully small or nonexistent. Unfortunately, much that is labelled 'school improvement' is merely the implementation of a single, isolated strategy selected from a menu of canned educational innovations. Many schools have adopted 'fixes' that have had no real history of fixing anything. Many of the strategies have constituted no more than someone's best guess as to what ought to work, and have been seen mainly as means to reduce community pressures to accomplish more meaningful—and perhaps more uncomfortable—changes. After a year or two of trying, many school systems have abandoned the new strategies, or been content with very modest results.

> **KEY POINT:** *A close examination of our classrooms reveals that not much has changed. But recent efforts to improve education have created a reservoir of new knowledge, which can be drawn upon to formulate a coherent strategy for radical change. However, change will occur only if educators are willing to question their current practices and to replace them with more effective practices.*

Even the most casual observer could list dozens of so-called innovations in education, and may wonder why any more could possibly be needed. In spite of some serious efforts, most innovations have not worked. Although there are several reasons for failure, two stand out:

First, many of the changes have been piecemeal. They did not reflect the complexity of the schools, and did not belong to an integrated strategy driven by a coherent vision. So they didn't take into account the need for all facets of school operations to be simultaneously involved in any change. There was no understanding that ways had to be found for systems to support individual schools, and that the focus of all change had to be to improve student outcomes. Merely changing curricula, decreasing class size, or decentralizing decision-making may be necessary, but do not amount to a serious school improvement program.

Second, in most cases where new programs have been tried, they have been layered on top of, rather than replacing, existing programs. Here is a good example of this 'educational layering':

We recently observed a classroom which contained five networked computers. This particular teacher had been lauded by the principal for her exemplary use of computers for improving instruction. However, as soon as we entered the classroom, we noted that next to each computer was a five-minute timer which the students were required to start when they began working on the computer. At the end of five minutes the timer rang and the students returned to their desks and were replaced by other students. At the conclusion of the class we asked the teacher to explain the use of the timer. Without hesitation or the slightest embarrassment, the teacher explained that if she allowed the students to remain on the computer for longer periods of time, they would get ahead of her lessons and the textbook.

Layering, or mindless eclecticism, is so common that we cannot resist citing another example:

Co-operative learning, a process which involves children learning from other children, was developed as a means of having children at various instructional and developmental levels helping each other. That is, it was conceived as supplanting traditional grouping practices. We recently observed a classroom in which the teacher was applauded for implementing co-operative learning. As soon as we entered the classroom, it was evident that the students were grouped for reading in the traditional manner: a high group, a mid-level group, and a low group. Two of the groups were at their desks completing worksheets and copying materials from the board. The teacher was working with the third group, apparently using legitimate co-operative learning strategies. But the teacher was using them *within* a homogeneous group of students. The building principal and the teacher had just layered co-operative learning on top of ineffective classroom practices. They failed to realize they had to undo what did not work before they installed a new approach.

Although most efforts to improve the schools have been disappointing in practice, these numerous efforts have created a valuable reservoir of new knowledge—knowledge about what works and what doesn't. It is now possible to take the best ideas from a variety of sources and integrate them into a coherent strategy for transforming America's schools.

We can now state the minimum prerequisites for ensuring the success of school improvement programs. These prerequisites are:

- That the school board, superintendent, and senior staff must publicly acknowledge that they expect all children to meet high standards, and that they will not tolerate any inequities in the organization or lack of delivery of educational services. They must provide information to the

parents and the public, revealing the nature of their problems, and demonstrating the system's progress in achieving the standards;
- That the system's leaders must take ownership of their problems, through a series of concrete actions which focus on changing all of those policies and practices that restrict educational opportunities. They must re-allocate existing resources to help implement these policies and practices;
- That there must be extensive training programs for all levels of staff, accepted by staff as part of the job;
- That community advisory committees must be formed to provide a mechanism for reviewing all plans and procedures, and to monitor the school system's progress as it executes the plans.

Introduction: Further Reading

Carnegie Forum on Education and the Economy. 1986. *A Nation Prepared: Teachers for the Twenty First Century.* New York: Carnegie Corporation.

Council of Chief State School Officers. 1989. *Success for All in the New Century.* Washington, D.C.: Council of Chief State School Officers.

Cremin, Lawrence, A., 1989. *Popular Education and Its Discontents.* New York: Harper and Row.

Educational Testing Service. 1990. (Prepared for the National Center for Educational Statistics), *America's Challenge: Accelerating Academic Achievement.* Princeton.

Educational Testing Service. 1987 National Assessment of Educational Progress (NAEP). *Literacy: Profiles of America's Young Adults.* Princeton.

Finn, Chester E., Jr. 1991. *We Must Take Charge: Our Schools and Our Future.* New York: The Free Press.

Hanushek, Eric A. 1991. Will More Spending Fix Unequal Schools? *Detroit News,* October 30.

Hornbeck, David W., and Lester M. Salamon (editors). 1991. *Human Capital and America's Future.* Baltimore: The Johns Hopkins University Press.

Johnston, William B., and Arnold H. Packer. 1987. *Workforce 2000: Work and Workers for the Twenty-First Century.* Indianapolis: Hudson Institute.

La Pointe, Archie, Nancy Meade, and Gary Phillips. 1989. *A World of Differences: An International Assessment of Mathematics and Science.* Princeton: Educational Testing Service.

National Center for Children in Poverty. 1990. *Five Million Children: A Statistical Profile of Our Poorest Young Citizens.* New York: School of Public Health, Columbia University.

Ravitch, Dianne, and Checker E. Finn Jr. 1987. *What Do Our 17 Year Olds Know?* New York: Harper and Row.

Schorr, Lisbeth B., and Daniel Schorr. 1988. *Within Our Reach: Breaking the Cycle of Disadvantage.* New York: Anchor/Doubleday.

Simons, Janet, M., Belva Finlay, and Alice Yang. 1991. *The Adolescent and Young Adult Fact Book.* Washington, D.C.: Children's Defense Fund.

The Secretary's Commission on Achieving Necessary Skills. 1991. *What Work Requires of Schools: A SCANS Report for America 2000.* Washington, D.C.: United States Department of Labor.

United States Center for Educational Statistics, 1991. *Digest of Educational Statistics: 1990.* Washington, D.C.: U.S. Government Printing Office.

United States Department of Education. 1991. *America 2000: An Education Strategy.* Washington, D.C.: U.S. Government Printing Office.

CHAPTER ONE

CHANGING ROLES IN THE TRANSFORMATION PROCESS

The trouble is that everyone talks about reforming others, and no one thinks about reforming himself.

                        Saint Peter of Alcantara

ISSUES

The new roles:
    Boards of education
    Superintendents
    Principals
    Central office staff
    Government
    Business
    Families

Preparing principals
Preparing teachers
Recruiting tomorrow's principals
Finding time

If schools are to become effective, they must be transformed, and if schools are to be transformed, there has to be a transformation of the working lives of everyone connected with the schools. Transforming the schools cannot be accomplished painlessly, or without disturbing some of those involved. *Everyone* has to be ready to adjust to change, or has to be ready to go.

After all, this goes without saying for any business, and it goes without saying for any active military organization—especially (to make the analogy with the schools somewhat closer) one that has suffered a humiliating series of defeats.

Naturally, it is not a matter of change for change's sake. It is a matter of redeploying all the school system's resources—especially its human resources—to get the best results.

I. The New Role for the School Board

Study upon study has demonstrated the failure of our American system of public education, and study upon study has attempted to locate the causes of that failure. Blame has been placed on a myriad of factors, ranging from the poor quality of leadership, to inadequate or inappropriate teacher preparation, to a lack of parental involvement, to a reduction in standards, and so forth. To our knowledge, not a single study has looked at the role that school boards may have played during this tumultuous period of decline. Is it possible that part of the responsibility lies with those who govern?

We have found that an increasingly large proportion of individuals who sit at the board table focus on quick-fix solutions. Their need to participate in carefully thought out long-range planning often gives way to their perceived need to respond quickly to a complaining constituent. The same impatience also frequently manifests itself in administrative intrusion. This short-sighted approach to governance most often results in actions that do not support sound educational policies and practices. Teachers and principals become confused about their roles and responsibilities. The edicts from on high change at a rate they cannot keep pace with, and the lack of logical consistency leaves those in the trenches wondering about those in command.

If we are to transform our schools into institutions that provide equal access to quality learning experiences for all children then we must be willing to revisit the roles and practices of those at the top; and when it is determined that the board is an obstacle, the board must be willing to change.

The board's role is not only to set policy. The board must also be initially involved with establishing standards of performance for all staff and students, and with judging whether or not those standards are being met. The actual daily implementation is to be left to a quality administrative staff led by a superintendant selected by the board.

In the early stages of implementing new policies, the board needs to show its support for the superintendent. If the policies show signs of beginning to work effectively, and the school system looks like making headway, or if the system is manifesting significant, measurable improvement, then also the board should back up the superintendent. If the system fails according to its pre-announced, objectively measurable goals, the board needs to reconsider the status of its leader. The evaluation of the superintendent is an important function of the board, and that evaluation should reflect the extent to which the board's goals for the school system are being met.

To effectively discharge their responsibilities, boards of education must:

a. Establish a Vision. The board reviews data about the performance of its schools. It surveys parents, the business community, schools of higher education, and the general public about their perception of the system and their desires for future direction. Then, working with staff, the board defines a governing mission or vision that will serve to direct the energies of the organization.

b. Create a Plan of Action. The board clearly defines the mission for the general public. The board then has its professional staff develop a plan of action, to move the system from where it is now to where it should be, as defined by the Vision. This action plan is clearly defined and explained to the public, and specific measuring devices are instituted to publicly monitor fulfillment of the plan.

c. Examine Resource Utilization. The board keeps in mind that 'more' is not always the answer. The board carefully examines how current resources are utilized. For instance, local business experts may be hired to analyze the system's administrative structure, check on its cost-effectiveness, and suggest improvements.

Teaching staff are surveyed to determine what they see as barriers standing in the way of accomplishing the board's mission. Removing many of these barriers may reduce costs.

d. Be Publicly Accountable. The board annually reports back to the public the tangible progress that has been made towards implementing the Vision. The board's report focuses on outcomes that can be defended and have been identified in advance. Specific benchmarks are announced as the district progresses towards its goal, and the public is made aware of whether these benchmarks have been met. The board ensures that each school's data are analyzed to determine how effectively learning outcomes are being met. A review is also made of the quality of staff evaluations prepared by executive staff and the relationship of those evaluations to student outcomes.

e. Evaluate Itself and its Superintendent. These evaluations carefully weigh the extent to which each contributed to the conditions ensuring success, as well as the extent to which success was achieved.

II. The New Role for the Superintendent

Superintendents who help to transform the public schools must, first and foremost, be visionaries. These men and women must have a powerful sense of a system that, if working properly, would provide an effective education for all children, and prepare each and every one of them to be productive members of society.

Given that vision, superintendents must have the political guts to make difficult decisions. They cannot expect to please everyone all the time.

Although superintendents don't have to be expert in every area, they have to be able to make critical judgments concerning all decisions made by their subordinates. They have to face the fact that many staff will resist change and seek a comfort level consistent with past practices. It is the superintendent's responsibility to force the staff to constantly re-assess their performance, and move it to new and higher levels. This is a frustrating but vital job, and ultimately a rewarding one.

Superintendents have to be the educational leaders, not only of their school systems, but of their entire community. They must project the system's mission, goals, and achievements to the wider world, as a means of gaining support for the public schools. Superintendents' vision and commitment to the education of all students should be reflected in their daily management style.

To be effective, superintendents need the following skills and capabilities:

a. Educational Leadership. Superintendents must clearly define the school system's mission, based on the philosophy that all children will learn.

Working with boards of education and staff at all levels, superintendents have to develop strategies to achieve that mission. The mission should convey expectations of high performance to all staff and students. Effective superintendents require loyalty and commitment from all staff, and must sensitize them to the need to do whatever it takes to bring about improvements. "Whatever it takes" means discarding or modifying daily habits and practices established over years or decades.

> **KEY POINT:** *Superintendents have to work closely with boards of education to reinforce the boards' role as guardians of academic standards.*

As the system's educational leader, a superintendent has to make the instructional program the focus of all board action, and initiate procedures to routinely examine instructional practices. An effective superintendent will keep the board well-informed about the current state of education, new relevant research findings, and new instructional trends. Most importantly, the superintendent will establish a quality control system that automatically keeps the board informed of instructional progress.

Superintendents should not permit any confusion between the board's policy-setting role and the superintendent's responsibility to administer the policies. The superintendent must not permit political interference with the system's mission. To be effective, superintendents have to stand tall and prevent the self-interest of individuals or groups from influencing critical decisions that have to be made.

b. Executive Leadership. Boards of education have every right to expect from their superintendents leadership that is at least equal to that provided by chief executive officers in industry.

Among their leadership functions, superintendents must clearly define the responsibilities and expected capabilities of school principals. Superintendents have to develop and disseminate a set of roles, goals, and standards that all principals are obliged to adopt and master. They also have to ensure the provision of training for principals and future principals.

Many of our public school systems are as large as major corporations. Even smaller districts have budgets and staffs that compare in size to local industry. Superintendents have a responsibility not only to be experts in their professional field, but also to possess those skills that a finely-tuned business enterprise expects from its leader. Among the attributes of such a leader are:

- The vision to continually re-assess the system's progress, moving the organization in new directions when necessary;
- The ability to delegate authority to maximize productivity;
- A leadership style that promotes loyalty and fosters creativity, enthusiasm, teamwork, and confidence among staff in order to achieve system goals;
- An understanding of the needs and motivations of employees, and the ability to inspire employees to higher goals;
- The ability to translate goals into clear, observable, verifiable results, so that progress in attaining the goals can be objectively measured;
- The ability to focus staff on identified problems and their solution;
- The ability to provide the board of education and the public with periodic briefings on the system's financial status. These briefings must reflect an awareness of the utilization of resources and staff;
- The courage to fight for the system's mission, and to defend it at all costs.

Superintendents, and those who aspire to the superintendency, should go into it with their eyes open. Change always upsets someone, especially in public organizations where individuals are tempted to view whatever has become customary as an entitlement. For every bold and courageous effort to reform the existing structure, there will be naysayers, schemers, and chronic dissidents, who will use every strategy imaginable, moral or immoral, to fight change. The two most conspicuous groups will be: 1. Those who feel—perhaps rightly—that their jobs or their comfortable persistence with what they have always done are in jeopardy; and 2. Those parents who feel—mistakenly—that ambitious programs to help the disadvantaged will somehow harm their own, comparatively advantaged, children.

The superintendent who does not arouse furious opposition from some individuals is very likely not doing his or her job properly. The superintendent must from the outset mobilize community leaders and media to isolate and combat these reactionary opponents of change. The superintendent must also make clear to the board that strenuous opposition from some quarters is fully expected, and cannot be allowed to deflect the system's plan in the slightest—subject to the ultimate test of actual results. (Naturally, not all discontent stems from obstruction to change, and complaints can sometimes be remedied without compromising the system's goals.)

c. Instructional Leadership. Superintendents have to be able to assess the educational condition of the system, guide the staff and the community in determining instructional goals for the future based on the system's mission, and put in place a long-range plan that will enable the goals to be attained within a reasonably short, and pre-specified, time period.

As school systems embark on the implementation of the plan, superintendents have to give direct leadership to the professional staff, by:

- Guiding the curricular and instructional practices of the system, with sharp focus on the specific skills needed to improve student performance;
- Initiating an evaluation plan for all staff members, to ensure professional growth;
- Initiating viable in-service programs for principals and teachers to focus on identified instructional and staff weaknesses;
- Advocating a firm, fair, consistent program of discipline and student expectations;
- Strongly promoting an ethos of academic excellence based on high standards;
- Encouraging a strong professional commitment by principals and teachers to a success-oriented school climate;
- Meeting frequently with principals to exchange ideas and to be able to respond to their concerns;
- Meeting with representative teachers to keep abreast of their views and reactions.

d. Effective Communication. Superintendents should, effectively and continuously, communicate the school system's mission, goals, programs, and requirements, both to everyone directly involved in the system and to the wider public.

Superintendents have to understand the organization and its programs so that they can communicate effectively with the community, public officials, and journalists. Superintendents must keep fully up-to-date through reports, briefings, and frequent personal visits to schools and program sites.

Superintendents have to represent the interests of their school system, and of public schools in general, and to encourage enhanced public support and funding. At the same time, they have to accept without question that the community is making a huge investment in public schooling, and is fully entitled to see some results for its money. Without reservation, the superintendent owes the public, the media and the legislators a convincing explanation and defense of the school system's current activities and future direction.

The public affairs function within the district should report directly to the superintendent and aggressively work to transmit the system's message to the public. Superintendents need to involve community leaders in improving programs and in supporting the system as a whole.

> **KEY POINT:** *Change always upsets someone, especially in public organizations where individuals are tempted to view whatever has become customary as an entitlement. For every bold and courageous effort to reform the existing structure, there will be naysayers, schemers, and chronic dissidents, who will use every strategy imaginable, moral or immoral, to fight change. The superintendent who does not arouse furious opposition from some individuals is very likely not doing his or her job properly. The superintendent must from the outset mobilize community leaders and media to isolate and combat these reactionary opponents of change.*

III. The New Role for the Principal

The school improvement literature is filled with rhetorical calls for the principal to take charge and become all things to all people. Although research and experience certainly document the need for a more active principal's role, this cannot be accomplished by waving a wand or by hectically rushing about.

Effective principals are willing to give some of the job away: they have to fight the tendency to retain absolute control. Instead, they will empower staff to become active players in decision-making and problem-solving. The principal's sacrifice of immediate control helps to ensure that staff members can assume ownership of broad educational issues, rather than being passive recipients of their influence. Teaching staff should be accorded substantial freedom of action—and then held accountable for student outcomes.

In an age of transformation, the effective principal does not try to fix everything personally, but maintains an inner confidence born of a knowledge of where the school is going and how it will get there. A synergy develops among staff in the context of that confidence and that knowledge.

The mission of ensuring that all students acquire the knowledge, skills, and work habits required to make them productive members of society is pursued most directly by bringing excellence to each school. The extent to which that mission can be accomplished depends on the performance of building principals. They must provide positive learning climates characterized by high expectations for all, effective instructional leadership, and a management system which gives staff overall direction along with considerable autonomy.

Principals have to keep abreast of research and theoretical discussion in the educational field. They should possess a good grasp of what is known about effective and ineffective educational practices, rather than passively accepting a 'conventional wisdom' or educational folklore based on prejudice and uninformed gossip. Principals lead staffs in the great task of maximizing student learning and development. All of the principals' effective leadership behavior is informed by their professional knowledge of effective schooling. Principals must be equipped to help classroom teachers to identify and utilize the most effective instructional strategies.

The role of the principal is very broad in scope and encompasses many skills and qualities in management and educational theory. If we are to see effective principals become the norm rather than the exception, then superintendents have to ensure that they provide leadership training for principals in each of the following nine areas:

> a. **Instructional Leadership.** Principals must know how to organize the available human and material resources in a way that maximizes their impact on student learning.

Merely being knowledgeable about effective instructional strategies without having the courage to shake up the school, change its governance structure, and change teachers' strategies, will not have the desired effects. Principals must be responsible for monitoring student progress on a regular basis and ensuring that appropriate changes are made on the basis of that monitoring. Principals must be able to help teachers apply state-of-the-art techniques in the delivery of educational services.

> **b. Planning for School Improvement.** Principles should make sure that staff are involved in key decisions within the building, and should implement procedures to ensure that this involvement occurs.

In concert with their staff, principals have to develop a school mission which supports the school system's mission and simultaneously meets the particular needs of the students in the school. Principals ensure that all staff are involved in the development of specific improvement plans which serve the school's mission, establishing both long- and short-term objectives, with dates and unambiguous criteria for determining success or failure. The observations that principals make of teacher performance should focus on whether or not teachers employ strategies designed to achieve the plan's goals.

> **c. Administrative Leadership.** Principles have to competently perform a wide range of administrative tasks, including financial management and analysis, facility planning and management, scheduling, and personnel evaluation.

Effective principals use resources optimally within the prescribed limits. The best use of resources is ultimately determined by the best interests of the students. Principals should know how to use personnel evaluations to signal strengths and weaknesses to each employee, and should be ready with concrete suggestions for improved performance whenever the planned improvement in student outcomes is not achieved.

> **d. Organizational Ability.** Principles must be knowledgeable and flexible enough to grasp the relationship between the school and the classroom organization, on the one hand, and program effectiveness and staff morale, on the other hand.

Principals must work co-operatively with all staff to ensure their meaningful involvement in key school issues and then ensure that the energies of staff really are focussed on achieving the school's mission.

> **e. School Environment and Climate.** Principals see to it that learning is the central focus of the school, and that the environment

is safe, orderly, and conducive both to teachers' sense of professionalism and to students' love of learning.

Whatever is needed to build a sense of family among teachers, students, and their families, must be the principal's priority. Pride should be the watchword and, although it is difficult to quantify, should be used as a major criterion in judging a school's effectiveness. Principals have to maintain buildings that are secure, safe, and inviting places in which to learn.

f. Communications. Good principals understand that open communication is beneficial, and will not occur unless staff trust each other, share common goals, value diversity, have access to the same knowledge base, and believe that risk-taking will be rewarded.

Although principals need to communicate their expectations to school staff, students, and the community, principals must often be ready to subordinate their own beliefs to the collective and individual professional wisdom of their staff members. Managing a school system or a school by edict, or with the assumption that "there's only one right way", is no longer acceptable.

g. Community and Public Relations. Principals must assume a major role in creating and maintaining positive school-community relations—including those with parents, local businesses, clergy, and civic organizations.

It is desirable to involve as wide a constituency as possible in accomplishing the school's mission. And, although principals should be sensitive to the needs of individual school board members and other elected officials, they must keep in mind that their job is to achieve the objectives specified by the system. Principals should never respond to other persons or groups in a manner that is contrary to the system's mission.

h. Professional Development. Principals are responsible for staff development of two very different types.

First, principals continually identify areas in which their staff require training, and do everything possible to see that such training is provided. Where staff development resources are limited, principals should provide the training themselves, or identify teacher experts in the schools to deliver training to their peers. Second, principals must be introspective and sensitive to their own weaknesses, and seek out opportunities for self-improvement.

i. Personal Qualities. Principals should serve as role models to all staff, students, and other members of the school community.

The values and assumptions that characterize the school system had better be reflected in every action taken by the principal, even the most trivial of daily interactions. The principal must continuously exude enthusiasm, optimism, self-confidence, respect for all employees, and reverence for the students' potential.

Administrators may have difficulty recognizing all the roles and responsibilities delineated above, and adapting to them. However, as schools and school systems undergo strategically planned restructuring, new roles and commitments will replace the more traditional ones. Administrators should be prepared to challenge the status quo, continually re-evaluate the way things are done, and seek alternative ways to do them more effectively. Being a risk-taker is fundamental to this process. Effective principals will not blame existing policies and procedures for lack of progress, but will strive to break out of bureaucratic strangleholds, bureaucratic mind-sets, and institutional lethargy.

IV. The New Role for Central Office Instructional Staff

Our emphasis on school-based management and on expanding the role of principals does not imply that central office staff are let off the hook. These staff have the capacity to support new innovations or to thwart them by clinging to practices of the past.

In the new, emerging paradigm for school reform, all school system personnel—the superintendent, central office staff, and building principals—must redesign their activities *to support the classroom teacher.* All staff exist to assist teachers be more effective, by facilitating change, by helping teachers cope with the stresses of change, and by being pro-active in addressing changes in curriculum design, teaching practices, and training.

The superintendent who is serious about transforming the schools will confront and combat the traditional theory that the role of central office staff is to direct the professional life of school-based employees. The prevailing attitude is that school-based employees carry out central office directives. Instead of this old viewpoint, the superintendent has to convince central office staff that it is their job to fulfil the requirements of all school-based staff. The proper attitude of central office toward the schools is: How can we help?

A new culture needs to be developed in which it is apparent to everyone that the priorities of the system are at the building level. To reinforce this message and leave no doubt about it, the annual evaluations of central office staff should be based in significant part on how helpful they have been to school-based employees.

Central office staff are there to help schools solve their problems, *as the school staff themselves define these problems.* The reforming superintendent who comes to a school district managed on traditional lines will make some changes at central office. The central office's staff development function will be largely abolished, for example. The initiative for staff development will come instead from the schools, who can shop around for the services they require. Central office may retain some role as a broker in this process, for example, helping a school find an expert on teaching dyslexic children. But central office is not there to provide all the training services from its own ranks.

Since schools are being made more accountable for their results, and at the same time given the freedom to innovate and experiment, it is not helpful to have central office imposing standard procedures on the schools. In only a few surviving instances will there be occasion to have staff development programs which are the same for all schools in the district: training in the use of a new textbook series, or new computer software, for example.

> **KEY POINT:** *In the new, emerging paradigm for school reform, all school system personnel—the superintendent, central office staff, and building principals—must redesign their activities* to support the classroom teacher. *All staff exist to assist teachers be more effective, by facilitating change, by helping teachers cope with the stresses of change, and by being pro-active in addressing changes in curriculum design, teaching practices, and training.*

Under the old paradigm, the role of central office was perceived as that of keeper of the gate, maintaining quality control—most typically by slowing down the creative process or by directly intervening in site-level program decisions. In the new paradigm, superintendents and their executive staffs must work closely with central office personnel to identify ways in which they can function as catalysts, rather than inhibitors, of change.

As schools are in process of transformation, there are two vitally important roles which can be played by central office:

> **a. Program Development.** Central office instructional staff should try to ensure that all central office policies and practices actively support the school improvement effort.

Central office staff should continuously seek state-of-the-art information about their program area, and make that information available to school staff. Central office staff should be relentless in ferreting out any educational practices which do not support the goals of the school system, and once these practices are identified, ensure that they are eliminated.

> **b. Program Implementation.** Central office instructional staff should ensure that information about present program or student performance and the effectiveness of new approaches or strategies that may be used by teachers is disseminated in a timely manner throughout the system.

Teachers are often lamentably ignorant about the findings of new research as it bears upon particular areas. For example, there have been exciting developments in research on reading over the years, but most teachers of reading are largely unaware of many important findings about how children learn to read. Comical as it may sound, for many teachers the most authoritative source of news about research findings is the textbook salesman's spiel! It is as if the only news physicians received about treatment methods was from pharmaceuticals salespersons, without the countervailing influence of teaching and research hospitals (which have no real counterparts in education).

Today most central office research departments are themselves quite ignorant of current educational research. They should be given the job of becoming aware of relevant findings and conveying these in digestible form to all staff within the system, particularly teaching staff.

As well as disseminating the most up-to-date information about what works to teachers and principals, central office staff should provide training programs as requested by the school staff, arrange for and provide observation and assistance for new, non-tenured, and out-of-field teachers, and provide information on student, classroom and school performance to be used in data-based decision-making.

V. The New Role for Governments

The transformation of schooling calls for bold new governmental initiatives. First among these must be to care for our impoverished pre-school children. Many of our public school system failures are directly related to problems that precede formal schooling, and unless we address these realities, we will continue our downward spiral. We should combine our internal reform strategies with complete support for those community efforts designed to improve the readiness of children to attend school.

Education has taken a serious beating in the press for its failure to compete internationally, yet we rarely see reports that cite our failure to take care of our babies and appropriately prepare them for school. The United States has a higher infant mortality rate than any industrialized country other than some of the nations of the former Soviet Union.

Marian Wright Edelman, President of the Children's Defense Fund, powerfully voices the challenge:

> Children must have their basic needs for health care . . . and nutrition met if they are to be prepared to achieve in school. A child with an undiagnosed vision problem, or without the means to get glasses once a problem has been diagnosed, can hardly learn to his potential. A child whose intellectual development is stunted by lead poisoning cannot excel in the classroom. . . . Nor can a hungry child . . . All of this is common sense. Any parent, any teacher, any doctor, any politician, understands these connections. The puzzling thing is why we can't do what we all know makes sense, giving all children the essential and cost-effective early investments they need to prepare them to achieve.

The school system can organize in several ways to work cooperatively with government agencies to tackle these concerns. First, we can provide education for all our graduates to prepare them for the serious work of parenting. Second, we can open parent centers in each of our schools, and encourage parents of new born babies and school-age children to avail themselves of parenting skills services and services designed to help them reinforce at home what is taught in our schools. Third, we can extend our organization beyond K-12, to include classes for three- and four-year-olds. And fourth, we can provide quality prenatal care for those teens who are pregnant. This care must be part of the regular school day, and be designed to keep pregnant students in school. This will necessitate nurseries for their infants, prenatal services, and supportive environments for the teenage parents. A complete school experience for these students will be a strong incentive to discourage repeat pregnancies and eradicate the frightening cycle of teen mothers and 30-year-old grandmothers.

As Patricia Graham puts the point in *Sustain Our Schools:*

> There is plenty of room for state and local initiative in educational reform, but the fundamental problems of poverty, single-parent families, inadequate health care, and hopelessness that affect many of our children are in the domain of the country as a whole, not of a beleaguered town with an inadequate tax base. Since the problems are inherently national in scope, federal actions are in order.

All school administrators should read *Sustain Our Schools* as well as *Ready to Learn* by Ernest Boyer, to acquire a fuller understanding of the seriousness of the problem, and enlightened suggestions for action.

VI. The New Role for Business

The most common expectation for business-school collaboration is the adopt-a-school program or school-business partnerships. These programs involve relationships between the school and a local business or industry, and typically result in the school's receiving financial support for special projects. In some cases, company employees volunteer time to serve as tutors or mentors for schoolchildren.

Such programs are valuable, and represent a good beginning, but they will not bring about the desired change that business and the nation want from their schools. When we are asked about what business can do, our response is: We don't want your financial contributions as much as we need your clout. Business must first and foremost become an advocate for education. To date, education has not had an advocate. We have had a great deal of political rhetoric, but no follow-up support. Business can force action, and that should be its primary role at all levels of government. Instead of Calvin Coolidge's dictum, "The business of business should be business", we contend that the business of business should be education. The very survival of our economy depends upon it.

We are not suggesting *carte blanche* advocacy, without a return. As we point out in detail in this book, accountability for results is critical.

Business can work with our schools, and at the same time demand that the schools turn out a quality product. Recently, we were engaged in a school-business relationship that provided a guarantee program for all graduates. Business outlined the skills needed for entry to the workforce, and our schools guaranteed not only to teach those skills, and test for mastery, but also agreed to take back any graduates who lacked important skills during the first year on the job.

Business can also help by providing time for employees to visit with their child's teacher during the work day, and by encouraging competent leaders to run for school board seats.

Business leaders have been very effective in advocacy for our colleges and universities, resulting in the best higher-education system in the world. It seems reasonable that the same degree of advocacy for public schools will have a similar result.

VII. The New Role for Parents

Our society has turned over to the schools many of the functions traditionally performed by families—including basic education about sex, drugs, race relations, nutrition, and many other areas. Each time a societal need is perceived, we tend to assume that the schools can address it, rather than the family or other community institution. We have piled more and more on our teachers' plates, while at the same time we expect them to improve their students' academic preparation.

There is a limit to what the schools can perform. Parents have to take a more active role in dealing with the total development of their children. They can begin by joining forces with the school to make education a priority in the child's life. Homework must take precedence over television viewing, space should be provided at home for study, and close contact with the child's teacher should be maintained.

Yet the separation between home and school has not been exclusively the fault of the home. Many of our parents feel uncomfortable in the school environment, for various reasons. Educators often fail to explain their programs and strategies in clear and comprehensible terms. We launch creative new approaches to instruction, foreign to the experience of parents, and then question their capacity for understanding. Careful attention should be paid to communicating with parents.

Schools, with their middle-class assumptions, also have a tendency to alienate poor parents. One of the best methods for dealing with this problem has been developed by Dr. James Comer. The Comer process helps teachers understand the subtle messages they unintentionally send parents, and assists with strategies to overcome these problems. The result is a much happier and more enthusiastic parent community.

Schools can also signal a welcome message by providing space for a parent center in each school building, and if resources permit, employ a home-school co-ordinator to keep in regular contact with parents concerning their need to stay involved with their child's education.

Parents are a child's first teachers. In the short run, we need a national effort to educate parents about the importance of their role and to empower them with the knowledge and skills required to enter into that role. In the long run, we need to ensure that children leave our high schools with those values that will enable them to be productive and supportive parents. That message can start in our classrooms.

VIII. Preparing Staff for New Roles

Research findings strongly support the view that school systems cannot be effective in today's conditions unless:

- Superintendents implement leadership training programs, to strengthen the capacity of existing principals and to provide opportunities for those who aspire to be principals;
- Principals stay current on educational issues, trends, and practices, and simultaneously provide leadership in administrative and instructional matters;
- Teachers are up-to-date on both subject-matter content and methods of instructional delivery.

In traditional systems, training and staff development programs can often be characterized as one-shot information dissemination sessions. Information is usually delivered in lectures to large audiences, who are then expected individually to apply in the classroom what they have learned in the lectures.

But research on coaching techniques suggests that this is one of the feeblest methods of imparting new techniques. Effective individual or institutional behavioral change is unlikely unless there are repeated opportunities for subjects to reinforce the new techniques and strategies, by monitored practice, and by knowledgeable criticisms of ongoing performance from trained observers. The recent proliferation of the peer coaching model, in which peers observe and critique one another in the field, is also a useful vehicle, to be taken up and implemented by the creative administrator.

Really worthwhile staff development programs will not put dozens of people with varying needs into a large lecture hall and expect that this alone will produce satisfactory results. Programs must be adapted to the specific needs of the participants, and should focus on those staff-identified priorities that are consistent with the system's goals and plan.

There are five key components of effective training programs that can form the infrastructure of staff development:

- Readiness. The administrator should avoid any tendency to mandate training. Staffs should participate in training experiences they perceive as relevant to their professional lives. In this way, training should evolve naturally from a school's plan, and from the staff's motivation to find the best ways to improve student outcomes;
- Preparation. Staff members who are asked to develop and co-ordinate effective training programs must be given time and resources to ensure that the program will be adequate and relevant;
- Training. Training sessions themselves should be active and experience-based. All current research in this area indicates that merely disseminating 'cold' information is of limited effectiveness. Hands-on, practical, and practitioner-based models prove far more efficacious, particularly if they are followed up by peer coaching sessions;
- Implementation. Implementation should include peer coaching options. Individuals must work with fellow-practitioners to explore how well strategies and methods are being applied in the field. Ongoing evaluations of training methods should also be a key part of the process;
- Modification. No training program should be sacrosanct or immune from revision. Like the operation of the schools and the delivery of curriculum, training programs should be continually honed and polished, and reconceived if this seems appropriate. We should be suspicious of any training program that is not modified periodically.

IX. Staff Development for Principals

Most principals were socialized to manage a school that functioned in a relatively centralized school system. Policy directives were forged in central office, and principals were then charged with the responsibility for implementing them. Teachers and other school-based staff were managed to ensure that they complied with policies and practices handed down from on high. The incentives for compliance with directives were stronger than the incentives to improve student outcomes.

> **KEY POINT:** *Where would our major corporations be if they treated middle management in the same apathetic way that public schools have treated their principals? Principals are indeed the key to success, and have to be nurtured and developed to carry forth the school system's mission.*

This management philosophy and the corresponding management style ought now to be considered defunct. Principals should be expected to manage a decision-making process in which they are participants, rather than the sole conveyors of instructions from the bridge. Principals should now be team-builders and catalysts for creative energy.

Principals need high-caliber diagnostic skills. They ought to find ways of ensuring that all school staff employ the most suitable and most effective strategies, matched to specific student needs. Principals also need to compare the achievement rates of their students by disaggregating data frequently, and if they find disparities in performance, develop an instructional action plan to eliminate them.

Although the need for these skills should be clear, most educational administrators still have little or no opportunity to receive meaningful training in these areas. Prospective administrators are taught how to schedule and manage their time, how to evaluate staff, and how to keep track of the varied policies of central office. They are rarely taught the analytical skills required for diagnosing a program's strengths and weaknesses, understanding data, and making trade-offs among competing programs.

Furthermore, building principals have not been expected to be critical of their own programs. They have been viewed as custodians of the central office's program. They have been evaluated and rewarded on the extent to which they implemented central office mandates, not on the extent to which they improved or developed their own programs on their own initiatives. In short, the system has manifested all the classic hallmarks of bureaucracy.

> **KEY POINT:** *Everyone involved in staff development and training should understand that all principals are not the same: they do not have the same strengths or the same weaknesses. Generally, it is unwise to conceive of 'training' in too broad or generic a fashion, tacitly seeking programs which will meet the needs of all principals. It is doubtful if many such programs exist.*

The recognition that specialized training must be supplied to school administrators has to be matched by the system's commitments to provide that training. Unfortunately, most administrative training programs in schools of education are not relevant to the present needs of principals. An occasional course in a nearby university, or an infrequent guest speaker, will not suffice. Consequently, local school districts must perforce assume the responsibility for improving school-level administration. The university can send candidates with a well-rounded preparation for the job, but refinement, adjustment to current conditions, and continued growth must be addressed at the local level. The superintendent is responsible for creating the appropriate learning opportunities for principals. In most cases this has been a neglected area.

Where would our major corporations be if they treated middle management in the same apathetic way that public schools have treated their principals? Principals are indeed the key to success, and have to be nurtured and developed to carry forth the school system's mission.

Training programs for today's principals should:

- Be long-term and involve monthly contacts;
- Focus on what works, and how to make it work;
- Be planned in part by principals themselves;
- Reinforce the goals and mission of the school system.

Seminars and workshops should feature experts in educational management and instructional leadership who can share their conclusions about current educational reforms and can offer strategies for principals to adopt, to bring about positive changes.

Emphasis should be placed on implementing and evaluating specific school-based plans using criterion-referenced testing or other assessment procedures as tools for instructional management. Training programs should also be provided to correct individual weaknesses as identified in the annual evaluation of principals. Each year the training should culminate in an annual summer institute—an intensive retreat devoted to reviewing the previous year's program, selecting a theme for the coming year's training activities, and planning for the future.

During the school year following the summer retreat, there should be regular meetings where principals can address follow-up issues related to the main theme developed at the retreat. The best format for such meetings is to have a speaker for an hour or so, followed by principals meeting in small groups to discuss the speaker's message, followed by a question-and-answer period between speaker and principals.

Everyone involved in staff development and training should understand that all principals are not the same: they do not have the same strengths or the same weaknesses. Generally, it is unwise to conceive of 'training' in too broad or generic a fashion, tacitly seeking programs which will meet the needs of all principals. It is doubtful if many such programs exist.

If we are serious about upgrading the capacity of principals, we need to provide special training to remedy the special deficiencies of some principals. To help provide this training, we can draw upon the expertise of principals whose strengths lie precisely in the areas concerned. The evaluation of principals should be tied to an individual growth plan, developed by the principals and their supervisors.

X. Staff Development for Those Who Aspire to be Principals

One of the sad contributing factors to declining morale in our public schools has been that many employees have, not without reason, seen the system as closed, with few opportunities for advancement.

Although the training of existing principals is important, the long-term health and success of the public school system depends on the quality of future principals. It is therefore advisable that the system invest time and resources in the identification and training of its future leaders. A training program for future principals should be open to all school employees, teachers, instructional supervisors, and vice-principals. There should be a visible, open, career ladder program for those who would like to qualify for principals' jobs.

Teachers and other system staff who choose to take part in a pre-leadership training program after school hours should be exposed to an intense series of lectures, seminars, and written and oral assessment, that details the requirements of principalship and provides information on recent research and reform. Applicants who can demonstrate the ability to reach logical conclusions, to make high-quality decisions, to identify educational needs and to set priorities should move on to a series of more in-depth administrative training activities.

XI. Staff Development for Teachers

There is a pressing need for teachers to be helped to digest new information coming from the world of research and new practices developed by their peers. The single greatest obstacle to this form of staff development is the scarcity of time in which to provide it. The traditional approach of bringing in outside experts to meet with teachers for half a day three times a year, or meeting for an hour or so at the end of a school day, is not effective. But—many argue—the school day is already filled up with other tasks.

As schools undergo restructuring, they must re-arrange the school day to provide meaningful opportunities for staff development. Instead of the wholesale workshop approach, where teachers arrive *en masse* for a one-shot session, without regard to their particular areas or problems, staff development must be provided when and as needed, and, most preferably, from within the school building. For instance, in a school system where there is a new policy to expose more students to algebra, math teachers in each middle school can be trained as staff developers to provide ongoing assistance to their colleagues. Such assistance ranges from state-of-the-art instructional techniques to exposing weaknesses in classroom instruction. Of course, the daily teaching schedule has to be changed to provide the in-house mathematics staff developer with the time required to meet with and observe their colleagues. Can this extra time be found?

XII. Finding Time for Staff Development and Instruction

Virtually all schools in America use their time in the same way. In elementary schools, classroom teachers are required to be in front of students for almost the entire day. It is extremely difficult to make time for them to develop and polish their lessons, to attend professional development sessions, or to meet and plan with their colleagues.

In the secondary school, the major problem is the way time is used for instructional purposes. Students are required to take six to eight periods of instruction a day for about 50 minutes per subject. This allocation of time almost requires that lectures be the dominant instructional delivery system, that knowledge gets broken into small, digestible pieces, and that meaningful discussion, analysis, and debate are difficult to generate.

Many people have proposed that the problem of time shortage be tackled by lengthening the school day and the school year. However, few school systems are doing anything about this, and we cannot expect any such increases in total schooling time, desirable though they may be, to become the norm within the next few years. However, we need not wait. There are ways in which the present ration of time can be used more effectively. To accomplish this, educators will be required to view time as a flexible, redeployable resource, and not to restrict its use in ways dictated by habit or custom.

XIII. Changing the Elementary School Day

At first glance, the school day appears to be full. Little time appears available for new activities, and teachers surveyed always say that one of their biggest problems is lack of planning time. This perception is accurate only if one refuses to challenge tradition by rethinking how the entire school day is used.

If the status quo is no longer set in stone, then other options open up. For example, a typical elementary school day is seven and a half hours for teachers and six hours for students. During the day, classroom teachers usually have about two and a quarter hours (including about 30 minutes for lunch) during which they are not responsible for children. However, the two hours and 15 minutes consist of about 15 minutes before the students arrive, 30 minutes for lunch, 30 minutes in the middle of the day, and an hour or so at the end of the day. This time is fragmented and therefore not available for intensive staff development, planning, or other activities which could enhance instruction.

Challenging the current use of time and traditional staff roles can uncover better ways of utilizing the available time. Consider, for example, a revision of the elementary school day in which all non-classroom staff function to support the activities of the classroom teacher. Could such an arrangement provide classroom teachers with sufficient time for staff development, planning, and meaningful student involvement?

Although schedules will vary by the size and staffing configuration of the school, there are creative ways that staff and time can be used to increase direct instructional time for students and provide time for teacher staff development and planning. The following illustration is based on a school which has 450 students, 16 classroom teachers, one principal, one vice principal, one physical education teacher, one music teacher, one guidance counselor, one reading resource teacher, one media specialist, one computer aide, two classroom aides and four parents who are paid to monitor lunch and recess activities. Rather than using these staff and time in a traditional manner, principals might consider the following in which both the use of time and staff are changed. The following illustration is not meant to be copied as is. Rather, it is an example of one way in which staff time and roles can be adjusted to maximize student learning and, just as importantly, to provide more planning and staff development time for classroom teachers during the school day. The example is based on the following assumptions:

- All adults in the school building are available to provide direct instructional services;
- All core courses are taught by classroom teachers in the morning;
- All non-core course staff (music, art, foreign language, media, and physical education teachers) assist classroom teachers for a total of two and a quarter hours in the mornings in reading and/or mathematics, making it possible to provide individualized or small group instruction;
- A combination of non-classroom teachers, aides, administrators, and parents who are paid to do so, monitor lunch and recess;
- All non-core courses are taught after lunch.

Given these assumptions, the following schedule could be adopted. The net effect of the schedule change is reflected in the 12:45–3:00 P.M. time slot now available for staff development and other purposes.

Time	Function
7:30–8:00	Teachers and students arrive
8:00–9:30	Language arts (reading, writing, and spelling): one half of the non-classroom teachers assist in the classrooms language arts

Time	Function
	instruction (**Non-classroom teachers have one hour of planning time between 8:00 and 11:15; the balance of their time is used for helping classroom teachers**
9:30–10:30	Mathematics: one half of the non-classroom teachers assist the classroom teachers
10:30–11:15	Science, social studies, health (rotated, daily, weekly, or quarterly)
11:15–12:15	Lunch: students receive thirty minutes for lunch with the balance for recess
11:15–12:15	Non-classroom teachers eat lunch for thirty minutes and monitor recess or lunch for thirty minutes
11:15–11:45	Classroom teachers eat lunch
11:45–12:45	**Classroom teachers provide remedial services to small groups of students with special needs. (These students miss recess).**
12:15–2:00	Students in physical education, art, music, media, computer labs, foreign language, and special project rooms. One day per week teachers at a given grade level are responsible for staffing the special project rooms assisting non-classroom teachers (for example, on Monday, all first grade teachers assist, on Tuesday second grade teachers, and so on). The two aides also assist the physical education and music teacher since they have somewhat larger classes than usual.
12:45–3:00	**For four days per week classroom teachers have a block of two hours and fifteen minutes for staff development, planning, or student mentoring. On the fifth day, one grade level's teachers cover the special project room.**
2:00–3:00	Students and teachers dismissed

This type of schedule illustrates the following three important lessons:

- First, significant changes can be made within the existing school day to provide more instructional time for students through the redefinition and redeployment of staff roles and time.
- Second, these changes can be made without extending the school day or year, or increasing overall costs.
- Third, it is possible to create more co-operative teaching and learning environments.

Nothing within an institutional structure occurs in isolation. Changes made in role delineations and staff development will inevitably affect all other aspects of school operations. New positions and duties, for example, will necessitate that administrators be allowed to eliminate outmoded or counterproductive ones. This planned obsolescence should be integrated into the change process. Similarly, finding time and financial resources for effective training programs with peer coaching components will necessitate that resources be reallocated from other aspects of school operations. The balancing or juggling act demanded of administrators can be a prime source of both confusion and stress, two fundamental realities that the new age administrator must confront and attempt to be pro-active about.

> **KEY POINT:** *The new scheduling options require that administrators and their staffs approach the use of time through a new paradigm, a paradigm that allows for diversity, program-specific choice, and redeployment of staff.*

XIV. Changing the Secondary School Day

Secondary school students should be exposed to an instructional delivery system which encourages discussion, debate, and analysis of problems and events. The present mode of delivery, within a series of 55-minute classroom periods, does not encourage such activities.

Re-organizing the secondary school day can be accomplished in a number of ways.

These changes require strong will and strong leadership in that they require teachers to teach differently, to encourage enquiry and experimentation. Fortunately, workable models for alternative allocations of time in the secondary schools have been developed and effectively implemented. Here are a few examples of some of the most successful methods:

a. The Copernican Model: This addresses the need for more extended time devoted to core subjects. The Copernican model compacts major courses such as English, social studies, science, and mathematics into half- or full-day sessions conducted over shorter periods of the year. For example, instead of students taking an hour a day of English for a full year for one credit, they may take a quarter's worth of English by being enrolled for a full day for two or three weeks. The depth of the model compensates for its inherant limitations. This model is cited by Sizer's Coalition for Essential Schools and other restructuring initiatives, based on the proposition that depth, rather than mere breadth, is desirable for effective delivery of a core curriculum.

b. Modified Block Scheduling: This allows schools to block core subjects such as English and Social Studies into extended periods. Two teachers might be assigned a cohort of 30 students in these two subjects; the students can then be configured in whichever way the two teachers see as most effective. If an extended lecture is considered appropriate, the full complement of 60 can be assembled as a full group. If separate sessions are required, then students can stay for a full two hours with either teacher. Co-operative learning cohorts can be assembled for some fraction of the period, and then larger cohorts can be re-assembled for full- or partial group processing and debriefing.

c. Modular Scheduling: This embodies a college-type scheduling matrix, in which short and long periods can be balanced. The scheduler can configure time in such a way that classes meet for extended periods only once or twice a week, instead of five times. The modular schedule allows for creative use of time in such options as mentoring, tutorials, and activity and class planning sessions. At present, this model is mostly used in private and parochial schools where the student populations are smaller and more homogeneous.

School size remains an important issue, which should not escape attention because it cannot be changed overnight. Most urban schools are far too big. The Conant model was created to ensure economies of scale, but as most districts implemented these economies, they did so at the expense of one of Conant's most important recommendations: the small school-within-a-school. Our failure to create intimate learning environments within our large schools has contributed to the deterioration of many of these schools. Administrators, particularly in the largest high schools, should look seriously at the feasibility of creating schools-within-schools.

The new scheduling options require that administrators and their staffs approach the use of time through a new paradigm, a paradigm that allows for diversity, program-specific choice, and redeployment of staff.

Current models of secondary school scheduling are typically rooted in an industrial age notion that bureaucratic streamlining and consistency should take precedence over creativity, divergence, and individualization. The creative secondary school administrator, like his or her elementary school counterpart, ought to begin to use the time available during the school day to allow for site-based training and staff development.

Chapter One: Further Reading

American Association of School Administrators. 1988. *Challenges For School Leaders.* Arlington, Va: American Association of School Administrators.

Benis, W., and B. Namus. 1985. *Leaders: Their Strategies for Taking Charge.* New York: Harper and Row.

Boyer, Ernest L. 1991. *Ready to Learn.* Princeton: Princeton University Press.

Cohen, Deborah L. 1990. Parents and Partners: Helping Families Build a Foundation for Learning. *Education Week,* May 9.

Comer, James. 1980. *School Power: Implications of an International Project.* New York: Free Press.

Edelman, Marian Wright. 1987. *Families in Peril: An Agenda for Social Change.* Cambridge, Ma: Harvard University Press.

Edelman, Marian Wright. 1990. *S.O.S. America! A Children's Defense Budget.* Washington, D.C.: Children's Defense Fund.

Goodlad, John, et. al. *The Moral Dimensions of Teaching.* San Francisco: Jossey-Bass.

Grady, Marilyn L., and Miles T. Bryant. 1991. School Board Presidents Tell Why Their Superintendents Fail. *The Executive Educator,* May.

Graham, Patricia Albjerg. 1992. *Sustain Our Schools.* New York: Hill and Wang.

Hoyle, J., F. English, and B. Steffy. 1985. *Skills for Successful School Leaders.* Arlington, Va: American Association of School Administrators.

Kearns, David T., and Denis P. Doyle. 1988. *Winning the Brain Race: A Bold Plan to Make Our Schools Competitive.* San Francisco: ICS Press.

Konnert, M. William. 1990. *The Superintendency in the Nineties: What Superintendents and Board Members Need to Know.* Lancaster, Pa: Technomic.

Murnane, Richard J. 1988. Education and Productivity of the Work Force: Looking Ahead. in Robert E. Litan, Robert Z. Lawrence, and Charles L. Schultze, eds., *American Living Standards: Threats and Challenges.* Washington, D.C.: Brookings Institution.

National Association of Secondary School Principals. 1985. *Performance-Based Preparation of Principals.* Reston, Va.

Olmstead, Patricia P., and David P. Weikart, eds., 1989. *How Nations Serve Young Children: Profiles of Child Care and Education in 14 Countries.* Ypsilanti: The High Scope Press.

Peters, Tom, and N. Austin. 1985. *A Passion For Excellence.* New York: Random House.

Shannon, Thomas A. 1990. The Educational Administration Professor. *Vital Speeches of the Day.* October 15, p. 26.

Shannon, Thomas A. 1991. Board Training: A Lesson From Richmond. *School Board News,* July 23, p. 2.

Sizer, Theodore R. 1992. *Horace's School.* Boston: Houghton Mifflin.

Snyder, Karolyn J., and Robert H. Anderson. 1986. *Managing Productive Schools: Toward An Ecology.* Orlando: Academic Press.

Snyder, Karolyn J., and Robert H. Anderson. 1990. Tenure of Superintendents. *Education Week,* November 14.

Stevenson, Harold, and James W. Style. 1992. *The Learning Gap.* New York: Summit.

Timpane, Michael P., and Laurie Miller McNeill. 1991. *Business Impact on Education and Child Development.* New York: Committee for Economic Development.

CHAPTER TWO

SETTING THE STAGE WITH EFFECTIVE POLICIES AND PRACTICES

The perfect bureaucrat everywhere is the man who manages to make no decisions and escape all responsibility.

Brooks Atkinson

ISSUES

Policies that support change
Practices that support change
Committing staff to change
Assuring implementation of policies and practices

I. Educational Policies that Support Change

One of the most ignored but potentially most useful documents in a school system is its official policy manual. The policies in these manuals should reflect the philosophies and programmatic objectives of boards of education and superintendents. These policies should be designed to send clear signals to all staff and members of the community that all that is done in the school system should be directed to providing the highest quality education to all students. However, policy manuals are often not viewed as useful tools in the school improvement process. Typically, school system policy manuals are:

- Familiar to very few staff in central office and even fewer in the schools are likely to be aware of their existence. Rather than guiding practice, the policies are typically used only as a means of justifying an action;
- Seriously out of date and need to be revisited;
- Virtually silent about the need to provide quality education for all students with a special emphasis on the performance of minority students.

It is recommended that all superintendents revisit their policy manuals to ensure that existing policies support and do not hinder school improvement activities. Here is a list of recommendations arising from the effective schools research that can be used to craft a set of policies to support school improvement programs.

Recommendation 1: *Develop a policy statement that conveys the school system mission statement to the public and to all staff.*

This policy should require:

- that the system and each school be responsible for meeting the educational needs of every child and that special attention be paid to ensuring that all groups of students, particularly those based on race and gender, participate equally in courses and programs. The policy should make it clear that where students show evidence of not learning at grade level, the schools must be responsible for modifying the content and/or delivery of instruction to maximize the students' chances of learning at appropriate levels. It is not sufficient to imply that equal educational *opportunities* are the goal. Rather, the goal should be equal educational *outcomes*.

The following two mission statements are provided as guides for the development of others.

> The school system believes that all children can master the system's essential curriculum and that it is the responsibility of the system to modify and adjust its instructional program to ensure such performance. The system further believes that such modification and adjustment will lead to the elimination of disparities in performance by race and gender.

or

> To assure that all students become responsible citizens, effective participants in our economy, and able to adapt to the rapidly

CHAPTER 2 Setting the Stage with Effective Policies and Practices

changing world through the acquisition and application of skills and knowledge.

Recommendation 2. *Develop policies and procedures that demonstrate the long-term commitment of the school board, superintendent, and other administrative staff, to improved student performance outcomes.*

These policies should require that:

- Instructional practices be designed to improve the performance of all students and acknowledge that disparities in outcomes by race, socio-economic status, and gender are unacceptable. These policies should further state that in those cases where improvement does not occur, it is the responsibility of the system, the principals, and the teachers to make appropriate adjustments in the delivery and/or content of instruction and not to assume that such differences are a consequence of the backgrounds of students;
- A community advisory committee be established to provide a mechanism for monitoring the progress of the school system in improving student achievement;
- The roles of central office instructional staff focus on keeping principals and teachers informed of the most effective instructional practices and responding to school staff needs as defined by those school staffs;
- A school calendar be developed including time for teacher training and school improvement meetings. The policy should emphasize that such staff development be tailored to the needs of a given school's staff and that the traditional cookie-cutter approach to staff development is not acceptable;
- All new curriculum and instructional materials be reviewed for their multi-cultural context, sex and race fairness, and appropriateness for students representing a broad range of abilities.

Recommendation 3: *Develop policies that focus on low achieving students.*

These policies should require that:

- The highest priority of the school system be to ensure that all children achieve subject mastery in all academic areas. In those cases where such achievement does not occur, it is the responsibility of the system, the principals, and the teachers to make appropriate adjustments in

the delivery and/or content of instruction and not to assume that such differences are a consequence of the backgrounds and/or characteristics of students;
- Teachers utilize a wide variety of instructional strategies. In those cases where students are not achieving, it should be the responsibility of the teachers and principals to make appropriate adjustments in the delivery and/or content of instruction;
- Principals be responsible for comparing the academic performance of their students by race, gender, and socio-economic status on an annual basis. If there are any disparities in performance, principals must develop an instructional action plan to ameliorate such disparities and to facilitate the training of their staff in the implementation of the plan. Principals must meaningfully involve their professional staff in the development of such plans;
- The superintendent annually review the academic performance at each school and, if there are disparities in performance by students of different income levels, sexes and races, or by other identifiable groups, to require building principals to develop appropriate action plans to remedy the discrepancies;
- Principals identify students who need to improve their achievement and must assume responsibility for such remediation. Remediation should be viewed as short-term interventions designed to move all students to a point where they can, at the very least, perform grade-level work;
- Principals and teachers continually try new, proven and creative ways of educating students;
- Principals be expected to play the major instructional role in their school. The system must, however, recognize its responsibility to provide relevant and sufficient training to principals to enable them to play such roles;
- All children receive the maximum amount of direct instructional time during the school day and anything that interferes with direct instructional time should be minimized;
- Performance evaluations of principals be linked to their efforts to create instructional environments that support educational improvement and student performance outcomes in their schools;
- Performance evaluations of teachers be linked to those instructional practices which are most likely to result in high student achievement;

CHAPTER 2 Setting the Stage with Effective Policies and Practices

- Teachers be required to move as many children as possible from one level of instructional grouping to another and principals should periodically monitor this activity. The policy should require the principal to periodically review the student instructional grouping in each class. Racially identifiable grouping should not be permitted. Long-term instructional grouping should be minimized. Short-term developmental reading or skill level grouping should be encouraged.

Recommendation 4: *Develop policies and procedures related to grouping and the use of instructional time.*

> **KEY POINT:** *The odious practice of grouping children by ability using standardized norm-referenced tests as the criteria should be eliminated and replaced by performance grouping. Such performance should be assessed by more relevant instruments such as criterion-referenced tests which would result in grouping students separately in each discipline, rather than in whole-class ability groupings. When students are assigned to lower-level performance groups, they should not be exposed to lower-level curriculum and standards. Instead the same rigorous rules and standards that apply to the highest performing groups should apply to all, with the understanding that some may take longer than others to master the curriculum. A measure of accountability for the principals and classroom teachers should include the number of students who legitimately progress from lower to higher groups during the course of the year. The constant focus should be to stretch children to higher levels of performance.*

A key to improving educational effectiveness is to maximize the amount of time in which students are actively engaged in relevant learning experiences. A variety of strategies and instructional approaches can be used to maximize learning time, including short-lived skill groupings and whole-class instruction. We have relied far too heavily on long-term ability and achievement-level grouping which results in almost all students not receiving direct instruction for a significant part of the instructional period. Appropriate student grouping policies should require that:

- Whenever homogeneous grouping does occur, it is short-term and every effort is made by principals and teachers to move children from one level of instruction to another. *Long-term membership in low-level groups or classes is not acceptable;*
- Scheduling and grouping practices ensure that the maximum feasible amount of direct instruction is provided to students;
- Extra time be provided for those students who fall behind. Such time could be provided during school hours, after school, during the summer, and at home;
- Wherever feasible, children be exposed to heterogeneous groups incorporating strategies such as co-operative learning, peer tutoring, mentoring, or independent study—strategies that can benefit all students;
- Schools be responsible for increasing the number of students in higher-level performance groups, classes, and programs, and for decreasing the number of students in lower-level performance groups, classes, and programs;
- Student placement be evaluated continuously during the year and that, using appropriate evaluation data, students are moved to higher levels of learning;
- Appropriate and adequate teaching resources be provided to students at all academic levels;
- Meaningful instruction continues until the end of a school year. If it is not possible to begin a new book or unit, alternative instructional activities and groupings (not busy work) should be utilized. This additional work should be designed to qualify students to be given higher levels of instructional material in the next school year;
- Procedures be developed to assist schools to involve the home in reinforcing student achievement in reading;
- Teachers utilize, at all times, a wide variety of instructional strategies. In those cases where students are not achieving on grade level, it is the responsibility of the teachers and principals to make appropriate adjustments in the delivery and/or content of instruction, and not to assume that such achievement is a consequence of the backgrounds of students.

The odious practice of grouping children by ability using standardized norm-referenced tests as the criteria should be eliminated and replaced by performance grouping. Such performance should be assessed by more relevant instruments such as criterion referenced tests which would result in grouping students separately in each discipline, rather than in whole-class ability groupings. When students are assigned to lower-level performance groups, they should not be exposed to lower-level curriculum and standards. Instead the same rigorous rules and standards that apply to the highest performing groups should apply to all, with the understanding that some may take longer than others to master the curriculum. A measure of accountability for the principals and classroom teachers should include the number of students who legitimately progress from lower to higher groups during the course of the year. The constant focus should be to stretch children to higher levels of performance.

Recommendation 5: *Develop policies and procedures related to monitoring student achievement outcomes.*

These policies should require that:

- Disaggregated school-based performance and participation data be collected and analyzed by principals and their staffs;
- Each school develop a school improvement plan based upon an analysis of annual school performance and participation data;
- A school improvement co-ordinator be appointed to annually review academic performance at each school and assist building principals and school improvement teams to develop appropriate instructional plans, identify training needs, and implement training;
- School principals and their staffs develop programs tailored to the needs of that staff;
- Principals and supervisors provide meaningful and timely feedback to teachers whenever they conduct performance observations.

Recommendation 6: *Develop policies and procedures related to curriculum, textbooks, and materials.*

These policies should require that:

- All new curriculum and associated materials be reviewed for their multi-cultural content, sex and race fairness, and appropriateness for students representing a broad range of abilities;
- The school system establish a broad-based committee, consisting of school employees and members of the public, to advise the system on the adoption of new textbooks, curriculum and materials. The

committee's task will be to comment on the extent to which the curriculum and materials contain sufficient relevant multi-cultural materials, are race- and gender-fair, and reflect high academic standards.

Recommendation 7. *Develop policies and procedures related to staff development.*

These policies should require that:

- The school system commit itself to providing all necessary staff development. It is not reasonable to increase educational expectations and standards without improving the capacity of staff to meet those expectations and standards;
- Principals designate one teacher in elementary school and one in each core subject area in secondary school to keep abreast of educational practices which are most likely to be effective with students who have traditionally been underachievers. These teachers should be expected to act as lead teachers to the staff in their buildings.

Recommendation 8: *Policies and practices related to student assessments.*

These policies should require that:

- There be an increased focus on using frequent and varied assessments of student progress as the primary means for placing and moving students in instructional groups. These assessments should be viewed as tools of the teachers and not as accountability tools in the broader sense;
- Assessments include the use of criterion-referenced tests, teacher made tests, student projects, writing samples, and the results of teacher team meetings;
- In no case should performance on norm-referenced achievement or ability tests be used as key criteria for placing students in or moving students from one instructional level to another.

Recommendation 9. *Develop policies and procedures related to teacher and principal evaluation.*

These policies should require that:

- As principals and others observe teachers, they focus on the teachers' use of time for direct instruction;
- Principals assess how much teachers contribute to meaningful student

growth during the year as measured by the percentage of students who meet the performance standards;
- The extent to which teachers in a school use effective instructional practices be employed as a criterion in evaluating the performance of principals;
- Student outcomes including performance on criterion-referenced and other performance assessments, the number of students who moved from one instructional group to a higher level group, the number of students on the honor roll or receiving special awards and the extent to which students' performance improved from one year to the next, be used as criteria in evaluating the performance of principals;
- The extent to which principals involve teachers and other staff members in the development of instructional and management strategies, and encourage staff to implement innovative practices without fear of failing, be used as a criterion in evaluating the performance of principals.

Recommendation 10: *Develop policies and procedures to foster parent involvement.*

These policies should require that:

- The principal convene at least three meetings during the year of all parents and school staff for the purpose of describing the school program, outlining grouping philosophies and strategies, including criteria for changing instructional groups, and strategies that parents can use at home for reinforcing what is learned in school. Given the location and personal circumstances of many parents, many of them have difficulty attending such meetings. In these cases, principals should be required to go the extra mile by arranging for the meetings on Saturdays, conducting the meetings in the parents' neighborhood, or using school buses to bring the parents to the school;
- Every teacher be required to meet with every parent at least twice during the year. At those meetings teachers should be prepared to explain to parents the extent to which their children are mastering the appropriate grade-level instruction, the efforts that the school is making to improve or accelerate student progress, and strategies for the parents to use at home to improve their children's school performance. It is important that not all contacts between school staff and parents be negative. Teachers should be encouraged to contact parents by letter or telephone to convey good things about their children's performance and progress.

Recommendation 11: *Develop policies and procedures related to the guidance program.*

These policies should require that:

- Guidance counselors play a pro-active role in identifying students whose interpersonal skills or personal circumstances endanger their academic performance. Once such students are identified, guidance counselors should either provide direct services (such as talking to students and/or parents) or referrals to appropriate agencies;
- Guidance counselors in middle and high schools be responsible for working with students and parents concerning course selection and the relationship between these courses and careers, college, and the military.

II. Educational Practices that Support Change

Although the development and dissemination of appropriate policies are necessary prerequisites for school improvement, their mere existence will not guarantee improvement. The policies must first be *converted* to effective everyday practices. It is the administrator's responsibility to ensure that these practices are in place. This section presents two case studies of ways administrators can use observations to determine whether effective practices are actually being implemented in schools and classrooms. To be able to make sound judgments about the presence or absence of effective practices, however, administrators must know them when they see them. Without such knowledge they are most likely to revert to meaningless bean counting (for example, judging a teacher's performance by whether or not the teacher writes the instructional objective in the top left hand corner of the blackboard).

The primary question that administrators should ask as part of these observations is—Are the classroom teachers, specialists, and guidance counselors performing their jobs in a manner which exposes students to a high-quality and challenging education? This question differs from the ones which are most typically asked, for example, Are teachers using the elements of a good lesson or, are the students well disciplined and paying attention or, are staff following the policies established by the principal or central office?

Identifying Exemplary Practices: Two Case Studies

The remainder of this chapter presents summaries of observations that focussed on two important issues: problems associated with teaching reading in elementary school and difficulties associated with the relatively low enrollment of minority students in higher-level courses. The reading study was conducted to discover why the reading achievement of many elementary school students, particularly minority students, was so poor. The observations were conducted in 15 classrooms, in four different schools, and involved about 450 students. The study focussing on the inadequate enrollment of minority students in upper-level courses was conducted by examining the characteristics of students enrolled in higher-level courses, an analysis of the formal policies governing such enrollments, and an identification of the informal practices that occur in assigning students to these courses.

The major point of these case study summaries is to sensitize the reader to the kinds of questions that should be posed when the focus is on assessing the effectiveness of educational programs. As the case studies unfold, the relationship between policies (real and perceived), existing practices, and what we know works from the world of educational research becomes apparent; as do remedies to correct the situations.

CASE STUDY 1

Identifying the Presence of Effective Elementary School Reading Practices

Summary of the Results of the Examination of the Elementary School Reading Practices

Based on the classroom observations it was concluded that the very grouping practices employed in the schools almost *guaranteed* that black youngsters who begin school with academic deficits will end their careers in a deficit position. The practices

CASE STUDY 1 *continued*

ensure that students are tracked early in their careers and make it virtually impossible for a student to move from one track to another. Students are grouped for reading on the basis of the level of reading book that they are using at the end of a school year. Virtually no other criteria are used. Once a school year begins and students are placed on the basis of the reading book they used the prior year, teachers rarely do any re-grouping during the year. Of the 450 students observed, only 30 were moved to a different reading group at the end of the year. *This surely represents a closed system of the worst type.*

Whether it is official policy or not, the teachers believe that such changing of groups is not or would not be supported by the central office supervisory and/or administrative staff. Combined with the rigidity of the reading grouping is the belief that activities in reading which require students at different ability levels to work with one another should be discouraged. Teachers are apprehensive about engaging in cross-grouping or co-operative learning activities which would cause the mixing of children at different levels. Many examples of what teachers called co-operative learning were occurring but most were either conducted within a single-level reading group or in a subject other than reading. Once again, whether or not this is official written policy or part of the culture, the effects are invidious. Children are tracked early, are not moved to higher groupings, and are not exposed to students who are higher achievers. It should be noted that in those classes where several black children were in attendance, those black children were invariably in the lower groupings. And because of these continuing practices, they are likely to remain in those low level groups.

A paradox emerged in discussions with and observations of the teachers. It is clear that the one thing that teachers would like to have more of is time for instruction. However, the system's policy (or, in this case folklore, which tends to have the same effect as official policy) is that if a group completes a book

CASE STUDY 1 *continued*

and in the teacher's opinion there is not sufficient time to complete at least a half of the next book before the end of the school year, then a new book cannot be started. An effect of this policy is that substantial numbers of students spend the last month or two of the school year doing busy work or worksheets rather than learning those things for which they are later to be tested. One group that was observed completed its last book in mid-April and would spend the last seven weeks of school in much less productive activities. All of this while school systems throughout the nation struggle to find ways of extending the school day and the school year!

In practice, a school system's reading curriculum is its textbook. This may be because someone believes that the textbook represents what ought to be taught in reading. However, not many reading experts would agree that any single text is broad enough to cover the wide range of skills and competencies that need to be taught. Teachers report that if they have special instructional problems, such as students who may be weak in phonics, they have few if any non-textbook resources at their command. They are textbook-dependent. It is likely that the reliance on the textbook provides teachers with a management tool for creating and maintaining the groups of students.

Recommendations

Although the above account depicts a situation where children are grouped in a way which impedes their academic progress, it is neither feasible nor desirable to dismantle the present system of tracking and ability grouping immediately. Such a change requires careful forethought and intensive staff development. Accordingly, we recommend that a set of short-term strategies be adopted which will increase student movement vertically from one level instructional group to another during the year, as longer-term grouping policies and strategies are developed. The possible short-term strategies are:

CASE STUDY 1 *continued*

- The development and dissemination to teachers of a policy which makes it clear that they should do everything within their means to move as many children as possible from one level of instructional grouping to another;
- The required evaluation of student placement three times during the year and, based on the evaluation, moving students from one group to another;
- The establishment of an accountability system that focusses on upward placement as one outcome measure;
- The identification of students who, with special attention such as peer tutoring, mentoring, co-operative learning, or independent study, could possibly move from one level group to another. Teachers, however, must be trained in these procedures;
- The provision to teachers of a wide range of reading-instructional resources that they can use for students at all levels of the reading spectrum;
- The development of instructional policies which do not halt meaningful instruction toward the end of a school year just because a particular textbook is completed. It may be that if it is not possible to begin a new book, co-operative learning or other cross-grouping activities can be utilized.

KEY POINT: *The practices described above are not for the benefit of underachieving minority students alone. The practices have been found to be successful for all students since they are designed to allow students to proceed as far as possible without the artificial ceilings that many of our grouping practices imply.*

CHAPTER 2 Setting the Stage with Effective Policies and Practices

CASE STUDY 2

Analyzing Minority Enrollment in Higher-Level Classes

An analysis of the characteristics of students who were enrolled in higher-level classes in middle and high schools disclosed that relatively few minority students were enrolled. Discussions with teachers, principals, and central office personnel revealed that they believed that this was the case because most minority students were unprepared to do the higher-level work. Assuming that they were correct, these respondents seemed to ignore the fact that *they* were somehow responsible for the students not being able to compete in the higher level classrooms.

As a means of improving our understanding of why more minority students did not move on to higher-level classes, a separate study was conducted to focus on how students were assigned to pre-algebra classes in the seventh grade. Pre-algebra was selected because it is the 'gatekeeper' course to algebra and to other advanced-level courses that students have to complete to have a chance to be accepted at a good college or to qualify for a good job directly from high school. The policy of the school system was to admit students to pre-algebra based on the recommendation of their sixth-grade mathematics teacher and the seventh-grade guidance counselor. Initial discussion with teachers and guidance couselors elicited the statement that the assignment of students to pre-algebra was based on criteria designed to identify the "strongest" mathematics students. This notion of "strongest" is a bit strange if one assumes that the course should be available to any student who may be able to benefit from it.

As discussions continued, it became clear that an elitist attitude permeated the ranks of the middle school guidance counselors (and through their acquiescence, the principals) who believed that the pre-algebra courses were available for "the best and the brightest". To complete the cycle, two criteria were established which guaranteed that only a few students would

CASE STUDY 2 *continued*

enter the courses. First, norm-referenced achievement test scores that the students took in the fall of their fifth grade were used to determine whether or not the student leaving the sixth grade should go into pre-algebra. Imagine, two-year-old test scores on a test which did not even measure the prerequisite skills needed to succeed in algebra!

The second criterion was the unwritten requirement that a student had to achieve an A or high B in sixth-grade mathematics to be recommended for pre-algebra. Given many of the grouping problems cited earlier, and the difficulties in providing an effective education to many minority students, it was not surprising to find that only a small percentage of students, including very few minority students, were able to meet these criteria.

Given our commitment to improving the education of minority students, and given the assumption that as many children as possible should be exposed to higher-level instruction in higher-level courses, new criteria were developed and incorporated in a formal school system policy. The new policy had two parts. The first addressed the requirements for entrance into pre-algebra. Students had to meet two criteria. They had to score at least 70 percent on an end of the sixth grade mathematics criterion-referenced test, and achieve a "C" or better on their report card in sixth-grade mathematics. If they met these requirements, they were automatically enrolled in pre-algebra in the seventh grade. No additional criteria had to be satisfied.

The second part of the policy was critical. It was feared that if the only thing that happened was an increased enrollment in pre-algebra while teachers still believed that the course was for the best and the brightest, many students would still fail, thus reinforcing the teachers original false notions. Accordingly, middle schools were required to modify the delivery of their pre-algebra courses to accommodate the particular learning styles of their 'new' and somewhat non-traditional students. They could change everything except the standards of the course. Those standards had to remain *equally high for all students*. In response to these new freedoms some schools

CASE STUDY 2 *continued*

doubled the length of the pre-algebra period for some students, others held Saturday classes, while others used computers and peer coaching extensively.

Concurrent with the issuance of the new policy for middle schools, middle-school mathematics teachers were provided with extensive staff development and a special mathematics resource teacher was trained in each school. It is anticipated that the net effects of the policy and the new practices will triple the number of students enrolled in pre-algebra and result in a distribution of grades similar to the distribution that characterized the more elitist pre-algebra student body of the past.

Implications

Based on the experiences gained in this case study, to encourage higher enrollment and success in higher-level courses, the following practices were immediately implemented:

A. Criteria for placing students in courses will be performance based. For example, a student who receives a C or better in the sixth grade in mathematics should be enrolled in the highest-level mathematics class in the seventh grade, or, a seventh-grade student receiving a C or better in seventh grade English, should be enrolled in the highest-level eighth grade English class. (Participation in talented and gifted classes could be exempted from this practice.) In no case should performance on standardized norm-referenced achievement or ability tests be used as an important factor in placing students.

B. From the sixth grade on, by no later than January, students and their parents should be provided with information about the nature and *levels* of all courses that are available to the students in the next school year, as well as the eligibility criteria for each. Teachers and/or guidance counselors should offer to meet with students and parents to discuss all scheduling options and to clarify the links between level of classes

CASE STUDY 2 *continued*

completed, and likely success in school, college, and career. If the school determines that the child has limited parental counseling with regard to these issues, an appropriate mentor should be assigned the task of guiding the child.

C. For those students who are enrolled in higher-level classes but who, under previous class assignment procedures, would not be in such classes, extra help must be provided to improve their chances of success. This help could be in the form of increasing the length of the courses; conducting special tutorial sessions during the day, evening, or weekends; peer tutoring; or the use of computers as instructional tools.

D. During the year prior to entering middle school and high school, parent meetings will be held to discuss scheduling and course options that are open to students. Parents will be provided with descriptions of all courses and, most importantly, will be made aware of the relationship between the courses that a student completes and his/her career, higher education, military, or other options.

Recommendations

Based on the information described above, it was concluded that a series of steps should be taken to promote long-term restructuring in the secondary schools as it relates to mathematics in particular and other courses more generally. These steps included:

1. Conducting Dialogues on Secondary Restructuring

The first system-wide step in secondary school restructuring requires meetings of groups of secondary principals, teachers and the superintendent for a series of dialogues about how to make secondary school programs more responsive and academically challenging for all students. At the completion of these dialogues, secondary principals and teachers would be

CASE STUDY 2 *continued*

asked to continue discussions of restructuring options at the local level, and begin planning restructuring models appropriate for their students.

2. Developing Secondary Restructuring Models

The second system-wide step toward secondary restructuring is the development of creative restructuring models designed to meet the needs of students in individual schools. Examples of options include:

- Assignment of students to cross-disciplinary teams with support for their social and emotional growth;
- Heterogeneous grouping enhanced with co-operative learning and faculty mentoring support;
- Continuous progress models based upon a continuum of skills or objectives;
- School-within-a-school models;
- Specialty programs based upon student interest.

3. Developing New Mathematics Placement Procedures

The third system-wide step toward secondary restructuring is raising expectations for student achievement in mathematics, making Algebra I an expected course for all students or, as has been recommended by the College Board, geometry. The new mathematics placement procedures make it possible to implement this option.

4. Changing Types of Data Used for Student Placement

A fourth system-wide step in secondary restructuring is to change the types of data used to group students for instruction. The use of group standardized achievement and ability test scores for instructional placement of individual students will be replaced by use of a variety of achievement indicators, including

CASE STUDY 2 *continued*

criterion-referenced test results, projects, writing samples, and student grades in specifically designated courses.

5. Phasing Out Traditional Leveling Practices

A fifth step toward secondary school restructuring is phasing out the traditional leveling practices used in middle and high schools and replacing these procedures with more heterogeneous grouping alternatives. There is ample evidence from research to suggest that long-term homogeneous grouping, particularly the tracking of students within low ability groups, is a major cause of low teacher and student expectations, academic failure, and high dropout rates. Students assigned to low ability groups tend to receive an education which is based upon skills taught in isolation. Moreover, they tend to have less access to a core curriculum which stresses higher-order thinking skills.

Although initial steps toward the elimination of traditional leveling practices may involve simply a reduction in the number of levels, a systems long range goal should be to implement more heterogeneous or flexible grouping procedures which will enable all students to have access to rich and challenging curricula.

KEY POINT: *Merely reducing the number of different ability level groupings is not an end in itself. Rather, students in lower-level groupings should be given instruction that will prepare them for successful participation in higher-level groupings or classes.*

III. Reinforcing Policies and Practices through Concrete Staff Assignments

Establishing appropriate policies and practices is only half the battle. Procedures have to be established to signal to administrative staff that they are expected to monitor the extent to which the superintendent's policies and practices are implemented. Senior staff are given assignments which make this responsibility clear.

The following is an example of an assignment that can be given to regional or area superintendents and other senior staff responsible for representing the superintendent and for monitoring the progress of schools, staff, and students. The memorandum was designed to help maintain a focus on issues important to the superintendent.

Hypothetical School System

Memorandum

To: Area Administrators
From: The Superintendent

Subject: Monitoring current initiatives

There are four issues that I would like you to attend to as soon as possible:

- Assessing the extent to which the time available for instruction is used for direct instruction;
- Describing our most innovative attempts at providing pre-algebra/algebra instruction to the increased numbers of students enrolled in these courses in middle schools;
- Improving our understanding of our high rate of student suspensions and;
- Planning for the possibility of reallocating staff as a means of improving our instructional program.

First, the issue of direct instructional time. As you know, the single most valuable resource that we can control is time. Our experience, as well as recent research, indicates that student achievement is a direct function of the amount of instructional time provided to students. Based on my observations, I believe that too much of the time that is spent in our classrooms does not focus on direct instruction. The use of worksheets, dittos, copying from the board, and so on, does not represent good practice. My initial interest in this area is on reading instruction in the elementary school. I want you to identify three schools in which direct instructional time for reading is maximized and describe, in detail, how such instruction is occurring. Such descriptions should include at least:

- Classroom organization and student grouping;
- Scheduling for reading instruction;
- Strategies for using time most effectively and;
- Technology as a tool for improving reading ability.

I would think that a major criterion for selecting the schools is that reading performance has recently improved or has remained at a high level for several years. The descriptions should be about three pages for each school, should be based on your personal observations, as well as any other information that you deem necessary, and should provide insight into what is happening and how others may adopt the practices.

Second, as we now come to the end of our first year of the new mathematics placement policy, I am interested in identifying those middle schools which have developed sound procedures for meeting the needs of students who would not normally have enrolled in pre-algebra or algebra. Therefore, please identify the two middle schools in your area which have the most innovative practices and describe the nature of their programs in detail. These descriptions should be about three pages in length and should provide the reader with a sense of what is happening and how they can make it happen.

Once completed, and assuming that the descriptions are sufficiently detailed and reflect meaningful attempts at educational improvement, I intend to distribute them to all elementary and middle school principals. Since I would like to distribute the materials before the end of this school year, please provide me with your contributions by no later than April 30th.

Third, I remain disturbed by the large number of high school suspensions that we have for fighting. I have a sense that in order to get a handle on the issue and develop more effective strategies for reducing these suspensions, we must improve our understanding of what is happening. Accordingly, I want you to conduct a number of case studies (about 15 to 20 in number) of suspensions that have occurred in the last month for fighting. As part of these case studies I want you and your staff to interview all relevant school staff, students, and anyone else who is relevant to the issue. I am interested in descriptions of the initial event which triggered the fight, the ways in which staff responded, the movement of the issue from the staff member who initiated it to the person who issued the suspension, alternative strategies which had actually been tried, and so on.

I would also appreciate your professional opinion as to whether or not the suspension was appropriate and, if not, what you would have done differently. Each case study should be approximately three to five pages in length. I want you and your staff to conduct the studies. Be sure to conduct the case studies in several different high schools. I want to see the case studies by April 30th so that I can review the findings and develop and disseminate any new procedures before the end of the school year.

And fourth, as part of our efforts to more effectively deploy central and area office personnel, I want you to ask each principal to meet with his or her staff to discuss staff deployment and to provide me with recommendations for future actions. As you undertake this assignment, think through its implications for every part of central office, not just those divisions which relate more directly to instruction. I am particularly interested in the principals' beliefs about the following:

- Are there any central or area office positions which are supposed to be helpful but, in fact, are not?,
- Are there any central or area office positions that should be

eliminated with the resulting vacancies redistributed to the schools? If so, what are they?
- Can central or area offices be reorganized to (a) provide more effective services and/or (b) result in smaller staffs with the reductions being re-allocated to the schools?

I understand that, faced with requests such as this, staff often hesitate to respond in a forthright manner. It is often difficult to get beyond the fact that we have friends and acquaintances throughout the system and do not want to imply that they may not be doing their jobs. However, in times of scarce resources we must constantly re-assess the way we do business and continue to adjust our organization so as to maximize effectiveness. Accordingly, I would appreciate it if you would meet with your staff and send me any recommendations that you and they believe are relevant.

KEY POINT: *Assignments such as these are designed to achieve three basic purposes. First, to keep all senior staff focused on those issues which the superintendent believes are most important. Second, to ensure that senior staff, and their respective staffs, visit schools regularly and observe the extent to which those activities that are designed to achieve the goals are actually present. Third, to provide a steady flow of information to the superintendent concerning the extent to which progress is being made toward the accomplishing the goals.*

IV. Ensuring Implementation of Policies and Practices

Once appropriate policies and practices are in place, the responsibility of the superintendent and senior administrative staff is to ensure that meaningful change is actually occurring. Administrators must constantly overcome the pressures to focus exclusively on short-term crises and matters of the day and keep their eyes on the bigger picture. Here are two ways that administrators can maintain the big picture focus. First, they can ask a series of questions whose answers will reveal whether or not meaningful change is happening. Superintendents can ask the questions of the leadership in their school system or even of themselves. The answers to these questions will provide a sense of how serious the school improvement effort is being taken in the school system and in each school. The indicators of change that superintendents should search for are described below.

Second, the hypothetical memorandum presented above represents the kinds of assignments that could be given to senior administrators as a means of reinforcing the superintendent's philosophy, goals and priorities.

V. Questions and Indicators: Determining the Extent to Which Meaningful Restructuring Is Occurring

Question 1. Do you allow schools to exercise flexibility in determining how they organize themselves, time, and instruction? In other words, is the locus of control placed at the school rather than the central office level?

Typical Indicators

- Effective schools process serves as a controlling philosophy;
- School-based management has been implemented;
- Central office staff development funds are allocated to the schools;
- Central office edicts on instruction and staffing do not exist;
- Central office staff development serves a brokerage role to find help for schools to address problems that the schools identify.

Question 2. Have you provided all of your staff—principals, administrators, teachers, and others—with training—ongoing training—on what works in education, and ways in which they can make it work in their schools?

Typical Indicators

- Issues and skills-oriented pre-leadership training is in place;
- Internships for intensive pre-leadership training experiences exist;
- Issues and skills oriented leadership training is in place;

- Staff development needs are defined and addressed at the building level;
- Staff development budget is decentralized;
- Staff development is issue oriented.

> **Question 3.** *Have you helped your schools to conduct self-analyses to determine their strengths and weaknesses? Have you helped staff develop the ability to disaggregate data as a means of understanding and evaluating (a) what they are doing and (b) the effects of their programs?*

Typical Indicators

- Outcome data are used to assess student achievement;
- Outcome data are used to develop school improvement plans;
- A system to provide relevant and timely information to school staff is in place;
- Release of system- and school-level data by race and gender is a common practice;
- Audit teams to assess the extent to which change is actually occurring are in place and operating;
- Staff training in the use of outcome data is provided.

> **Question 4.** *Have you developed a core curriculum with clearly identified standards for student performance? Do those standards ensure that all students master skills and knowledge at a satisfactory level? Are there also standards that identify goals for excellence for all?*

Typical Indicators

- System identifies the core components of every course and establishes short and long term indicators of success in mastering the coursework;
- Data are analyzed to compare annual growth rates.

> **Question 5.** *Have you evaluated your grouping and student placement procedures to determine whether or not they accelerate or hinder student participation in a rigorous curriculum? What kinds of students—by race and gender—are in your higher-level performance groups? Is participation in higher-level classes viewed as being 'for the best and the brightest', or is it encouraged as a goal for all students?*

Typical Indicators

- The most rigorous standards apply to all levels of the curriculum;
- Time and resources are used flexibly to ensure that all children will master high-level curricula;
- The number of lower-level courses is minimized with a corresponding increase in student enrollment in higher-level classes;
- There is movement toward more meaningful grouping practices;
- Administrators' goals focus on instructional improvement;
- There is an increased number of students in gateway and higher-level courses;
- There is an increased number of students assigned to higher-level instructional groups.

> **Question 6.** *Have you provided training to teachers to help them modify and deliver instruction to accommodate students individual strengths and needs in both the cognitive and affective domains? Moreover, has staff been trained to use methods that engage students as active rather than passive learners?*

Typical Indicators

- System level training programs in co-operative learning, multicultural education issues, working with at-risk populations, teaching thinking skills, using technology, and grouping strategies are in place;
- There is evidence that teachers are using effective questioning techniques and a variety of instructional strategies;
- There is building-level training to reinforce identified teacher staff development needs.

> **Question 7.** *Do you require the use of assessment instruments which result in appropriate student placement and the capacity to regularly monitor, adjust, and change the level of instruction for students?*

Typical Indicators

- There is a shift toward the use of performance assessments;
- There is a shift toward student/curriculum-centered programs and criterion-referenced testing.

Question 8: *Are you engaging parents and community leaders in an ongoing dialogue to identify their concerns and to solicit their support for school system initiatives?*

Typical Indicators

- Representatives of business and industry are involved in an advisory capacity;
- School/university collaborations are common;
- Ethical citizenship and multicultural task forces serve in an advisory capacity;
- More parents participate in PTA's and school programs.

Question 9. *Have you provided students who need support and guidance with that help? Have you increased students' and their families' access to a wide range of supportive services?*

Typical Indicators

- There are co-operative projects with relevant social agencies to meet the needs of students and their families;
- Guidance counselors are deployed to work closely with students as opposed to doing clerical and administrative work;
- There is an adequate student/counselor ratio;
- There are flexible working schedules for counselors and other school resource positions.

Question 10. *Have you modified your teacher, principal, and administrator evaluation systems to ensure that they include performance criteria that we know are directly related to improved student performance?*

Typical Indicators

- Standards for effective teaching and leadership have been established;
- Teacher and principal evaluations are based on effective practices and student outcomes;
- Student outcome and participation goals for each school have been set;
- Personnel evaluations contain reasonable growth and self-improvement plans;

CHAPTER 2 Setting the Stage with Effective Policies and Practices

- Programs have been established to personalize staff development based on individual needs.

> **KEY POINT:** *Once an assessment is made of the big picture, administrators then can focus on the specific changes that must be made in the content, organization, and delivery of education in their system and schools. In the next chapters the specific pieces of the puzzle that need to be fit together will be reviewed.*

Chapter Two: Further Reading

Haggerson, Nelson L., and Andrea C. Bowman. 1992. *Informing Educational Policy and Practice through Interpretative Inquiry.* Lancaster, Pa: Technomic.

Hall, Gene E., and Shirley M. Hord. 1987. *Change in Schools.* Albany: State University of New York Press.

Hickman, Craig R., and Michael A. Silva. 1984. *Creating Excellence in Managing Corporate Culture, Strategy, and Change in the New Age.* New York: New American Library.

Hill, John C. 1992. *The New American School: Breaking the Mold.* Lancaster, Pa: Technomic.

Fiske, Edward B., Sally Reed, and R. Craig Sautter. 1991. *Smart Schools.* New York: Simon and Schuster.

Kaufman, Roger. 1990. *Strategic Planning in Education: Rethinking, Restructuring, Revitalizing.* Lancaster, Pa: Technomic.

CHAPTER THREE

PIECES OF THE PUZZLE: THE ELEMENTS OF SCHOOL IMPROVEMENT

The history of man is a graveyard of great cultures that came to catastrophic ends because of their incapacity for planned, rational, voluntary reaction to challenge.

Erich Fromm

ISSUES

Restructuring   Effective schools
Accountability   School-based management

KEY POINT: *Improving the quality and output of schools is not easy; it cannot be accomplished overnight or as a quick fix response to community pressures. The demands for quick fixes must be balanced with the knowledge that meaningful change takes time. The good news is that everything we know from research and from emerging practices gives us confidence that we now have many of the answers. The bad news is that creating the conditions appropriate for change is the toughest issue of all. A commitment to improvement means a commitment to more than rhetoric. It means that fundamental policies that guide the behavior of school system staff must change,*

> *and the ways in which staff actually practice education must also change.*
>
> *Improvement cannot happen if central office staff merely tell school staff that they have the freedom to make things better. The very organization and role of the central office staff must be redefined so that it supports and reinforces the needs of schools.*

Although it would be comforting to believe that some grand plan has guided the school improvement movement during the past decade or so, it would also be deluded. The movement has generated a wide range of approaches; some related to one another, and some not; some well thought out, some not. There has not yet been a careful description of a balanced program of school improvement combining the various components that really make a difference. As we develop such a description we must understand that we cannot pick and choose those discrete pieces of the school improvement process that feel comfortable or are easy to implement.

Transformation is highly ramified and involves changes at every level of the system. Although most school systems advertise the fact that they are meaningfully involved in a school improvement program, their participation is often marked by activities that are piecemeal, or trivial, or otherwise not well-conceived. The purpose of this chapter is to identify and describe the most effective elements of school improvement and integrate them into a coherent system that educational leaders can study and modify to fit their particular needs.

I. The Concept of Restructuring

The organizing principle that provides the 'glue' that defines effective school improvement programs is that of restructuring. To the extent that school improvement can be reduced to a mathematical formula it could be viewed as consisting of the following components:

School Improvement = principles of effective schools + school-based management + staff accountability

Selecting just one of the components is insufficient. Meaningful change involves employing what we know works from the effective schools literature, giving staff freedom to use their talents to bring about changes in a school-based management system, and establishing procedures to hold staff accountable for student outcomes. The concept of restructuring recognizes that there is no easy answer to school improvement and that it must be a system-wide priority. It is a process involving the systematic examination and renewal of all aspects of school operations, including governance and management structures, organizational patterns, and the critical areas of curriculum and instruction. The process also requires that staff be involved in extensive collaboration and site-based decision making and problem solving.

Effective school restructuring requires that the following basic principles be embraced. (Each of these principles is discussed in detail in later chapters). **If recent experiences have taught us anything it is that successful restructuring efforts leave no room for choosing among these principles. One either buys into all of them or none at all.**

Principle 1: *Change must be recognized as a stressful process.*

> **KEY POINT:** *The initial stages of change will inevitably involve some anxiety and confusion. They cannot be avoided.*

It is hard to imagine a serious school improvement program that does not create some anxiety among some staff, particularly among those who are part of the problem and do not recognize that fact. Yet many of those who are frustrated with the early stages of a school improvement plan can become converts to the cause if administrators involve them in the process and empower them with information about how to do their jobs more effectively.

Principle 2: *School system policies and practices must be guided by a clear, compelling and controlling mission statement.*

> **KEY POINT:** *Although the implementation of change takes time, the creation of a school system mission statement which signals the direction of those changes and the commitment of the system to the changes, must be done as a first and very public step.*

The mission statement should be simple and clear. For example:

The school system believes that all children will master the system's essential curriculum and that it is the responsibility of the system to modify and adjust its instructional program to ensure such performance. Such program modifications and adjustments will lead to the elimination of disparities in performance by race and gender,

or

To ensure that *all students* become responsible citizens, effective participants in our economy, and able to adapt to the rapidly changing world through the acquisition and application of skills and knowledge.

While mission statements do not have magical qualities in and of themselves, the pledge that all students will learn *places the burden to improve on the schools,* as well as on the students. Given a clear and accepted mission statement, a set of improvement goals around which the system and all of its components can organize must be developed. This step is designed to align the mission, on the one hand, with the activities of all school employees, on the other hand.

School boards and superintendents must assume responsibility for establishing the mission and for ensuring that all goals, curricula, staff behaviors, and student and staff assessments are designed to contribute to that mission.

Principle 3: *Learner outcomes must be clearly understood and assessed regularly, and staff evaluated on the extent to which the outcomes are achieved.*

It is virtually impossible for schools to produce students who are able to compete in a global economy and who are otherwise self-assured and productive citizens, unless the schools clearly specify what it is they want their students to know and do when they leave the 12th grade. For example, it may be important that students are able to apply mathematics problem solving strategies to complex real-life situations, or that they are able to have a reasonable discussion about the origins of the United States Constitution and its implications for contemporary events.

Once standards of what students are expected to know and do are developed, it is necessary to establish specific benchmark goals for every school, grade level, and subject. These goals serve three purposes. First, they provide the basis for judging the performance of schools and reporting those judgements to the public. Second, benchmark goals reflect the expectations that the system has for student performance. Third, benchmark goals enable the system to track its progress over a period of time.

The goals can be simple but ambitious. They should be designed to encourage staff to focus on student outcomes and not on how well they are complying with district rules and procedures. The goals could include:

- Increasing the number of students who meet grade and subject area standards as measured by portfolios and other assessment strategies;
- Reducing the achievement and program participation gap between advantaged and disadvantaged students, while showing overall gains;
- Increasing the percentage of students at each grade level who attain essential instructional objectives as measured by criterion-referenced tests;
- Increasing the percentage of students who enroll in and are successful at higher-level or advanced placement courses;
- Increasing the percentage of students who meet or exceed the emerging national proficiency standards;
- Increasing the performance of students on any norm-referenced achievement measure;
- Reducing the number of suspensions, retentions, and discipline referrals while maintaining a safe and orderly environment.

Against the backdrop of the goals, all school-based staff should annually develop plans which reflect the strategies and programs that they will deploy to ensure that the goals are achieved. It is equally important that all school-based staff understand that achieving the goals is possible only if all of the staff members work together as a team.

KEY POINT: *It is virtually impossible for schools to produce students who are able to compete in a global economy and who are otherwise self-assured and productive citizens, unless the schools clearly specify what it is they want their students to know and do when they leave the 12th grade. For example, it may be important that students are able to apply mathematics problem solving strategies to complex real-life*

> *situations, or that they are able to have a reasonable discussion about the origins of the United States Constitution and its implications for contemporary events.*

A school system which embodies clear standards and goals, and requires that plans be developed to specify how those goals will be achieved, must embed these activities in an accountability system that measures the progress of each school as it strives to achieve the goals set for them. These goals should *reflect* the school system's mission and the specific increment of gain expected for each school should be based on that school's present level of effectiveness. In fact, the further behind a school is on a given measure, the higher the increment of expected gain. The increment of expected gain on the goals should not be trivial; they should force staff to stretch toward a higher level of performance. An integral part of this process should be a reward system that provides financial bonuses to all employees in a school that successfully meets its goals.

The heart of the accountability system is the use of appropriate assessment tools. The assessment tools should include both norm- and criterion-referenced tests, as well as data reflecting program participation and performance. The test scores and program data should always be disaggregated in ways that would reveal any differences among groups of students (for example, by socio-economic status, race, and gender) that are not benefiting from the school's efforts.

The final step required to operationalize this principle is the creation of a system for effectively evaluating staff at all levels of the organization. These evaluation systems should document and account for the extent to which each employee contributes directly to achieving the goals or otherwise makes it possible for others to do so.

Principle 4: *New school structures must be characterized by a process of decentralization.*

The primary focus of control as it relates to the organization and delivery of instruction is the school, not the central office. To help achieve this objective, *school-based management* represents an effective approach. School-based management can occur only through collaborative processes and not by fiat. Local school autonomy in no way reduces the need for strong accountability measures established and implemented by the central office.

> **KEY POINT:** *The mere decentralization of decision-making does not ensure that the quality of decision-making is better than in a centralized system. Administrators must do whatever is necessary to improve the capacity of their staff to make better decisions by acquainting them with knowledge about 'what works' and 'how to make it work.'*

The most important element of a school-based management program is collaborative decision-making. Such decision-making capacity can be developed through collaborative meetings involving teachers, administrators, parents, and other community members. These meetings or dialogues require participants to define and share their vision for their schools and specify topics for full staff discussion and debate, including: How should the school be organized? How should curriculum be designed and instruction delivered? What are the barriers or impediments that stand in the way of effective teaching?

School-based management programs can only work if both school system management and teachers' associations support the effort and are able to stand back and let staff run the schools.

Principle 5: *Educators must be effective instructional leaders and change agents.*

> **KEY POINT:** *The training of school leaders should be an ongoing process and a regular part of the principal's routine. Educators should not assume that college of education graduates will have the knowledge necessary for reforming schools.*

High-quality leadership is a major prerequisite to effective restructuring. Principals must be change agents, facilitating the change process rather than mandating it. They must assume responsibility for creating those changes that will lead to high levels of student achievement. Similarly, all central office supervisory staff must assume the role of consultant and facilitator, supporting schools to address fully the needs of the students they serve. They must understand that the change process demands that teachers be direct participants in all aspects of school operations, including curriculum planning, defining staff development needs, and hiring staff.

Principle 6: *Outmoded or inappropriate curricula must be restructured to accommodate student needs.*

> **KEY POINT:** *Meaningful, high quality, and relevant curriculum must be delivered to all students. It is the responsibility of staff to find ways of enabling all students to take advantage of such curricula.*

A first step in this direction is the development of an integrated and meaningful course sequence which specifies what children should know and be able to do at the end of every grade and course. Lower-level courses in all subjects should be phased out and invidious grouping methods in elementary schools and tracking or levelling in secondary schools had better be stopped. Various heterogeneous and performance grouping configurations combined with appropriate co-operative learning strategies and the infusion of instructional technology should *replace* some of our older practices.

Principle 7: *High expectations must underlie all aspects of the school improvement process.*

> **KEY POINT:** *Expectations for what many students are expected to learn must change. Staff must be disabused of the notion that students from certain social, economic, or ethnic groups are somehow less able to benefit from a high-quality education.*

All classroom instructional and grouping strategies, assignments to levels of classes, and behavior and discipline referrals should be reviewed regularly to ensure that certain children are not tracked in a way that will later minimize their life chances. All staff should understand that while some children may come to school with more needs than others, it is the staff's responsibility to adjust their teaching and organizational styles so that all children will have access to programs of excellence. Superintendents and others have to ensure that staff constantly monitor data to assess student performance and access to educational programs and experiences which embody high standards and rich curricula.

Principle 8: *Restructuring must be data-driven.*

> **KEY POINT:** *Central office and school staff must be data literate. They must be able to accurately diagnose problems, determine how the best allocation for scarce resources should be allocated, and how to assess the extent of student learning.*

There must be ongoing scrutiny of educational outcomes through the appropriate collection, analysis, and reporting of relevant data. Without the capacity to conduct such analyses, superintendents, principals and their staff cannot accurately assess program effectiveness, identify instructional needs, and make appropriate instructional modifications. Although observations and anecdotal records are valuable supplements to the development of restructuring efforts, the primary evaluative tool must be the analysis of disaggregated data concerning student performance and its relationship to instructional interventions.

Principle 9: *Educational leaders must have constant feedback concerning the condition of education in their schools.*

> **KEY POINT:** *Superintendents and other administrators must have access to critical data concerning the state of affairs in their system and in their schools.*

Although data are usually collected routinely by the central office, there are some issues that require on-site visits to individual schools. These visits—or audits—can be used to address two types of issues. *First,* to determine the extent to which programs are implemented as originally intended, and are truly the product of broad staff involvement. *Second,* to troubleshoot actual or reported problems in a given school building. Trained teams of principals and teachers from other schools could visit designated schools to interview the principal and staff, visit classrooms, review data, and prepare a report to the superintendent or other administrator. These reports should lead to the development of plans which specify all necessary corrective actions that must be implemented by school staff.

> **KEY POINT:** *If the reader takes away only one point from these principles, it is that a successful school improvement program must incorporate every one of them. None can be sacrificed for the sake of cost, convenience, or easy acceptance.*

II. Accountability as a Motivating Principle

As educators attempted to improve their schools during the past decade, public dissatisfaction with continuing unsatisfactory outcomes grew at an alarming rate. Public, political, and business support for public schools waned. School bonds were defeated in large numbers. Education became the profession of last resort. At first it was thought that the problem was essentially one of resources. Many believed that all that schools required was more of something: more teachers, more books, more field trips, and so on. As it became clear that more was not, in and of itself, the answer, attention focussed on the need for new instructional procedures and/or organizational arrangements. Unfortunately, no matter what the innovation, the experience was the same. *Merely changing instructional procedures or arrangements was not sufficient to improve the quality of teaching or the character of learning.*

> **KEY POINT:** *Accountability should not be the only thing that school system staff think about when they begin the improvement process. They cannot hold others accountable for improvement without making them aware of what research says works and how to make it work. After all, if they do not have a sense of what's possible, they cannot be expected to change their practices.*

After a period of flailing about for answers, commentators, policy-makers, and a few educators began to look at the entire educational system to determine what was wrong and what required fixing. Most did not deny that additional resources were required, nor that new instructional arrangements were needed. However, they did conclude that it would be wasteful to dump these added resources and new programs into school systems and schools whose leadership and management styles would not maximize the chances that they would have the desired effects. More new wine in old bottles was not seen as the answer.

As educators and others tried to turn the tide of declining achievement, public attention shifted to finding ways that schools could more effectively use rewards, sanctions, and their existing resources to achieve better outcomes. The movement embodying these thoughts was dubbed the 'accountability' movement. This focus on accountability shifted the attention from educational inputs to educational outputs—reflecting the view that education was a business and a big business at that. Following this line of logic, educational accountability was conceived as consisting of three general components; outcome goals, measurements of those goals, and strategies designed to achieve those goals. The consumers (represented by parents, the school board, and school system central office staff) should determine the first two components and after appropriate dialogue with all parties, school staff should determine the strategies.

So far, most accountability efforts have been characterized by only the first of the three components—setting student outcome goals. Inappropriately, accountability in many districts is used as the two-by-four that will bring about educational improvement. Many accountability proponents fail to understand that the very structure and organization of schools, combined with the limited knowledge that many educators have about school effectiveness, creates barriers which militate against taking risks and trying new approaches. *Merely* setting clearer and tougher goals, and threatening staff to make them achieve those goals, does not amount to an effective school improvement strategy.

Since most school systems have not linked accountability with steps to improve the knowledge base of staff and the organization of schools, the concept has yet to make much difference to individual school and classroom practices. Many administrators have not yet recognized that accountability—as characterized by goal setting and measuring—does not by itself get at the root of what's wrong in our schools. *For schools to be truly effective, administrators must combine goal setting with:*

- A staff that is knowledgeable about what works and how to make it work;
- Fundamental changes in the ways in which schools are organized, in what they teach, and in how they teach students with differing needs.

Accountability should not be the only thing that school system staff think about when they begin the improvement process. They cannot hold others accountable for improvement without making them aware of what research says works and how to make it work. After all, if they do not have a sense of what's possible, they cannot be expected to change their practices.

III. The Effective Schools Literature as a Guide for Action

A lesson that many educators must still learn is that those strategies which were effective with the student body of the 1950s do not work with many of today's students. More students are coming to school from impoverished families and communities, often without the advantages that many middle-class children bring to school from the moment they enter kindergarten. This does *not* mean that separate or lower standards, embodying different expectations for some students, are required. The same high standards should apply to all students. It is the school system's obligation to use a mix of instructional strategies to increase the chances that all students will meet those high standards. If some students in a given class receive a different or additional treatment than other students, that is all to the good, as long as the expectations and standards are the same for all students.

Earlier efforts to identify the factors that account for effective education, particularly for disadvantaged students, are now embodied in what is known as the *effective schools movement*. The representatives of this movement spent time at schools in which large numbers of 'at-risk' students were enrolled. After detailed sets of observations and intense data analysis, they concluded that effective schools embodied a combination of specific characteristics, characteristics that are positively correlated with improved student performance. Unfortunately, it has become relatively simple for some educators merely to pay lip service to these characteristics and adopt them in a way which does not require them or their colleagues to change their everyday policies and practices. It should also be noted that this early effective schools research focussed almost exclusively on individual school buildings and did not address the positive and negative influences that a school system's central office policies and practices could have on school improvement.

There are two important points to recognize concerning the effective schools literature. First, it is not in and of itself a school improvement program; it does *not* address such issues as how to create change. Second, it *does* provide a wealth of information about what works, and therefore serves as a point of departure for administrators and teachers to begin examining their own practices. The effective schools orientation is especially important because it constantly reminds us that all innovations and initiatives must be made with the best interests of students in mind. The framework also helps unify and give coherence to different activities which otherwise may seem fragmented.

Recent experiences in school systems provide important insights in how to convert the descriptive correlates of effective schools into discrete educational practices. One of the most important lessons learned is that the objectives imbedded in school improvement plans must not be trivial. Administrators must signal that they expect the changes to be significant, aligned with the district goals and fundamentally change the practices in a school building. Having a spaghetti dinner as a response to meaningfully involving parents in schools, or distributing more awards as a means of enhancing student self-concept, are insufficient to make significant impacts on the correlates.

Administrators should be sensitive to the failed efforts of the past including efforts in which school systems:

- Trained their staffs in what works only to find that principals and teachers do not have the self-confidence or skills required to make necessary changes;
- Embraced school-based management as a means of allowing school-based staff to make more crucial decisions, only to discover that staffs do not have the technical information to make such decisions;
- Trained staff in what works and provided them with discretion in making decisions, only to experience more failure because central office policies and practices presented major barriers to change.

Although the 'effective school' characteristics are categorized somewhat differently by various authors, we now list those for which there is a consensus, and we offer some clues as to how they may be converted from mere description into concrete policies and practices.

IV. The Characteristics of Effective Schools

Characteristic 1: *For a school to be effective it must have and act upon a clear and focused mission statement.*

Effective school systems are those in which the *school system leadership* proclaims that:

- Their essential mission is effective teaching for learning for all students;
- It is the responsibility of the school system to identify students who are not achieving, and *do whatever is necessary* to change the content or delivery of education to improve that achievement.

> **KEY POINT:** *It is critically important that all staff at every level of the organization be involved in developing the mission. It is equally important that the wording of the mission statement not be overly general and that it clearly state that the system is responsible for finding ways of delivering effective educational services.*

Once the school system mission is developed and accepted by the local board of education, every organizational unit in the central office and every school building must develop a mission which supports the system's mission. For example, if the *school system* adopts either of the mission statements:

> The school system believes that all children will master the system's essential curriculum and that it is the responsibility of the system to modify its instructional program to ensure such performance. Modification will lead to the elimination of disparities in performance by race and gender,

> or

> To ensure that all students become responsible citizens, effective participants in our economy, and able to adapt to the rapidly

changing world through the acquisition and application of skills and knowledge.

then the Division of Instructional Services could develop the following mission statement:

> The mission of the Division of Instructional Services is to ensure that the nature, quality, and delivery of all curriculum, materials, staff development, and instructional strategies are designed to help students meet rigorous academic standards.

Individual schools could then develop mission statements of the following type:

> The mission of this school is to ensure that all school staff are engaged in providing high-quality direct instruction to all students and that they regularly monitor and adjust that instruction to guarantee that all children will be high academic achievers.

It is critically important that all staff at every level of the organization be involved in developing the mission. It is equally important that the wording of the mission statement not be overly general and that it clearly state that the system is responsible for finding ways of delivering effective educational services.

Characteristic 2: *For a school to be effective it must create a climate of high expectations for all students.*

KEY POINT: *It is difficult for many educators to admit that their expectations for some students are lower than for other students. In many cases when teachers are asked to develop strategies that demonstrate higher expectations for students, they typically design activities whose purpose is to reward students for successful performance with the hope that such success will increase the expectations that students have for themselves. Educators must realize that this does not get to the heart of the expectations issue. Rather, they—the educators themselves—***must change*** *their expectations for the performance of their students.*

Many principals and teachers tend to 'blame the victim' when things do not go well. Faced with declining test scores or other indicators of poor performance, the most common explanations given by principals and teachers include: the student has a low IQ or ability level, or comes from a poor background, or has only one parent, or does not have parents helping him or her at home, or has been in the low reading groups too long. Imbedded in each of these excuses are expectations that students with these characteristics are doing what they can do, and that to expect more is unrealistic.

If school administrators accept these excuses as reasons for poor performance, they are buying into low expectations and virtually guaranteeing that these students will be tracked accordingly for their entire school careers. If administrators doubt this, they should understand that the vast majority of students who are grouped in lower-level reading groups in the second or third grade stay in these low-level groups for most of their school careers. There seem to be only two reasonable explanations for this invidious tracking system, either

- Children come to the school from socio-economically deprived backgrounds and do not have the capacity to do higher level work; or
- The school system, government agencies, and parents have failed to effectively address the deficiencies that children bring to school.

Fortunately for the future of our society, evidence is accumulating that the second explanation is the more appropriate; merely using the same instructional strategies that were used years ago with primarily middle class students is not likely to work with today's at-risk students. This does not mean that one should expect less from these students. *It means that we need to use different instructional strategies that can compensate for whatever shortcomings students bring to the school, while simultaneously maintaining the same high standards that we have for all students. It is difficult for many educators to admit that their expectations for some students are lower than for other students.* In many cases when teachers are asked to develop strategies that demonstrate higher expectations for students, they typically design activities whose purpose is to reward students for successful performance with the hope that such success will increase the expectations that students have for themselves. Educators must realize that this does not get to the heart of the expectations issue. Rather, they—the educators themselves—must change *their* expectations for the performance of their students.

Characteristic 3: *For a school to be effective the principal must provide aggressive leadership to staff on a wide variety of matters, particularly in the area of instructional leadership.*

To be effective, principals must demonstrate competence in each of the following five areas:

- *They must be good diagnosticians.* Principals must be able to analyze the effectiveness of the school's instructional program, identify those students who are successful and those who are not, and know which staff are effective and which are not. They must have the capacity to collect, organize and analyze information about the educational processes used in the school and the performance outcomes demonstrated by the students;
- *They must be aware of 'what works' for those students who come to school at different starting points.* Principals must expect the teachers' repertoire of instructional strategies to be varied and must ensure that the correct educational package is provided to each and every student;
- *They must understand how to make things work.* Principals must be familiar with the many organizational, cultural and other barriers that often stand in the way of change and they must be willing to take on the 'status quo'. An effective principal is going to constantly challenge the objections to change that are often voiced by the nay-sayers in every school system;
- *They must learn how to be effective 'coaches'.* The principal as instructional leader must provide teachers with assistance in improving their skills. They must be up to date on effective organizational and teaching strategies and spend significant amounts of time imparting that knowledge to teachers;
- *They must have the management skills necessary for convincing teachers who have been doing things the same way for several years to change their ways.* Principals must do whatever is necessary to re-educate or remove those staff who do not have the capacity or motivation to improve.

Educators cannot assume that it is the responsibility of colleges and universities to train school principals. Rather, it is the responsibility of the school system to provide such training. Private businesses have long argued that they want the colleges and universities to provide them with people who can think, who can synthesize information, and who are analytic. Given such people, they argue, they can then best train them to do the specific tasks associated with any position in the organization. The case is no different for school systems.

> **Characteristic 4:** *For a school to be effective, the amount of appropriate direct instructional time provided for each student must be maximized.*

Schools which are unusually effective maximize the time used for the direct instruction of students. This finding is one which appears with the most regularity over the past 20 years of educational research. *Direct instruction* is defined as the time in which a student is individually or in a small group interacting with a teacher, or with an interactive learning aid such as a computer. *Completing worksheets, dittos, and copying from the board do not qualify as direct instructional time!*

Increasing direct instructional time does not always imply that the time allocated for a given subject is increased. For example, if 90 minutes per day is available for reading instruction, but a student receives only 30 minutes of direct instruction because of inefficient use of time, the issue becomes one of increasing that direct instructional time within the 90-minute period. Although most educators agree with the need to increase direct instructional time, this has been difficult to implement in many schools and classrooms. More than any other of the effective school characteristics, this one requires principals and teachers to make significant changes in the way they plan for instruction, organize classrooms, and teach students.

The time that students do not consume through direct instruction is most typically spent completing worksheets, beginning the next day's homework, or copying spelling or other lists from the board. This use of time is one which has been prevalent in our country for decades and, as some will point out, was successful in the past. When one explores why these procedures once worked but are not now effective, a fascinating picture emerges. In the past when a higher percentage of students came from families less impacted by the culture of poverty, those students came to school with a foundation that enabled them to use the 'indirect' time as a positive learning experience. These students actually taught themselves; they worked through the assignments and thereby reinforced those lessons that they were already taught.

On the other hand, many students are now coming to school having been raised in families that were socio-economically deprived and have not developed the foundations or work ethics necessary to allow them to take advantage of the indirect instructional time.

> **KEY POINT:** *The fact that students from advantaged and disadvantaged backgrounds often come to and continue in school with different foundations and learning styles does not mean that one group is more able to learn than the other group. Rather, it means that the same 'treatment' may not be appropriate for both groups. It is the responsibility of the school and teacher to tailor instruction to compensate for any deficiencies that students bring to school while simultaneously maintaining equally high expectations for each and every student. This tailoring requires that schools and classrooms organize their time and resources differently.*

Beyond the issue of time on task within the context of the classroom, administrators must confront the need to restructure the use of time itself within schools. Schools as institutional structures currently conform to an industrial paradigm with strict six- or seven-part divisions of days and yearly calendars extending from an even earlier agrarian period. The creative and visionary administrator must work with his or her staff to discover creative uses of time so that necessities such as site-based staff development and opportunities for enrichment experiences for students can be integrated into the school day. Central office mandated policies and procedures ought not to be allowed to guide the scheduling process; rather the needs of student learners and staff members as instructional leaders should define the nature of the schedule.

As administrators review the efficacy of their *elementary* school programs they should focus on ensuring that:

- Instructional standards that define what children should know and be able to do are internalized by all staff;
- Grouping in elementary school is minimized and characterized by short term skills groups that have short life spans;
- Frequent classroom assessments are conducted so that teachers know exactly where students are academically before they fall behind;

- Extra help is provided as needed during classroom time, after school, and on Saturdays.

The fact that students from advantaged and disadvantaged backgrounds often come to and continue in school with different foundations and learning styles *does not mean that one group is more able to learn than the other group*. Rather, it means that the same 'treatment' may not be appropriate for both groups. It is the responsibility of the school and teacher to tailor instruction to compensate for any deficiencies that students bring to school while simultaneously maintaining equally high expectations for each and every student. This tailoring requires that schools and classrooms organize their time and resources differently.

The issue in *secondary* school is somewhat different. By the time students are in secondary school, they are typically grouped or tracked into courses at various levels of difficulty. For example, some may be in a general or consumer mathematics class while others may be enrolled in algebra. In other cases, most typically with English classes, the name of the course may be the same (English 9), but the more advanced students are enrolled in higher-level English 9 classes while the less advanced students are enrolled in lower-level English 9 classes. Real progress will not be made in our schools until these low-level courses whose only purpose is to allow students to mark time and qualify for a diploma are eliminated. General or functional classes have no role to play in preparing students to compete in the twenty-first century.

Putting aside for the moment problems associated with grouping students in this manner, teacher expectations for students often differ in higher- and lower-level classes. It is often assumed that advanced students will benefit more from teaching which features discussion, problem-solving activities, seminars, and independent study, while the less advanced students require a lecture format, grill and drill procedures, and worksheet assignments. This assumption is unwarranted and must be challenged wherever and whenever it arises.

There is ample evidence that the more sophisticated teaching techniques and instructional arrangements are at least as effective with the less-advanced students. As a matter of fact, these techniques and arrangements may be the only chance that many of these students have to be successful in school. In addition, the adoption of these more sophisticated and higher-level instructional strategies signal teachers that more is expected of them and their traditionally lower-performing students.

> **KEY POINT**: *When assigning teachers, it is important that those assigned to teach less advanced students be as knowledgeable about instructional strategies and content as those who are assigned to teach more advanced students. Criteria such as seniority should not determine which teacher teaches advanced or less advanced students. The assignment to teach more advanced students should not be portrayed as a 'plum', or reward for past good performance. Principals must make it clear that equally effective teachers are required to teach all students and, in some cases, arguments can even be made that more experienced teachers are required for those students who display the most serious learning problems. Whenever a student is enrolled in a less advanced performance group, the ultimate objective must be to prepare that student for performing well in a higher level group.*

Characteristic 5: *For a school to be effective, teachers must regularly assess student progress and modify a student's instructional program based on those assessments.*

Frequent assessments can help central office staff, administrators, principals, and teachers in two ways. First, it can provide teachers and principals with information about how groups of students (whether the groups be based on such characteristics as race, sex, age, or achievement level) are performing and can identify those groups which are not benefitting from instruction. It is common to find teachers and principals genuinely surprised when told that students in their classes or schools, who share common characteristics, are performing significantly below average for their school. For example, it may be that black male students, or girls, or students who are in the lowest reading groups, represent the great majority of those students who receive a low grade on a standardized test. In these cases, this information encourages teachers to analyze what they have been doing for these students and often to try new instructional approaches. The information also enables administrators to identify those teachers who have difficulty educating particular groups of students and, therefore, serves as a basis for providing targeted staff development opportunities.

Second, it can provide information about the strengths and weaknesses of individual students that can be used for modifying instruction. Too often students are placed in instructional groups at the beginning of the year and end up in the same group at the end of the year. This is partly a function of not having appropriate and frequent assessments of student progress and partly because long-term grouping helps teachers organize and manage classrooms even though it may not contribute to maximizing student potential.

> **KEY POINT:** *Administrators must be aware that the appropriate use of assessments should result in fewer long-term homogeneous learning groups. If frequent assessments of students' progress occur, and significant regrouping or other instructional modifications are not made, then the assessments are not being used for instructional purposes.*

Characteristic 6: *For a school to be effective, it must have a safe and orderly environment which is conducive to teaching and learning.*

The most serious problem reported by teachers is that of discipline. They claim that students are unruly in school, in the halls, and in the classrooms, and that such unruliness stands in the way of learning. Administrators must ensure that behavioral violations are dealt with swiftly, and that such processes as 'moving in the halls' occurs without incident. First and foremost, administrators must be responsible for minimizing any distractions that hinder teaching and learning. At the very least, the school system should develop discipline-related policies designed to ensure that the school has an orderly and purposeful atmosphere, free from any threat of physical harm. Such policies need to be developed and implemented in such a manner as not to be oppressive and not to throw up barriers to teaching and learning. The policies should be embedded in a student code of behavior that is disseminated to every student, parent, and school system employee. At the very least the code should include:

- An overview of the system's philosophy of discipline including a careful description of all related policies and all behaviors for which students are to be held accountable;

- A description of the conduct which warrants disciplinary measures that would result in the denial of educational participation;
- A detailed description of administrative procedures associated with the implementation of disciplinary measures;
- An overview of the impact of non-school originating criminal charges and their potential impact upon students' participation in school activities;
- Clear student-directed procedures for the review and appeal of disciplinary measures. It is critical that students be helped to understand their responsibilities and rights as citizens within the educational environment;
- Options extended to students in the event of suspension, including such issues as the right to make-up work, tests and examinations, and access to school grounds;
- Modifications of policies and procedures to accommodate the needs of special populations, including students diagnosed as requiring special education services;
- Options for those students who continually disrupt the learning environment to be placed in alternative learning settings.

The mere development and distribution of a student code of conduct will not have the desired effect if all staff are not adequately trained in its meaning, implementation, and enforcement.

Although discipline problems must be met head-on and unambiguously, many behavioral problems are more a function of instructional programs that do not engage children, rather than an indication that the children are just bad and refuse to behave.

Some students may be bored while others may not be challenged by instructional content or its delivery. Others may be in a low group and receiving instruction which is repetitive and not mind stretching. And finally, some may not be able to handle the significant amount of non-direct instructional time to which they are exposed. Whatever the reason, whenever a child misbehaves in a classroom, the first assumption that teachers should make is that the students are not being engaged in the learning process. Given that assumption, a teacher's first response to a discipline problem should be to adjust the child's instructional environment so that it is more personal and more direct. Strong instructional programs will challenge almost all students and demand their full attention and energies, thereby minimizing discipline problems.

More and more students are coming to school from neighborhoods and cultures that espouse behaviors that conflict with those advocated by the school. The mere development of relevant school policies and staff and student understanding of the implications of violating those policies is not sufficient. Schools must also provide learning experiences that will correct inappropriate behavioral values and replace them with more acceptable ones.

Characteristic 7: *For a school to be effective, the role of parents as educators must be strengthened.*

Appropriate parental involvement is a prerequisite for successful student performance. Even though most schools involved in the effective schools process include this emphasis in their improvement efforts, they often unfortunately do so in a way that fails to take account of research findings. Most schools develop elaborate programs to involve parents in fund-raisers, back-to-school nights, and other social activities. Although these are indeed important, they do not respond to the research, which indicates that student performance is likely to increase if parents are meaningfully involved in the children's schooling.

A particularly exciting development in this field is the emergence of new models of school governance involving parents and community members in the decision-making and problem-solving process in the school. These models require that administrators relinquish absolute power and governance responsibilities in favor of more collaborative approaches using an ongoing oversight committee, generally composed of the principal, key administrators, representative teachers, support personnel, parents, and community members. Although this approach to governance and management takes more time and demands new forms of diplomacy from administrators, the collaborative decision-making process can prove invaluable for increasing staff and community ownership of education and all that goes into defining and shaping it.

For too long we have made parents feel like visitors in 'our' institutions. In an effort to eliminate the 'them' versus 'us' attitude of educators and parents, a sincere effort must be made to signal this new co-operative relationship. One way to do that is to reserve space in every school as a parent center equipped with appropriate work tools, such as desks, files, and computers, and staffed by a paid co-ordinator who can develop strategies for meaningful parent involvement and interaction with the professional staff in the school.

> **KEY POINT**: At the heart of such collaborative initiatives is the fundamental assumption that schools are institutions and as such exhibit an institutional culture and climate. Ideally, this culture should reflect norms, mores, and standards which encourage open communication, collegiality, and collaboration in all aspects of the schooling process. However, there is frequently a gap between the expectations and cultural experiences of school staff and the parent/student populations that comprise the school's population. Teachers from a middle-class, suburban background, for example, may have conscious or unconscious expectations about such issues as student behavior, attitudes, values, or parental roles and responsibilities, derived from their own experiences as students and learners. The clash of cultures that typifies many school settings today is a fundamental and frequently unrecognized issue that effective administrators must understand, and address through viable staff development and related interventions.

V. School-Based Management

If our schools are to be held accountable for the performance of their students, as we propose that they should be, then we must bestow upon the schools the authority to make those decisions that impact the key areas of learning, personnel, programming, and budget. The assembly-line model that represented this decision-making function in the past can no longer direct the destiny of our schools. If we are to be competitive in a global society, we must send forth graduates prepared to succeed in this demanding world, and as we look for new and daring solutions to take us to a higher road, we must recognize that leadership and wisdom exists beyond the walls of central office and the board room.

No longer can we govern a system with uniform plans that are forced on every classroom in the district. This 'lock step' approach has contributed to many of the shortcomings that exist in our systems today. Instead, we need to encourage our individual schools to experiment and to take risks. Clearly we should hold them responsible for the outcomes of schooling, but we must also respect their professional skills and give them the freedom to make their own critical decisions. However, as schools organize to promote co-operative decision-making, they must simultaneously focus on how well students are learning and what needs to be done for those who are underserved. They should be encouraged to try bold new ideas, and we should remove any barriers that stand in their way, provide them with valuable research information, and locate needed resources to implement worthwhile strategies.

The fundamental need will be to develop school-based teams to question the status quo, look for new answers, try new solutions, and think bold ideas. Administrators must ensure that these teams are allowed to operate as intended. They cannot become the province of the building principal. As we push power into the schools, the ideas that are generated by the teams will come to the fore. Staff will take ownership of these exciting new solutions, giving them a much greater chance for success.

As we move into this new arena of decision making, we must first start a training program to ensure the necessary skills for those engaged in the process. We must carefully develop policies that clear the way, and work with union or association leaders to understand the new relationship that needs to be established. While these groups will still represent teachers with respect to working conditions, the site-based decisions we are referring to deal with factors that govern the teaching and learning process and as such should not become entangled with collective bargaining. Our school-based needs need to focus on: What is currently being done in our schools? Is it working? Can we do it better? Who does what? How will we know if it works? As we establish this new culture of accountability and authority, we must also be aware of need for a culture shift at central office. Extensive work will need to be done to train those in former command positions to accept their new role as support staff.

Even the casual observer of the educational scene is cautious about any new movement designed to improve the enterprise. For years educators have 'created' new movements to fix their problems. And, as could have been expected, these movements have fallen by the wayside one after another. However, school-based management deserves special consideration. The essential core of school-based management is that *a school's staff should have the most sophisticated understanding of the students' problems and know the most effective ways of addressing those problems within the context of the school.* The purpose of school-based management is to unleash the energies of the staff, empower them with the ability to make key decisions and give them flexibility to use resources as they see fit. The school-based program provides principals with an opportunity to influence program and budget decision-making priorities at their schools through staff and parent involvement.

> **KEY POINT:** *A key feature of school-based management is shared power and collaborative decision-making by those staff within a school building. Often ignored, but critically important, is the reality that even in a system which practices effective school-based management, overall policies and educational requirements must still be established by the Superintendent and the board of education. Within that context, schools can be given the freedom to seek and implement their own strategies while still being responsive to these overall policies and procedures.*

School-based management has many of its foundations in corporate and management research. This research generated a series of principles upon which the movement was built:

- The ownership of problems and solutions related to teaching for learning should be assumed by those directly involved in working with students;
- People can be trusted and want to do a good job;
- People are more likely to change when they have a voice in defining the changes;
- Those who are the closest to where implementation will occur are in the best position to decide how implementation should take place;
- Decisions can be made more swiftly at the local level;
- If risk-taking is rewarded, people are more likely to change;
- When staff work together on common concerns, they tend to develop a sense of ownership and co-operation.

The school-based management process is a natural outgrowth of the effective schools literature. School-based management programs should only be implemented if those who are expected to make decisions are provided appropriate training. In a school-based management system, principals, with staff and community involvement must be allowed to realign the school's personnel and materials allotments with their perceptions of the kinds of programs that they deem appropriate for improving student achievement. Financially, school-based management is self-balancing; that is, it is structured to avoid net additional costs. Participants must operate within existing resources to develop and execute plans to improve the delivery and effectiveness of educational services in their respective schools. No 'bail-out' reserve should be considered. The process offers the potential for improved student-staff ratios and programming opportunities tailored to meet local students' needs. Principals and their staffs are fully accountable for the educational services in their schools.

Preconditions to Implementing School-Based Management

As school system leaders seriously consider adopting school-based management, they must understand that school-based management *alone* does not improve schools. Although the concept involves improving the capacity of local school staff to make decisions about the organization and delivery of education in the school, decentralizing decision-making is not the sole ingredient of school improvement. Decisions do not automatically become 'more right' just because they are made 'more locally'. As school systems commit to school-based management, they must understand that it is one of the *final* steps in an overall school improvement program and they must be willing to embrace a set of crucial preconditions. If any one of the following preconditions cannot be met, it may not be wise to proceed.

Precondition #1: There must be an agreed upon and widely disseminated school system philosophy which commits all system staff to delivering a quality education to all of its students. *Unless school-based management activities are in service of this philosophy, they cannot make a meaningful contribution to school improvement.*

Precondition #2: The school system must embrace an accountability system which specifies clear goals for all school system employees and establishes procedures for measuring progress toward those goals. *Without such a system, school-based management can easily* *generate activities which do not directly contribute to the overall goals of the school system.*

Precondition #3: The school system must provide all staff with meaningful training opportunities. *The absence of such training will guarantee that the quality of decision-making in any single school will not improve, staff will not be willing to be risk-takers, and most of the new efforts will be trivial in nature. At the very least training should be provided in the following areas:*

- Procedures to use in identifying local school needs;
- Knowledge of the effective schools process and the most effective teaching and instructional practices;
- Shared decision-making and long range planning;
- Strategies for co-operative problem solving;
- Technical knowledge as it relates to new tasks that staff must perform in a school-based management system including:
  - Policies related to personnel, funding, and program restrictions;
  - Transferring funds from one school system account to another;
  - Ordering materials and supplies;
  - Auditing and managing fiscal accounts;
  - Record keeping;
  - Positive customer relations.

Without a serious investment in staff development, school-based management cannot work and, worse yet, staff will suffer from low morale and increased frustration.

Precondition #4: The schools must devise a plan to involve parents in the educational process of their children and have parent representation on whatever group is charged with the responsibility to develop the school's educational plans and programs. *Without such meaningful parental involvement, the support required to try new approaches and to sustain change will be lacking.*

Precondition #5: The principals in the schools must share meaningful program decision-making authority. Although the final legal authority for decision-making rests with the principal, teachers and other staff must be involved in the review and evaluation of existing practices and the development and implementation of new ones. *In the absence of meaningful shared decision-making, creativity will be stifled and classroom practices are likely to remain unchanged.*

Precondition #6: The principals and their staffs must be given meaningful flexibility in the way their schools are staffed. Superintendents should consider changing the allocation of personnel from a system which relies on allocating the same 'mix' to all schools, to one which allows principals and their staffs the flexibility to trade in some personnel for others who have different and more needed expertise. (In the future it is likely that principals will be given a total number of full-time equivalent staff that they can hire based on their judgments of the competencies needed to meet the needs of their students.) Here are some brief examples of the kinds of 'trade-offs' that some schools have begun to make as part of their broader school-based management program.

> **School A:** Plans include redefining the role of the Reading Specialist to that of a Communications/Arts Specialist and trading the (.50) Media Specialist position, a (.10) Vocal Music Teacher position, and a (.20) Secretarial position to add a .50 Teacher and part-time support personnel to keep the media center open full time.

> **School B:** Redefined the role of the Media Specialist to that of an Instructional Technology Resource Teacher to enhance the media program through an emphasis on computer technology and resources. Traded the (.20) Instrumental Music Teacher position, a (.50) Secretarial position, and some instructional materials to add a .20 Guidance Counselor position and a .80 Instructional Aide position to expand support for students with special needs.

> **School C:** Traded a .20 Teaching position in each of Physical Education and Vocal Music and some instructional materials to add 1.5 Instructional Aide positions to facilitate team teaching and improve student time on learning. The role of the Instrumental Music Teacher will be redefined to include vocal music instruction.

> **School D:** Traded two teaching assistant positions for one teacher, to reduce class size and to increase direct instructional time for students.

Precondition #7: The central office should eliminate all policy, procedural, and contractual practices which function as barriers to the effective implementation of programming at the individual school. The central office ought to ensure that individual school system staffs can:

- Use personnel, time, and materials with as few restrictions as possible;
- Adopt or adapt instructional procedures that they believe are most appropriate to their students' needs;
- Rely on central office staff to help implement solutions to students problems (central office staff must be retrained to serve this technical assistance rather than directive role);
- Make the school based management and budgeting process relatively easy to use with minimal paperwork requirements.

Many school systems have considered adopting school-based management in response to pressures from the community to improve the quality of the schools. Unfortunately in some cases the commitment is 'a mile wide and an inch deep'. Often the decisions that school staff are allowed to make are limited. Sometimes they are (a) decisions that have little to do with school improvement (such as building maintenance and repairs) or, (b) decisions that are instructionally related but which must be made in the context of strong guidelines from the central office. Neither type of involvement will result in meaningful school improvement.

Chapter Three: Further Reading

Bailey, William, 1991. *School-Site Management Applied.* Lancaster, Pa: Technomic.

Benore, Lynn A., and Michael A. Boulus, 1990. What Districts Can Do to Provide Support for School Improvement. *Michigan Association of School Boards Journal,* March.

Cetron, Marvin, and Owen Davies. 1989. *American Renaissance.* New York: St. Martin's Press.

Cetron, Marvin, and Margaret Gayle. 1991. *Educational Renaissance: Our Schools at the Turn of the Century.* New York: St. Martin's Press.

Comer, James. 1980. *School Power: Implications of an International Project.* New York: Free Press.

Deal, Terrance E. and Allan A. Kennedy. 1982. *Corporate Cultures: The Rites and Rituals of Corporate Life.* Reading, Ma: Addison-Wesley.

Drucker, Peter. 1988. *Innovation and Entrepreneurship: Practice and Principles.* New York: Harper and Row.

Firestone, William A., Susan Fuhrman, and Michael Kirst. 1989. *The Progress of Reform: An Appraisal of State Educational Initiatives.* Washington, D.C.: Center for Policy Research in Education.

Graham, Patricia Albjerg. 1992. *S.O.S.: Sustain Our Schools.* New York: Hill and Wang.

Harrison, C., J. Killian, and J. Milatell. 1989. Site-Based Management: The Realities of Implementation. *Educational Leadership,* 46: 55–58.

Kirst, Michael W. 1990. *Accountability: Implications for State and Local Policymakers.* Washington, D.C.: Government Printing Office.

National Commission on Excellence in Education. 1983. *A Nation At Risk: The Imperative for Educational Reform.* Washington, D.C.: U. S. Government Printing Office.

O'Neil, J. 1990. Piecing Together the Restructuring Puzzle, *Educational Leadership,* 47: pp. 4–10.

Payzant, Thomas. 1989. To Restructure Schools, We've Changed the Way Bureaucracy Works. *American School Board Journal,* 176: pp. 19–20.

Purkey, Stewart C. and Marshall S. Smith. 1983. Effective Schools: A Review. *Elementary School Journal,* March, pp. 427–452.

Peters, Thomas J. and Nancy Austin. 1985. *A Passion For Excellence: The Leadership Difference.* New York: Random House.

Reavis, Charles, and Harry Griffith. 1992. *Restructuring Schools: Theory and Practice.* Lancaster, Pa: Technomics.

Siu-Rinyan, Yvonne, and Sally Joy Heart. 1992. Management Manifesto. *The Executive Educator,* January, p. 23.

Taylor, Barbara (ed.). 1990. *Case Studies in Effective Schools Research.* Dubuque, Iowa: Kendall-Hunt (National Center for Effective Schools).

CHAPTER FOUR

TRANSFORMING THE CONTENT AND DELIVERY OF CURRICULUM

Things do change. The only question is that since things are deteriorating so quickly, will society and man's habits change quickly enough?

Isaac Asimov

ISSUES

Redefining and renewing the basics (language arts, mathematics, science, social studies and the arts)

Enriched curricula
Technology
School dropouts
Choice

I. Rethinking the Curriculum

Unless curricular content and delivery are drastically improved, restructuring will not succeed. There are many who find it easier to change management structures or organizational arrangements than to change what gets taught and how it gets taught. Changing what gets taught and how it gets taught requires that careful consideration be given to identifying what students should know, providing the requisite staff development to teachers, and working with staff to change the ways in which they have been practicing their profession.

To make the necessary changes in curriculum, instructional staffs must be given extensive freedom to adapt their teaching to their particular groups of students. However, the effectiveness of the curriculum remains subject to system-wide accountability. It is unreasonable to assume that school-based staff can or should make key curriculum decisions unless the central office first develops, in concert with school-based staff, basic frameworks and standards for each course, and related implementation and assessment strategies. The frameworks should: 1. delineate expected student outcomes at all grades; 2. identify acceptable performance standards at both 'satisfactory' and 'excellent' levels; 3. include suggestions for instructional modifications necessary to ensure that a maximum number of students master identified outcomes; 4. include a profile of criterion-referenced assessment tools to measure student progress; and 5. include portfolios and related performance-assessment instruments.

> **KEY POINT:** *Our very system of assessment in the United States reinforces students' expectations that there is always a single right answer and that the goal of education is for the student to learn that answer. This mentality must change and be reflected in new assessment and instructional strategies that ensure not only mastery of subject matter but evidence of the capacity to use that information in a productive way.*

A fundamental and required process for any school system contemplating restructuring is the identification of outcome goals for all students. For example, the entire K–12 curricula should be committed to preparing students for success in post-secondary educational institutions and in the complex, change-governed contemporary world of work. At the completion of high school every student should be expected to master those higher-level skills identified by the College Board as necessary for success in both areas. Every student should also master the following higher-level skills identified by the College Board as necessary for success in the world of the 21st century:

- Analytical and critical reading;
- Speaking and listening;

CHAPTER 4 Transforming the Content and Delivery of Curriculum

- Writing in a variety of rhetorical modes and for a variety of audiences and purposes;
- Mathematical problem solving;
- Literacy in computer applications and related educational technology;
- Observation, including the ability to draw inferences and support conclusions with empirical evidence;
- Advanced study skills, including goal-setting, time management, research, and test-taking.

School systems must do everything within their power to ensure that all of their students graduate with the ability to think analytically and critically, to solve problems, and to make logical and coherent decisions. The business community continues to remind us that the worker of tomorrow must be able to think independently. He or she must also be able to tolerate ambiguity and cope with the change that seems to pervade our technology-driven world. Students must be more than passive recipients of pre-digested knowledge bites.

Our very system of assessment in the United States reinforces students' expectations that there is always a single right answer and that the goal of education is for the student to learn that answer. This mentality must change and be associated with new assessment and instructional strategies that ensure not only mastery of subject matter but evidence of the capacity to use that information in a productive way.

One of the most consistent elements of school improvement is the need to increase academic standards reflected in each subject taught in our schools. Further, it is critical that these new standards be delivered to all students in a delivery system characterized by sufficient time, quality instructional strategies, and relevance to the worlds of work and higher education. The SCANS report notes that:

> Tomorrow's career ladders require even the basic skills to take on new meaning. . . . future jobs will require employees who *read* well enough to understand and interpret diagrams, directories, correspondence, manuals, records, charts, graphs, tables, and specifications. . . . At the same time, most jobs will call for *writing skills* to prepare correspondence, instructions, charts, graphs, and proposals, in order to make requests, explain, illustrate, or convince. . . . and *computational* skills are also essential. Virtually all employees should be prepared to maintain records, estimate results, use spreadsheets, or apply statistical process controls as they negotiate, identify trends, or suggest new courses of action.

As administrators begin to pay more attention to issues of standards and curriculum, they must also begin to think through ways of redefining our courses to make them more rigorous and relevant to contemporary needs.

II. The Language-Arts Curriculum

> **KEY POINT:** *In spite of all of our new knowledge in the face of poor student performance in reading, most reading instruction has not changed in terms of its content, organization, or delivery. If school administrators and teachers are not willing to abandon the processes that we know do not work, there cannot be improvement. Even though most school administrators cannot and should not be expected to be experts in reading, they must be familiar enough with what constitutes good practice to allow them to make judgements about their programs, and be able to remove any real or perceived barriers that stand in the way of their effective implementation. Administrators cannot expect reading performance to improve if the basic delivery of such instruction remains more or less the same. They must be courageous enough to challenge current reading practices and to implement new methods and materials.*

An exploration of the role of reading instruction in the schools illustrates how each of the factors identified in this book are interrelated. Evaluation of current classroom practices and recent developments in reading and writing methods and classroom organization suggest that major shifts in reading and language-arts instruction must be accompanied by appropriate resources in the form of time, training, and materials. Moreover, new findings in reading instruction imply new approaches to instructional grouping practices, a development which impacts scheduling, administration, and staff allocation. Above all, the changes required in reading instruction should be supported and nurtured through viable instructional leadership, the kind identified as the key distinguishing feature of an effective administrator operating within the paradigm proposed in this document.

One would think that since reading has been an essential skill for our cultural and economic development for thousands of years, that all of our children would learn how to read and to accept reading as the most important skill for acquiring knowledge. However, practices that worked for a relatively small percentage of students in the nineteenth and early twentieth centuries no longer suffice where reading and a much higher level of literacy have become survival skills for each individual in our increasingly complex society of the 1990s and the decades ahead. Despite what seems to be an eternal debate concerning ways to teach students to read, educational research and effective classroom practices have clearly indicated methods and materials for effectively teaching all students.

> **KEY POINT:** *Today there is no longer any excuse left for not reaching all children. The issue now is to recognize what we know works, and find the will to change our current practices to make them work.*

As measured by norm-referenced achievement tests, reading achievement shows slight improvements in some cases. These tests are typically confined to the more mechanical aspects of reading, leaving the assessment of such skills as comprehension, identification of main ideas, and analysis woefully weak. Assessment of reading (and other disciplines) needs to move away from norm-referenced tests to criterion-referenced tests using a wide range of performance assessments reflecting the desired reading, writing, and educational goals. Experts in state and national assessment are moving in the direction of curriculum alignment, so that assessments will give a clear message to teachers—and in turn to administrators, parents, and students—as to what is really expected of all concerned.

There is now sufficient evidence to convince the most skeptical observers that there is a mismatch between many practices used to teach reading and the needs of many students. Reading instruction must be redesigned to use available time more effectively to increase direct instructional time for all students. Language arts programs at the secondary level should be redesigned to incorporate much of what current research reveals is both needed and wanted to ensure student success in this discipline. There should be a commitment to ensuring that challenging curricula are available for all students, not just an elite few. Through the students' study of literature, language, writing, and speaking/listening, they can be supported to become active learners who think critically and creatively. They can also be assisted to solve problems and make decisions related to human communication in a coherent, effective manner.

Efforts must be made to sort out the truly essential curriculum from a field that has become overcrowded and frequently disjointed. Moreover, the curriculum must have a multicultural focus, eliminating an exclusively Eurocentric or Western focus. We should help students to discover the history and contributions of major cultural groups within our society, particularly as they manifest themselves in literature and traditions.

Just as in the case of elementary schools, we ought to pay careful attention in our secondary schools to current research on reading, particularly from the perspective of cognitive psychology and schema theory. We now recognize that reading is a fluid, constructive process: meaning is created by the reader in response to the work, rather than simply being found in the work itself. Teachers need to pay careful attention to activating students' prior learning and knowledge, the schema structures they bring to the literary selections they study. This requires moving away from a micro-skills-based approach to literary selections for the at-risk student, for example, in favor of whole-text selections which are challenging and exciting as well as relevant. Reading instruction must be viewed as a fluent, strategic, and continuously developing complex of skills. Language arts teachers must actively pursue ways to engage student readers, to motivate them to make reading and thinking an essential part of both their academic and personal lives.

Similarly, writing instruction must be restructured in our schools. The writing-as-process model provides significant guidance in this area, with teachers encouraging students to view writing as a vehicle for communication and self-discovery. Much emphasis is placed upon the pre-writing phase in which students brainstorm and generate ideas, explore personal reactions and experiences, and use such cueing devices as free-writing, clustering/webbing, and related forms of advanced organizers to build idea fluency.

In the spirit of the writing-as-process model, students should be encouraged to become their own editors, rather than relying on the teacher's red pen. This process is further enhanced by extensive use of peer response groups during the initial drafting and later editing stages.

The critical importance of writing for an audience and emphasizing the importance of the writing process is reinforced through an emphasis upon student publishing, including student-generated anthologies, journals, classroom displays, and participation in local and national writing contests. This approach also suggests that we move away from a text-driven, grammar-in-isolation emphasis on language improvement, toward one which encourages students to approach grammar and usage within the context of writing itself. The effective implementation of the writing-as-process model will then make it possible to require exit essays at all transitional levels (elementary, middle, and high school).

Finally, there must be a significant emphasis placed upon students' oral communication skills. Speaking and listening, identified by the College Board as non-negotiable necessities, must become a fundamental part of the curriculum. Teachers need to make an active, ongoing effort to include both informal and formal speaking opportunities in all language arts classrooms. Co-operative learning structures such as diad and triad brainstorming, think-pair-share opportunities, formal debates, and seminars can be invaluable complements to full-group discussions. Oral defenses of theses or essays should be included as a key graduation requirement.

We next review recent research findings relating to the content, delivery, and evaluation of reading programs.

III. The Effective Teaching of Reading

The skill of reading is no longer seen as a discrete skill isolated from listening, speaking, writing, and the other language arts. Rather, reading is seen as an integral part of all language instruction and should therefore be integrated with all of the language arts, especially oral language development, and writing as a response to reading. If integrated imaginatively and creatively, and presented as a seamless whole, each is taught as a part of the daily lesson, in context with a clearly-stated purpose, and it reinforces all of the other language arts.

> **KEY POINT:** *A major conclusion of the research community and from effective teaching is that good literature and daily writing should form the foundation of all reading programs. More specifically:*

> - *The best of children's literature provides the appropriate models of usage and expression for children to become familiar with and imitate;*
> - *Writing is the most effective way for students to respond to our great literary heritage, to become active, creative learners, to integrate all of the language arts, and to learn how to think.*

Reading instruction builds essentially on oral language, and if this foundation is weak, progress in reading will be slow and uncertain. Therefore, it is essential to compensate for weaknesses in oral language, especially with at-risk children, and before formal instruction begins in kindergarten or first grade.

In place of the old assumption that a strong beginning reading program is sufficient, or that reading skills can be absorbed passively or intuitively, it is now recognized that *reading is an active, constructive process*. Therefore, the teacher who lectures continually is no longer seen as effective; rather, teachers are much more successful if they are coaches, modelling strategies of learning to students, and letting students assume responsibility for questioning, clarifying, predicting, summarizing, and leading the discussion, as is done in reciprocal teaching.

A systematic and complete phonics program is an essential element of beginning reading programs so that all students can learn the regularities of English at the very beginning and can internalize the logic of spelling and pronunciation by the end of the first grade. A solid and intensive phonics foundation at the very outset provides the fluency and automaticity required to make reading effortless and pleasurable.

A major conclusion of the research community and from effective teaching is that good literature and daily writing should form the foundation of all reading programs. More specifically:

- The best of children's literature provides the appropriate models of usage and expression for children to become familiar with and imitate;
- Writing is the most effective way for students to respond to works of great literary power, to become active, creative learners, to integrate all of the language arts, and to learn how to think.

One of the important findings of recent years is that schools benefit from cultivating very close working relationships with parents. Students are in the classroom for a relatively small portion of their time between birth and age 18, so parents must reinforce at home what is taught in the classroom. A major vehicle for such reinforcement is the assignment of sufficient and high-quality homework. Parents can ensure that such homework is effective through controlling time spent watching television, providing a learning environment for study, engaging in challenging dialogues with their children, and reading aloud to and with them at least daily. Schools had better assume the responsibility of helping parents perform these tasks.

There are five additional critical variables which influence the reading process and which should be present in all effective reading programs. School administrators ought to ensure that all of the policies and practices in their system are designed to expedite and not hinder the implementation of these new practices. These critical variables are:

- Sufficient time and effective use of time for reading instruction;
- Grouping in the reading program;
- Monitoring student achievement in reading;
- Strategies used in reading instruction;
- Materials used in reading instruction.

IV. Sufficient Time and Effective Use of Time for Reading Instruction

Perhaps the most obvious and consistent finding concerning effective teaching is that learning improves as direct instructional time increases. However, in spite of this finding, the use of time for reading is often characterized by activities that do not involve direct interactions between teachers and students, or computers and students, or students with students. Rather, much time is spent with students completing dittos and worksheets, copying from the board, allowing frequent interruptions of a non-academic nature, and getting a head start on the next day's homework. This inefficient use of time is primarily a function of the ways in which we group and manage our students.

Many schools allow 90 minutes per day for reading and language arts. In most cases the students are divided into three groups, each of which receives 30 minutes of direct instruction and 60 minutes of other activities (completing worksheets, dittos, homework, or visiting the library). These activities are of limited value and they are *not* effective in reinforcing or extending what was taught in the 30 minutes of direct instruction.

A typical response to the problems associated with the traditional three groups for reading is: 'I don't understand the issue. This three-group process worked for me when I was in school.' The truth is that it probably did work for many. However, the nature of our student population has changed. In those cases where the student body was primarily middle class, and came to school already having experienced learning in the home or pre-school environment, and had reasonably good work habits, they were able to take advantage of the 60 minutes of indirect instruction. They would actually work through the dittos and worksheets and use those experiences for positive learning. Today, on the other hand, many students come to school without the home learning or pre-school experiences and work habits that enable them to benefit from indirect instruction. Many of today's students have difficulty in maintaining a focus on indirect instruction because they are easily distracted and therefore often misdiagnosed as having serious learning or behavioral problems.

> **KEY POINT:** *The differences in learning styles between average middle class students and students from more disadvantaged backgrounds must not be interpreted as differences in ability, intelligence, or potential. Teaching styles that worked with students in the past do not work as well with contemporary students. It is the responsibility of the educator, therefore, to identify and implement those procedures which are most likely to be effective given the traits and conditions that students bring to school with them in today's society. It is also important to note that these new teaching styles must be implemented without minimizing or otherwise changing expectations for student performance.*

Although school administrators do not have to be experts in reading instruction, they should take the initiative to bring the best available practices to their school systems and to require the implementation of these practices. They must be able to counter the common response from many teachers who explain students' lack of progress in reading by blaming the victim, for example, 'The student has a rather low IQ score,' or, 'The student does not concentrate and seems to daydream while I am teaching.' The most effective way of countering these beliefs is to be armed with the facts and with knowledge of what is known to work. It must be recognized that *the extent of direct instructional time spent in reading must exceed the 30 minutes or so that we now provide in most of our classrooms.* Direct instructional time includes such activities as:

- Teacher-led whole class or small group instruction, including teachers reading aloud to students with emphasis on interactive dialogue rather than lecturing and directing the class towards the teachers' answers;
- Students working with classroom computers or in computer labs;
- Students participating in co-operative learning groups such as reciprocal teaching;
- Peer tutoring under teacher direction;
- Teacher-directed writing activities based upon responses to reading selections and other classroom activities;
- High-quality homework assignments such as writing assignments and book reports.

Once again, direct instructional time does not include completing worksheets or dittos, copying from the board, working on the next day's homework, or reading silently.

V. Grouping in the Reading Program

Traditionally, elementary classrooms have been organized in three instructional groups based on students' achievement levels as indicated by basal assessment tests or similar measures. Research clearly documents that students in lower groups tend to be perpetually assigned to low groups, and this low-group status is maintained throughout those students' school careers. A cycle of failure becomes established in which students fall further and further behind, never having an opportunity to learn the skills and concepts needed for higher achievement. Being in the bottom group leads to increased frustration, further failure, and eventually dropping out of school. Given that the three-reading-group organization *minimizes* the amount of direct instructional time that students receive, it should not be used. In its place schools should employ instructional strategies which create opportunities for students to advance to higher achievement levels. (See Appendix A for alternative grouping strategies.)

Students may be part of several types of reading instructional groups at the same time. For example, a student who needs to develop skill in identifying a main idea may be in a skills group with 'main idea' as its focus, while at the same time the student might be working with another group of students on a children's literature selection. Groups should not remain intact for an entire school year; they may last for a few days or weeks.

KEY POINT: *Grouping strategies which are designed to eliminate tracking or grouping stagnation and create opportunities for students to advance to higher achievement levels should be used. Flexibility is the key. Ways of organizing a class to promote flexibility include:*

- *Individual students working independently or with the teacher;*
- *A co-operative learning group as designated by reciprocal teaching procedures;*
- *Whole-class grouping in which the teacher must learn the skills to challenge and keep every child alert;*
- *Groups organized on the basis of students' special needs;*
- *Support groups of students who help one another;*
- *Tutorial groups, aided by students of high capability;*
- *Interest groups organized on the basis of common interest;*
- *Research groups organized on the basis of curiosity.*

The *traditional* three-group structure for organizing classroom reading instruction must be replaced. Alternative strategies should provide at least 60 minutes and preferably 90 minutes of direct instruction per day.

The Issue of Whole-Class Grouping

Many teachers believe that because of student differences, and the likelihood that they would have to be teaching 30 or so students, whole-class instruction would not be effective. They are both right and wrong. They are right if one assumes that their teaching strategies remain the same. They are wrong if one assumes that they incorporate more effective teaching strategies.

For example, whole-class instruction featuring co-operative learning groups is an appropriate organizational strategy for reading instruction. Most students are placed in grade-level material or, at least, the same material. Attention is given to students' individual differences through small-group instruction or skill groups related to objectives presented in the whole-class instruction. Where the discrepancy between reading ability and text difficulty is small, students engage in more independent trade book reading and work in co-operative groups under teachers' guidance and monitoring. In situations where the text and ability discrepancies are greater, teachers must provide more direct instruction, including modeling and interactive teaching.

Whole class grouping for reading is appropriate when:

- The objectives to be taught through the lesson are needed by all students, and,
- There is follow-up for students with special needs.

Examples of activities that are particularly adaptable to whole-group instruction are establishing prior knowledge, building vocabulary, reciprocal teaching and co-operative learning, practicing reading and studying strategies, introducing and discussing children's literature selections, providing background, and discussing content selections.

VI. Monitoring Student Achievement in Reading

Traditional ways to monitor student achievement in reading have included: 1. the rate of completion of basal readers; 2. the use of results from basal reader unit or placement tests; 3. the use of results from standardized achievement or ability tests; and 4. completion of class assignments and homework. These types of measures typically have resulted in the perpetuation of a three-group classroom organizational pattern, with little opportunity for students to demonstrate ability to work with higher groups.

Research indicates that the frequent monitoring of student achievement and the subsequent adjustment of instruction based on that achievement is most likely to lead to improvements in reading. Therefore, it is critical that teachers be provided with assessment instruments which allow them to make such adjustments. It is recommended that classroom feedback, criterion referenced tests (CRT's) and performance-based assessment tests be used for these purposes.

Feedback from daily instruction is the most effective way for teachers and students to monitor the progress of students. Assuming that teachers provide a diversity of feedback (such as dictation, proofreading, using the dictionary to check spelling, vocabulary, and usage), students will then know themselves what problems they have encountered, if any, and have the skills and strategies to correct their own errors of spelling, grammar, usage, and vocabulary.

If teachers monitor students' reading aloud, as well as their compositions, they can watch the progress of all students and help those who are falling behind before they have severe problems and become discouraged. Teachers should also provide special homework assignments so that these students can catch up. For those students who are indeed falling behind, special arrangements should be made to attend school catch-up sessions, Saturday school, and even during summer holidays.

If CRT's are used, they can be administered in September, January, and May. The September and January scores can be used for identifying students' specific strengths and weaknesses and can serve as a means of assigning them to groups based on their performance on specific objectives on the CRT. For example, if a third-grader achieves an overall score of 80 out of 100 but does not do well on the objective which measures inferences, that student could be placed in a skills group with other students who did not do well in inferences. The end-of-the-year (May) CRT's, on the other hand, can be used as a means of determining how much of the curriculum a student mastered during the year and can provide a description of the summary performance of an entire school.

> **KEY POINT:** *There are three ways to use CRT results for assigning students to groups:*
> - *Scores on specific objectives can be used to place students in short-term skill groups;*
> - *Scores on clusters of similar objectives can be used to place students in short-term skill groups;*
> - *Total scores can be used to place students in short-term skill groups.*

In addition to monitoring progress using CRT's, it is crucial that teachers use additional techniques for assessing reading. The assessment of basic reading proficiency can be obtained by ascertaining whether students can do the following:

- Read aloud unfamiliar but grade-appropriate material with acceptable fluency;
- Write satisfactory summaries of unfamiliar selections from grade-appropriate social studies and science textbooks;
- Explain the plots and motivations of the characters in unfamiliar grade-appropriate fiction;
- Read intensively during leisure time from books, magazines, and newspapers.

Although high test scores are a laudable and achievable goal for children from all backgrounds, that is not the ultimate goal—which is to provide an instructional program that introduces children to the best of children's books and writing; challenges children to read many of the great children's books; and encourages children to enjoy reading as much as sports or television viewing so that they develop the reading habit at an early age. Such a goal is not an impossible dream, but a practical and achievable reality! As *Becoming a Nation of Readers* stated in 1985,

> If the practices seen in the classrooms of the best teachers in the best schools could be introduced everywhere, improvements would be dramatic.

In the 1990s we know much more than we did in the 1980s, so that statement is accurate beyond any reasonable doubt. It is just a matter of tenacity, commitment, and implementation.

KEY POINT: *Create frequent opportunities for students to move to higher instructional levels.*

VII. Instructional Strategies Used in Reading Instruction

Traditional instruction in reading focuses on step-by-step use of the basal reader and the basal reader teacher's manual. Seldom is time given to direct teaching of comprehension skills; to using the writing process to reinforce and extend reading instruction; to the use of co-operative learning strategies; or to the employment of new technology to support instruction.

Research supports the use of specific strategies for reading instruction including, but not limited to, intensive phonics instruction in grades K–2; reciprocal teaching; teacher modeling or demonstration of specific reading strategies; the use of writing to reinforce reading comprehension; the use of graphic organizers; computer-assisted instruction; the use of co-operative learning strategies; and encouraging students to enjoy reading as an important source of information and pleasure. Students can be grouped into heterogeneous learning teams to work towards a shared group goal. Co-operative learning techniques are useful for working with heterogeneous groups of students, particularly in teaching literature and research skills.

> **KEY POINT**: *Flexibility in grouping and frequent and conscientious monitoring will prevent grouping stagnation. Reading instruction should utilize flexible grouping, provide opportunities for students to read a wide variety of materials including children's literature, and participate in writing activities that include responding to literature, keeping journals, creative writing, report writing and writing classroom stories and reports. An effective learning environment will also include listening and speaking activities essential in a language-rich classroom.*

Basal reading materials are the primary tool used in many reading programs. Although recent editions of basal readers are much improved in terms of reading selections and instructional guidance provided for staff, students must have experience reading from a wide variety of materials. Research clearly supports the need for incorporation of children's literature, content materials, and functional (real-life) materials in direct reading instruction. Therefore, in addition to use of the basal reader, reading materials employed in direct instruction with students should include literature books, texts and other selections on topics related to science, social studies and other content areas; reference materials; student-developed materials; and everyday reading materials.

Flexibility in grouping and frequent and conscientious monitoring will prevent grouping stagnation. Reading instruction should utilize flexible grouping, provide opportunities for students to read a wide variety of materials including children's literature, and participate in writing activities that include responding to literature, keeping journals, creative writing, report writing and writing classroom stories and reports. An effective learning environment will also include strengthened opportunities for listening and speaking activities essential in a language-rich classroom.

VIII. Indicators of an Effective Reading Program

There are three questions which school administrators must answer as they assess and monitor their reading programs: 1. Are appropriate oral language and introductory phonics activities given to kindergarten students to provide them with the proper foundation for later success in reading? 2. Are appropriate strategies in use for non-readers in grades 3–6? and, 3. What is being done to eliminate the decline in reading performance that typically occurs sometime after the completion of the third grade?

1. Are appropriate activities given to kindergarten students to provide them with the proper foundation for later success in reading?

Activities that will assist students in early language development include the following:
- Interactive discussions to develop oral language abilities;
- Reading aloud early;
- Phonics: awareness of names and sounds of letters and oral blending of sounds and syllables into words;
- Teaching integrated language arts;
- Using big books;
- Using predictable books;
- Using finger plays and songs;
- Using computers;
- Discussions;
- Integrating literacy activities into the content areas;
- Providing dramatic play activities.

2. Are appropriate strategies in use for non-readers in grades 3–6?

Students who are non-readers in grades 3–6 may benefit from the following kinds of instructional strategies:

- Integrated language arts with emphases on dictation and daily writing;
- Strengthening oral language capabilities;
- Reading aloud;
- Composing dialogue and script for picture sequences;
- Choral reading;
- Paired reading;
- Tutoring;
- Response journals;
- Interactive teaching;
- Reciprocal teaching.

3. What is being done to eliminate the decline in reading performance that typically occurs sometime after the completion of the third grade?

First of all, monitoring the student performance and making the necessary adjustments from the first through the third grades will all but eliminate the decline in performance at the end of the third grade. However, research has demonstrated that fourth-grade students who seem to have performed at a satisfactory level through grade three often experience difficulty and show signs of reading failure. Specifically, some of the causes of difficulty may be due to:

- Increase in the amount of required reading;
- Difficulty of vocabulary and concepts;
- Introduction of specific content;
- Increased amount and complexity of content reading;
- Shift from predominantly narrative to increased emphasis on expository text;
- Lack of sufficient prior knowledge to meet reading demands;
- Increased demands for students to read independently;
- Lack of appropriate study skills;
- Inadequate foundation in decoding and word attack strategies;
- Inadequate or inappropriate reading materials;
- Insufficient opportunities to read a variety of materials;
- Need for teacher training in use of a variety of reading strategies.

Suggestions for minimizing this decline in performance include:

1. **Teaching comprehension strategies through:**
   - Providing direct instruction in comprehension by explaining the steps to be used through teacher modeling and thinking aloud, along with providing information on why and how to use the strategy;
   - Teaching children to summarize;
   - Activating prior knowledge and having students use the writing process;
   - Teaching thinking skills to enhance comprehension;
   - Teaching text structure to help students differentiate among types of writing and become proficient at determining how materials are organized;
   - Teaching children to use predictions in reading;
   - Using graphic organizers to help students visualize relationships.

2. **Developing strategies for systemically teaching vocabulary, including:**
   - Independent reading;
   - Interdisciplinary projects;
   - Writing;
   - Word games;
   - Read-aloud activities;
   - Vocabulary instruction including analogies and antonyms.

3. **Teaching self-management and study strategies, including improving students abilities to study independently and to read efficiently. Self management and study strategies may include:**
   - Time management skills;
   - Study skills;
   - Tape recording lessons for review;
   - Using co-operative learning for study sessions, advance organizers, and reading guides.

4. **Using interactive teaching strategies such as reciprocal teaching and concept attainment.**
   - Identifying and assisting students who lack a foundation in decoding and word attack skills.

IX. Monitoring Your Reading Program

Whether you are a superintendent, central office staff member, or building principal, as a final step in monitoring the state of your reading program, keep asking the following questions of your teachers. Their answers to these questions should provide you with the necessary insights for making your own judgments as to your program's effectiveness.

1. How do you group students for reading?
2. How do you group your students at the beginning of the school year? What kinds of information do you use? Do you group based on instructional level or need? How many of your students are in higher level reading groups now than they were in September?
3. To what extent do you believe that students should move from one group to another during the year or would they learn more if they stayed in the same group for most of the year?
4. What kind of information do you or would you use to move a student from one group to another?
5. For how much time are students given *direct* instruction per day? Briefly describe what happens to those students not receiving direct instruction. How do they spend time? What materials do they use?
6. How often do you assign homework in reading? What kind of homework is given? Do all groups get the same amount of homework? How many hours do your teachers expect children to read at home, and do they convey those expectations to parents? How much writing (composition) homework is assigned?
7. How many minutes do students do worksheets per reading/language arts block of time per day? Per week?
8. Is there any difference between your reading basal text, the school system's reading curriculum, and the reading assessments, or are they more or less synonymous?
9. How are word attack skills typically taught to a group of students?
10. How are students typically taught to decode words?
11. What do you believe are the major reasons for differences in black and white or socio-economically advantaged or disadvantaged student achievement?
12. This year, what percent of your students will be performing below, at, or above grade level? What are you doing to reduce the percentage of those performing below grade level?

CHAPTER 4 Transforming the Content and Delivery of Curriculum

X. The Mathematics Curriculum

Rapid changes in technology and the skills required in today's work force have already reshaped conceptions of what it means to have 'basic skills' in mathematics. There is scarcely a single occupation that does not or will not one day require a relatively sophisticated knowledge of the application of mathematics to real-world situations. If anything, the mathematics skills required to be competitive in the work force will even intensify. The implication is clear: school systems are going to have to deliver high-quality mathematics programs to the vast majority of their students and ensure that those students succeed at math. The practice of responding to increasing mathematics standards by adding additional low-level mathematics courses to the curriculum must stop.

Standards and Guidelines

The Curriculum and Evaluation Standards for School Mathematics developed by the National Council of Teachers of Mathematics (NCTM) provide educators with the basic curriculum framework for mathematics. These standards are research-based and represent a consensus among leading mathematics educators. The issue of what our students need to know is no longer a matter of conjecture. Administrators must now ensure that these standards are embodied in the selection criteria for new teachers and in the professional development provided for current mathematics teachers, specialists, and supervisors.

> **KEY POINT:** *The NCTM standards document emphasizes that* higher level *mathematics must be viewed as a fundamental part of the essential curriculum for all students and that all curricula and associated staff development should be revised to reflect this fact.*

As the Council suggests, appropriate mathematics curricula should enable students to:

- Learn to value mathematics;
- Learn to reason mathematically;

- Learn to communicate mathematically;
- Be confident of their mathematical abilities;
- Be mathematical problem-solvers.

A careful review of the NCTM Standards implies a set of guidelines that administrators could use to evaluate and modify their mathematics programs. These guidelines could include the following:

- *Teachers and administrators must develop and/or use curricula based on the NCTM standards.* For example, the secondary school curriculum is typically separated into courses with a specific subject orientation (such as algebra, geometry, and calculus). The Standards now challenge educators to integrate mathematics topics across courses so that students can view major mathematical ideas from more than one perspective.
- *The Standards cannot be met by the use of most of the existing textbooks or worksheets.* It is important for all staff to be familiar with the new standards and ensure, perhaps with the use of outside experts, that all instructional materials and textbooks reflect those standards.
- *Tests must be used which measure problem solving and reasoning.* Continuing to use tests which focus primarily on computational skills will only ensure that a disproportionate amount of time will be spent on teaching those skills.
- *Instruction must be consistent with the vision implied in the Standards.* Teachers must assign appropriate project work, group and individual assignments, discussions between and among students and teachers, practice on and with mathematical methods, and exposition by the teacher.
- *Teacher in-service programs must help teachers to encourage students to reason, explore, and communicate.* They must also be designed to help teachers talk to each other about instructional strategies, problems, and solutions.
- *Calculators, software, and manipulative materials are required for the effective implementation of the Standards.* Relying on paper and pencils as the major instructional tools in our classrooms ought to stop. Teachers should integrate a wide range of materials into the classroom activities. Calculators should be available to all students at all times. Students should have access to computers for individual and group work, and students should learn to use the computer as a tool

for processing information and performing calculations to investigate and solve problems.
- *Mathematics instruction ought to emphasize problem solving rather than the memorization of facts and algorithms.* Resources which involve mathematics applications in the real world should be provided to teachers to support problem solving activities.
- *There should be increased, uninterrupted and carefully protected time spent teaching mathematics in the classroom.* About an hour per day is the desired target.
- *Departmentalization in mathematics beginning at least in Grade 4, to provide students with the best possible mathematics learning environment, should be seriously considered.* Departmentalization will also allow the exploitation of the talents of those teachers who have interest and expertise in mathematics.
- *The Standards are for all students, not just a few.* Principals and teachers have to find ways of varying the delivery of instruction to ensure that all students can learn challenging curricula.
- *Administration should not be permitted to restrict teaching by mandating* such things as the number of chapters to be covered in a textbook, providing insufficient time for instruction, or evaluating teacher performance according to factors that are not conducive to effective teaching.
- *Principals, guidance counselors, and teachers should give high visibility* to ideas that convey to both school and community that all students can and must learn mathematics, that knowledge of mathematics is important in all walks of life, and that mathematics is valued in this technological society. Guidance counselors, in particular, should be made aware of the relationship between the type of mathematics courses taken in the middle school and later success in high school.
- *School personnel must help all students to understand* that a knowledge of mathematics is needed to better prepare them for higher education and the world of work.

Setting System Goals for Mathematics Performance

To increase the chances that the NCTM Standards actually influence what gets taught and how it gets taught, superintendents should adopt a set of clear goals concerning mathematics. These goals should be ambitious and cause staff to stretch their capacities. When such goals are established, superintendents should be prepared to hear that such goals will cause morale problems and that they will be unfair to the many students who will not be able to cope. These reactions must be confronted directly. Staff must understand that such reactions are not compatible with the high expectations that most of them claim to have for every child. Central office staff must also do whatever is required to provide teachers with the know-how, materials, and time required to deliver the more advanced curricula to all students.

> **KEY POINT:** *Algebra should be considered the new minimum. Policies and practices should be implemented to ensure that the maximum number of students are successful in algebra prior to entering high school; even if it means that some students receive double periods of pre-algebra and/or algebra and do not take otherwise interesting but less important courses.*

Mathematics goals could include the following:
- By the end of 6th grade, all students will successfully master the mathematics skills and concepts necessary to enable them to enter pre-algebra in the 7th Grade;
- By the end of 8th grade, all students will successfully complete pre-algebra;
- By the end of 9th grade at least 90 percent of students will successfully complete Algebra I;
- By the end of 11th grade, all students will successfully complete Geometry as a minimum mathematics requirement;
- By the end of 12th grade, 70 percent of students will have successfully completed mathematics courses in each year of high school;
- College-bound students will enroll in calculus-track mathematics courses during each of their high school years;

Algebra should be considered the new minimum. Policies and practices should be implemented to ensure that the maximum number of students are successful in algebra prior to entering high school, even if it means that some students receive double periods of pre-algebra and/or algebra and do not take otherwise interesting but less important courses.

XI. Staffing for Improved Mathematics Performance

If teachers do not understand mathematics themselves, they cannot teach the subject. Schools of education and local school systems are going to have to be more aggressive in helping teachers and teachers-to-be to meet the NCTM standards. Administrators can ensure that the standards are met by aggressively supporting the following policies and practices:

- Mathematics specialists should be placed in every elementary school and should be responsible for teaching and providing professional development to other staff. At a minimum these specialists must possess a degree in elementary education with a strong minor in mathematics;
- Mathematics teachers should be required at the elementary, middle, and high school levels to satisfy high preparation/certification requirements at their respective levels;
- Elementary school teachers should successfully complete 15 hours of mathematics in college;
- Middle school mathematics teachers should at the minimum have minored in mathematics or mathematics education in college;
- High school mathematics teachers should have majored in either mathematics or mathematics education in college;
- Pre-algebra, algebra, and geometry teachers with elementary certification should take classes in those respective subjects.

Improving the Capacity of Mathematics Teachers

To ensure that today's students are prepared to meet the mathematics challenges of tomorrow, teachers have to upgrade their skills regularly. A sound staff development program for teachers of mathematics must be designed to improve teachers' subject mastery and skills in utilizing effective pedagogy. To accomplish this goal, school systems should:

- Involve all teachers in *ongoing* professional development to promote the use of instructional strategies and materials that increase student participation and success in advanced mathematics courses;
- Make time available during the school day (or by lengthening the school day) for ongoing staff development;
- Work closely with local universities and colleges to upgrade the skills

of currently certified teachers and to require teachers who are teaching out of field to receive the proper certification;
- Allocate resources and work with local universities and colleges to help teachers develop instructional strategies and materials that will facilitate teaching mathematics to all students.

> **KEY POINT:** *The focus of school mathematics is shifting from a dual mission—minimal mathematics for the majority and advanced mathematics for a few—to a singular focus on a significant common core of mathematics for all students.*

XII. Mathematics Instruction in the Classroom

> The United States must restructure its mathematics curriculum—both what is taught and the way it is taught—if our children are to develop the mathematical knowledge (and the confidence to use that knowledge) that they will need to be personally and professionally competent in the 21st Century. This restructuring involves more than producing new texts or retraining teachers. Replacing parts is not sufficient. What is required is a complete redesign of the content of school mathematics and the way it is taught. (National Research Council, 1990 *Reshaping School Mathematics*.)

The National Research Council and other recent sources suggest that the overall restructuring of the content and delivery of mathematics education in America's classrooms be changed in the following ways:

- *From an authoritarian model based upon "transmission of knowledge" to student-centered practice featuring "stimulation of learning". We can no longer act as if mathematics is a fixed and unchanging body of facts and procedures;*
- *From an assumption that effective mathematics instruction requires passively absorbing information and storing it in easily retrievable fragments as a result of repeated practice and reinforcement to the use of such information for solving problems that have practical relevance to students;*
- *From preoccupation with inculcating routine skills to developing broad-based mathematical capabilities;*

- *From primary emphasis on paper-and-pencil calculations to full use of calculators and computers.* Mathematics students should not spend much time calculating answers to problems using a specific catalogue of rehearsed techniques.

We can now be confident that effective mathematics instruction should be characterized by:

- *Students receiving ongoing instruction designed to improve their understanding of mathematical relations in a variety of contexts.* Such instruction helps students to reason logically and to solve a variety of problems, both routine and non-routine;
- *Students learning to read documents using mathematical methods and to express quantitative and logical analyses in oral and written form;*
- *Students using calculators and computers throughout the mathematics curriculum.* Such technologies allow for the de-emphasis of time-consuming algorithmic calculations and allow students to participate actively in the actual process of mathematics: in conjecture and argument, in exploration and reasoning, in formulating and solving, in calculation and verification;
- *Students using mathematical tools in contexts that mirror their use in real-world situations.* Mathematical ideas should always be presented and developed in the context of meaningful mathematical activities;
- *Students being involved as active learners.* No single teaching method nor any single kind of learning experience can develop the varied mathematical abilities. What is needed is a variety of activities, including discussion among pupils, practical work, practice of important techniques, problem solving, application to everyday situations, investigational work, and exposition by the teacher.

XIII. General Staff Development Procedures

A new curriculum suggests new pedagogy. New pedagogy, in turn, suggests the need for retraining and re-educating teachers. What sort of retraining and re-education is necessary? What implementation procedures are appropriate? What roles does the educational administrator play in these matters? These issues are addressed in a companion volume to the Curriculum and Evaluation Standards, also published by the NCTM and entitled *Professional Standards For Teaching Mathe-*

matics. To imagine the scope of the necessary re-education and training efforts, we can look at the five major shifts described at the beginning of the *Professional Standards for Teaching Mathematics*.

We need to shift:

toward classrooms as mathematical communities and away from classrooms as simply collections of individuals,

toward logic and mathematical evidence as verification and away from the teacher as the sole authority for right answers,

toward mathematical reasoning and away from merely memorizing procedures,

toward conjecturing, inventing, and problem solving and away from an emphasis on mechanistic answer-finding, and

toward connecting mathematics, its ideas, and its applications and away from treating mathematics as a body of isolated concepts and procedures.

Clearly, to make these shifts successfully and in a reasonable time will tax the leadership capabilities of school administrators. Where does one begin?

Hire Competent Mathematics Specialists: Mathematics specialists must be available to classroom teachers on a continuing and regular schedule. This is especially true for the elementary grades where most teachers are not strong in mathematics.

Identify Teacher Leaders: Those teachers who have backgrounds in mathematics, who are comfortable teaching it, and who understand the importance of mathematics (as distinct from arithmetic) in the lives of their students should be identified and used as school-based staff developers and mentors.

Establish Support Seminars: Teachers have to be able to share problems and solutions with each other. Creating procedures to organize and facilitate such discussion is essential. One good way to do this is to schedule seminars in which teachers can share problems and their solutions. Such seminars must be available regularly and must be led by carefully chosen and well-prepared professionals who are knowledgeable in mathematics, pedagogy and the art of interpersonal communication. The importance of knowledge in mathematics and pedagogy is fairly obvious; an understanding of interpersonal communication is important because the leader must be able to guide discussion and help teachers reach reasonable conclusions, not impose his or her views.

Establish First-Year Expectations and Subsequent Year Expectations: Don't expect the kind of curriculum reform called for by the NCTM standards to be accomplished in one or two years. That's not realistic. This doesn't mean that a schedule of year-by-year expectations should not be published and reviewed annually.

Make Use of Mathematics Teachers Conventions: The National Council of Teachers of Mathematics (NCTM) sponsors regional conventions throughout the country. These conventions are rich resources for teacher re-education and renewal. Establishing standard procedures for helping teachers to attend these conventions and report back to their colleagues can be an important ongoing activity. Calendars of upcoming conventions are maintained by the NCTM and published in their journals.

Make Teacher Journals Available: Many journals are published specifically for classroom teachers. They contain new ideas, communications from teachers, advertisements for new products, and much more. Two notable journals, both published by the NCTM, are devoted exclusively to the problems of teaching mathematics. *The Arithmetic Teacher* addresses elementary and middle school mathematics, while *The Mathematics Teacher* addresses middle school and secondary school mathematics. Having such journals available in teachers' lounges and school libraries for instructional leaders, and even for individual classroom teachers, can be a low-cost, effective way of keeping instructional personnel in tune with the latest professional developments. Special bulk subscriptions to these journals are often available.

Order Extra Teachers' Guides: A good curriculum will have teachers' guides that are essential for implementing content, pedagogy, long-range planning, and daily planning. Despite their central role, teachers often ignore the guides and focus attention on those aspects of the curriculum represented in the student books. Ordering extra teachers' guides so that every teacher can have one in school and one at home, will not only emphasize the importance of the guides, it will help teachers prepare lessons at home and, will be seen by teachers as a sign of caring and support for them.

Enlist Family Involvement: Parents can be important allies, but the sort of co-operation that is necessary does not happen without careful planning and frequent communication. Wise administrators enlist parental involvement in all stages of curriculum decision-making, beginning with the earliest stages of curriculum study and continuing through all stages of implementation. Communication can be achieved directly, by involving parents in curriculum decisions, through workshops, letters, and through homework assignments. All are important.

Parents and teachers must distinguish between two very different kinds of homework. Both are important. The first, traditional homework, usually takes the form of assignments based on work done in class and is most often used as a way of extending the school day. Wise teachers use this form of homework to meet the individual needs of each student, since not all students need the same kind or amount of skill practice, and individualized assignments can meet the needs of all students. Traditional homework assignments can also be used to communicate to parents about the mathematics topics being considered in class, as well as the performance of their children.

The second kind of homework is much more difficult to assign, for it often requires the active participation of other family members. Here we are talking about having youngsters do mathematics at home that relates to, and highlights the usefulness of, the mathematics being learned in school. Such homework might involve youngsters in decision-making at home, might have youngsters playing mathematical games with other family members, or might have youngsters explore connections between mathematics and other subjects in which they might be interested.

XIV. Indicators of Effective Mathematics Instruction (Questions that Administrators Should Ask)

Having begun the process of change, we are still faced with the question of how school administrators can monitor what is happening in the classroom. What happens as individual teachers implement new curricula? What should administrators and instructional leaders look for?

CHAPTER 4 Transforming the Content and Delivery of Curriculum   143

Since they can't know for sure without remaining in the classroom for long periods of time, are there clues one might look for during regular observations? There are indeed tangible clues.

1. *Does the teacher use the teacher's guide?* If your school has chosen a good mathematics curriculum, the teacher's guide will be the heart of the program. If a teacher is using only the student book, it is unlikely that he or she is implementing the curriculum effectively.
2. *Is the class well organized?* In an effective mathematics classroom, materials are well organized and there is very little time lost as students go from one part of the lesson to the next. Too much lost time and ineffective use of materials is a clue that a problem exists.
3. *Is discipline maintained?* A good mathematics curriculum will have youngsters discussing problems, co-operating on projects, interacting with the teacher and playing games without interrupting the learning of others. Are expectations for such behavior in evidence? If not, that is a sign of trouble.
4. *Does the classroom atmosphere promote inquiry, thinking, and enjoyment?* Do the interactions between teacher and students, and among students themselves, promote true inquiry, with alternative procedures and answers considered? Or, is there only one answer to a problem, with little or no discussion allowed? Are the students enjoying the mathematics lesson? Is the teacher enjoying the lesson? If not, there is a problem.
5. *Is the class proceeding through the school year on about the right schedule?* A good curriculum will allow teachers to proceed from lesson to lesson without necessarily achieving mastery of all of the material covered, because the material is taken up again in later lessons. Although this spiral type of curriculum is not a new idea, many teachers are uncomfortable with it, and, especially in the first year of teaching a new program, some teachers will tend to fall behind and not complete the curriculum. A good curriculum will have comprehensive teachers' guides that explain this sort of pacing. If the class is significantly off-schedule, there is a problem.
6. *Are all components of each lesson being used?* A good curriculum will have a typical 45-minute lesson subdivided into segments based on differing content and pedagogy. Typically, these will include games, activities, mental arithmetic exercises, stories, discussions, direct teaching, drill and traditional workbook exercis-

es. Although teachers should feel comfortable modifying a lesson to meet a particular need, if each lesson consists largely of traditional workbook exercises, there is a problem. Each of the other components mentioned here are likely to be essential as well, and a teacher who systematically excludes a particular type of activity must be re-educated regarding its importance.

7. *Are problem-solving activities emphasized, particularly involving problems with open-ended answers, problems solved in a co-operative atmosphere, and problems solved with the use of technology?* Learning experiences should be designed to help students reason mathematically, to make conjectures, to build arguments, and to gather evidence. Students should be encouraged to apply mathematical knowledge to new, unique settings, rather than through exclusive use of formulaic, exercise-based activities.

8. *Is there evidence of mutual interaction and feedback?* Good teaching requires continual interaction between teacher and students so that the teacher gets feedback on how well the lesson is going and the students get feedback on how well they are learning. A good mathematics curriculum will use games, discussions and special response exercises to achieve this. If a lesson does not elicit mutual interaction, and if there are long periods in which information flows only one way, then there is a problem.

9. *Are assessment procedures in evidence?* A good curriculum will provide daily opportunities for informal assessment, but also more formal procedures for diagnosing specific difficulties, measuring achievement, and monitoring student progress. Evidence that such diagnosis and assessment has taken place can usually be gathered from examining class record books or other management devices provided by the publisher.

10. *Is communication with parents effective?* Evidence that communication with parents is effective is suggested by one or more of the following: Is a regular pattern of homework assignments in place? Are parent volunteers used in the classroom? Are letters to or from parents in evidence? If none of this is in evidence, a problem exists.

XV. The Science Curriculum

Most experts agree that the quality and delivery of science education must be improved. The competitive position of America in the world is dependent upon the capacity of educators and others to make science education more relevant, attractive and available to all students, not just a few. The present sequencing of science courses, combined with the rigid tracking of students in different levels of these courses, makes it virtually impossible for many students to pursue careers in science. As noted by the National Science Teachers' Association (NSTA), students who do not enroll in algebra in middle schools are not even eligible for most high school mathematics or science classes. Consequently, they can never be in a position to major in science or engineering in college.

Recent research and experience provides four clues that can be used as guides for improving science instruction.

- *The first clue:* Science curriculum must be relevant to students' interests and related to the ways in which we organize science and mathematics instruction across grades. In Japan, China, Germany, and Russia, countries whose students outperform ours, course content is more closely linked to the requirements of modern technology. The major instructional approach is to teach an array of science concepts and skills over a period of years without regard to specific discipline (such as biology or chemistry). By contrast, the practice in this country is to take one science discipline for one academic year and then move to another science subject the following year without linking the materials to relevant technological needs.
- *The second clue:* The effectiveness of science and mathematics increases when they are integrated, a task recently simplified by the use of technology.
- *The third clue:* Science curricula must incorporate a common core of concepts and skills for *all* students. Second-class curricula yields second-class students. The National Research Council unequivocally states that today's high school graduates entering the work force and those going on to college need virtually the same skills and competencies—only the former have less time and opportunity to gain them (National Research Council. 1989).
- *The fourth clue:* The purpose of science instruction in secondary schools is to assist students in the transition from concrete facts to problem-solving or application skills. We know that students in science and mathematics courses emphasizing hands-on approaches, and utilizing appropriate computer software, become more inquiry-oriented, develop more positive attitudes toward science and mathematics, and gain higher-level intellectual skills such as critical thinking, creativity, and problem solving.

As administrators consider these clues they must also address several fundamental problems.

In Elementary Schools

- There is insufficient time allocated to teaching the sciences at all grades;
- There are too few teachers prepared to teach science classes;
- There are insufficient supplies available for most teachers to create meaningful hands-on experiences.

In Secondary Schools

- Courses are not co-ordinated. Biology, chemistry, and physics are taught as if they represented independent bodies of knowledge and bore no real-world relationship with one another. The following example described in the NSTA report illustrates a superior approach;

> During a certain number of class hours in one year, students in biology class explore the human heart and the circulatory system. In chemistry class, the same students investigate chemical reactions that involve oxygen and, in particular, such metabolic reactions as oxygen transport by hemoglobin. At the same time in physics class they study the kinematics and dynamics of fluid flow.

- Not enough time is spent teaching science;
- Incorrect or inappropriate pedagogy is used. There seems to be a basic but incorrect assumption that all students should be exposed to the same style of instructional delivery;
- Courses must be sequenced to emphasize the concrete and descriptive in the early years, the quantitative and empirical in the middle years, and the theoretical and abstract in the later years.

Although the initiative for many of the improvements must come from superintendents and their senior instructional staff, principals can make significant changes in the way science is taught in their schools. They must function as advocates and participants. As noted by the NSTA, they must make sure that their school's programs:

- Are well co-ordinated;
- Help students identify and solve problems;
- Enhance higher cognitive processes and skills;
- Integrate social issues with science subjects;
- Focus on the application of skills rather than on the acquisition of skills;
- Emphasize science in all grades (more specifically, emphasize factual and descriptive information, quantitative and empirically-based knowledge in the middle schools, and more abstract and theoretical information in the high schools);
- Minimize the distinctions among different secondary school disciplines (such as biology, chemistry, and physics) and develop an integrated, spiralled curriculum which addresses issues of science, no matter what the specific discipline.

XVI. The Social Studies Curriculum

Although most recent attention has focused on reforming mathematics and science education, serious and needed reform efforts have been initiated in the area of social studies. The Bradley Commission on History in Schools (1989) and the National Council on Social Studies in the Schools (1989) issued reports calling for the reform of social studies teaching.

- The knowledge gained from studying history is a prerequisite to good citizenship and must be required for all students. The kindergarten through 6th-grade social studies curriculum must be history-centered and students must be required to take at least four years of history between the 7th and 12th grades;
- The study of history and associated subjects goes far beyond the memorization of facts to the application of that knowledge to help inform analyses, judgments, and perspectives;
- The time that is available for the study of history must be increased significantly;
- Teaching must include the historical experiences of peoples from Africa, North, Central, and South America, Europe, and Asia and the history of women and racial and ethnic minorities;

The National Commission's report *(Charting a Course: Social Studies for the 21st Century)* suggested that more time be made available for social studies instruction and that schools use well-designed, integrated, and spiralled kindergarten-through-12th-grade curricula. More specifically, the Commission recommended that:

- The social studies curriculum help students to understand their roles as citizens and help them to learn to participate in democratic institutions;
- Content knowledge not be taught merely for the sake of learning the facts but rather as a means for understanding broader issues and events. The content knowledge should arm students with the capacity to question and to analyze;
- History and geography form the basis of any social studies curriculum but with concepts from economics, political science, and other social sciences used wherever appropriate;
- Other subject areas be infused with social studies to help students understand the inter-relationships among other disciplines;
- Social studies materials be varied. They should contain a mix of written materials including literature, essays, original sources, audio-visuals, and computer programs for analyzing social and economic data, and appropriate maps and globes.

XVII. The Arts Curriculum

Current national education goals recognize the need for all Americans to be literate and possess the knowledge and skills to compete successfully in a global economy. A major component of this emerging literacy is the critical need for students to understand and respect both their own esthetic and cultural traditions and those of others. Through a fine arts program that is designed to be inclusive, multicultural, and interdisciplinary, students can gain self-esteem and a capacity for self-expression. In addition, the arts (including music, dance, theater, and the visual arts) can become a wonderfully rich and productive backdrop for students to study aspects of their academic subjects.

Current research on learning style preferences, for example, suggests that many students would benefit from an enhanced concentration on the expressive, tactile-kinesthetic aspects of learning: through the generation of artistic products (such as artistic productions and performances), students can reinforce their understanding of basic and higher-level concepts and skills in such areas as English/language arts, social studies, mathematics, and science. Finally, there is an emerging body of research which confirms that students who have an arts background do better on their PSAT's and SAT's than students whose education has been more restricted or confined to what has been narrowly defined as academic subjects.

As administrators go about the business of improving their arts programs to reflect the expanded role that arts education can play, they must keep the following factors in mind and seek creative ways to overcome them:

- Major areas of arts education are either omitted from the curriculum or taught so infrequently as not to be effective. Theater and dance are addressed only tangentially. Elementary school art is taught only a few minutes per week.
- Arts instruction is de-contextualized, taught in isolation, and removed from any social or environmental location. Consideration should be given to viewing arts education as a complement to social studies and reading/language arts instruction.
- There is little or no cross-disciplinary concept development in the arts and academic areas. Arts programs must be integrated into students' academic studies so that the arts are used to complement and reinforce key academic skills and concepts. For example, when students look at ratios in mathematics, they can apply them as they study architectural forms.
- There are few opportunities for students to express themselves and to understand the use of the arts as a vehicle for communication. Ways must be found to assist students to operate effectively in group situations, expand self-awareness, improve self-image, and enhance their sense of future possibilities.

KEY POINT: *If administrators want to strengthen curriculum in every subject area, they must:*

- *Ensure that all students are exposed to course work that will require them to think;*
- *Ensure that thinking skills are developed through varied instructional modes;*
- *Ensure that thinking skills are integrated into the curriculum and not seen as the province of the talented and gifted;*

> *Ensure that, as curricula are revised, care is taken to make connections between subject matter courses and everyday experiences that students will have throughout life. This interaction is especially critical in courses like chemistry, biology, history, government, or vocational courses, all of which have clear connections to the worlds of work and higher education. The responsibility for making these connections should fall on the shoulders of curriculum developers, staff developers, and classroom teachers.*

XIX. Models of Enhanced Curricula and Instruction

We now outline some examples of curricula and instruction that represent significant improvements over most current offerings. These models embody high standards, require that time be used flexibly, and demand that existing teachers receive intense and ongoing staff development. The models also have profound implications for the qualities of new teachers that need to be hired.

The James Madison High School Curriculum

Recent efforts to reform curricula have focused on the secondary school. One of the more publicized attempts at reform has been the development of what is known as the James Madison High School curriculum, developed in response to problems cited in *A Nation At Risk* which concluded that:

> Secondary school curricula have been homogenized, diluted, and diffused to the point that they no longer have a central purpose. In effect, we have a cafeteria-style curriculum in which the appetizers and desserts can easily be mistaken for the main courses.

The report noted that a full quarter of credits received by general track high school students were for physical and health education, work experience outside the school, remedial math and English, and personal service and development courses. The report recommended that secondary school course requirements be revised to reflect what students had to know and do to meaningfully contribute to their own self-development and to the health of our nation and world. Building on these recommendations, the James Madison curriculum required that every student graduate from high school have completed:

- Four years of English (Introduction to Literature, American Literature, British Literature, and Introduction to World Literature);
- Three years of social studies (Western Civilization, American History, and American Democracy);
- Three years of mathematics (selected from among Algebra I, Plane and Solid Geometry, Algebra II and Trigonometry, Statistics and Probability—one semester; Pre-calculus—one semester; and Calculus);
- Three years of science (selected from among Astronomy/Geology, Biology, Chemistry, and Physics or Principles of Technology);
- Two years of a foreign language;
- Two years of physical education;
- One year of fine arts.

Although one may argue about the specific combination and number of required courses described above, it is important to note that the curriculum eliminates lower-level courses and expects the schools to find ways of delivering the richer, more in-depth courses to all students. As noted in the report,

> Most of our students are ready; some are not. But we should do what can be done now; we should aim high not low, and remember that children tend to perform according to our expectations of them.

The International Baccalaureate

While the James Madison curriculum represents a set of higher expectations for all students, the International Baccalaureate should be considered by administrators as an important option for schools preparing for world-class standards of achievement. The International Baccalaureate (IB) provides a broad course of studies culminating in rigorous, performance-based assessments; if students achieve an adequate level of performance, they will earn an IB Diploma which provides advanced credit at American universities (and as much as one year of college credit at some, such as Harvard); and which will provide an entrance qualification to almost any university in the world.

The IB program simultaneously offers both structure and options; some schools offer it for its international dimension, but most American schools offer it because of its academic rigor, to prepare students much more effectively for higher education. Although it requires that students demonstrate competence in the major modes of learning, the IB primarily sets high standards of performance so that the IB Diploma is roughly parallel to secondary certificates in Europe, Japan, and other countries.

All candidates for the full IB Diploma must meet nine requirements which are internally and externally assessed. The guidelines are carefully defined and can be found in the *General Guide to the International Baccalaureate*. Although the IB program takes place only at the junior and senior years of high school, it presupposes that students who wish to participate before the 11th grade already have a broad background in their native language, a foreign language, mathematics, world history and geography, the sciences, and some experience in the arts. As of 1991 there were 180 schools in North America which offered the full IB curriculum and examination; it provides a model curriculum as taught in 63 countries and examined by 1,400 examiners from countries around the world.

Students are required to select one course from each of the following groups:

- *Language A:* Ordinarily a course in world literature taught in the mother tongue; in America, so far, all Language A courses are offered in English only;
- *Language B:* A second language;
- *Study of Man in Society:* World history, geography, economics, philosophy, or other social science;
- *Experimental Science:* Chemistry, physics, biology, physical science, experimental psychology, environmental systems, and so forth;
- *Mathematics:* Mathematics, mathematical studies, mathematics and computing, and so forth;
- *Sixth Group:* A second foreign language or a second course from any of the above groups, any of the arts, or special courses developed by the International Baccalaureate network of schools.

Of the six courses, each student must select three at the higher level and three at the subsidiary level. The higher-level courses are approximately at the first-year college level or the Advanced Placement level or slightly above, and the subsidiary level courses are slightly below the Advanced Placement level courses. There are three other requirements to earn the full IB Diploma:

1. *Theory of Knowledge:* A course in elementary logic and philosophy about how one arrives at truths or judgments in science, social sciences, history, esthetics, and ethical behavior. The purpose is to stimulate critical thinking, to apply what was learned elsewhere to a wide variety of situations, and to develop the capacity to create knowledge through original thought and synthesis of other thoughts and beliefs.
2. *Extended Essay:* Each student must write an original 5,000-word essay in any of the subject areas listed above.
3. *Creative Activity, the Arts, and Social Service (CASS):* And finally, each student must demonstrate participation in one of the CASS activities such as the visual or performing arts or doing some type of community service.

Thousands of Americans are now earning their full IB diplomas each year. These students come from all socio-economic levels and because of higher expectations, that they have for themselves and others have for them, they *are* able to rise to the challenge. Instead of the usual one to two hours of homework, students willingly do three to six hours per day, and they learn to do serious academic work at an earlier age than is normal in America. Accordingly, they are much better prepared for higher education than other students.

In the industrialized countries, the national systems provide for basic academic needs, so that the IB mainly takes care of students who are abroad and who attend the international schools in most population centers throughout the world. By far more Americans participate and earn their IB diplomas than any other nationality.

High schools are best prepared to offer the full International Baccalaureate curriculum and examinations if they have had at least three to five years of experience with the Advanced Placement courses (or equivalent) in the areas of mathematics, foreign languages (at least one), and preferably English, history, and a science. The main criterion for acceptance into the IB family of schools is the commitment to encourage students to take the full IB Diploma (yet many students can and do take only a few IB courses), and the commitment to encourage continuing teacher training for IB teachers as they become familiar with the more challenging curriculum and higher levels of performance. Those schools that are interested in applying should contact the International Baccalaureate office in New York.

The Paideia Program

No discussion of curriculum reform is complete without making the point that the delivery as well as the content of what is taught must be improved. There is general agreement among educators that the traditional lecture approach to teaching is not effective. Yet, school systems are hesitant to advocate alternative procedures or train their staffs in them. As administrators wrestle with this problem, they should examine the potential of the Paideia approach. This approach to educational reform is designed to free talented and qualified teachers to teach effectively. It helps children learn to love learning, to take some of the responsibility for their own education.

The Paideia approach addresses education for all twelve years and treats it as an integrated unit, not grade by grade. The approach has the advantage of not containing a single curriculum. Rather, it provides a framework within which a curriculum can be modified to reflect the priorities and interests of any given school system. The course of study is very general, not specialized, vocational, or humanistic.

Perhaps the most intriguing part of the approach describes ways in which teachers can more effectively teach and students can more effectively learn. The following three inter-related styles of teaching practices are suggested for use by every teacher:

- Didactic practices designed to increase students' acquisition of information;
- Coaching practices meant to improve skills such as problem solving and writing;
- Socratic seminars which are designed to increase students' understanding of ideas.

Each of these teaching styles should be brought to bear on every body of knowledge that is transmitted or otherwise discussed in the classroom. The knowledge learned through lectures, through the didactic approach, must be reinforced by teacher coaching and by deeper understandings developed in the seminars.

The successful implementation of the Paideia approach requires that schools be restructured. Schedules must be redesigned to allow time to be used differently for instruction. (A set of 55-minute periods is not the appropriate model. While some lectures may fit into that schedule, seminars do not. They might require two or three hours each.) The notion that all subjects require the same amount of time is not supported by this approach. Time for staff training has to be made available. Teachers need to relearn much of their profession ethos and many of their everyday practices.

The Paideia program requires that administrators support its development and nurture its existence. More specifically:

- Superintendents should signal to principals and teachers that it is acceptable to depart from usual instructional practices;
- Superintendents and principals need to provide sufficient time and resources for staff training. A block of at least two weeks during the summer, prior to the first year of the program, and at least five full days during the school year itself, is required;
- Principals must ensure that their administrative staffs are flexible and willing to be innovative as they perform their duties;
- Ritualistic behavior cannot be tolerated. Administrators must encourage and allow leadership to spring from among the faculty members. The program cannot be implemented by outsiders;
- Superintendents and principals should acknowledge that meaningful change is complex and will take several years to accomplish.

Prerequisites for Curricular Restructuring

Curriculum restructuring is a complex process that requires tenacious administrators and curriculum specialists who are up-to-date and aware that the status quo is unacceptable. As new and enriched curricula are developed, administrators should ensure that the following prerequisites are in place.

- Essential curriculum has to be delivered to all students. Curriculum should identify fundamental learning outcomes expected of all students and should be demanding, intellectually stimulating, and relevant;
- All students must be equipped with critical thinking, creativity, and decision-making skills. Students must be taught (a) to make conceptual abstractions concrete and real through an exploration of their real-world applications and (b) to become knowledge generators and creators rather than passive recipients of predigested data;
- An organic, holistic model must guide the process of all curriculum development and delivery. Students must understand the interconnectedness of human knowledge through interdisciplinary units, spiral curriculum designs, and related forms of curriculum renewal;

- Students need knowledge of emerging technologies, including computer-assisted instruction, interactive television, CD-ROM's, and on-line search capabilities.

XX. Restructuring and the Use of Technology

The question associated with educational technology is no longer 'does it work?' Research and experience reveal that, properly implemented, technology can improve the availability, effectiveness, and cost-effectiveness of education. Administrators cannot undertake meaningful restructuring activities without exploiting what new technologies can do to improve student learning. There are three ways in which technology can be used for improving education. First, technology can be used to supplement the regular classroom curriculum. Computers can be used to deliver curriculum to some students while teachers can then work with other, smaller groups of students. Television, in both videotape and videodisc formats, can be used to provide students with a wide range of information. Both computers and television also offer an interactive mode in which students can explore and question the material and concepts that they are learning.

Second, technology can be used to deliver services where they are otherwise unavailable. For example, interactive TV can be used to:

- Deliver advanced placement courses from high schools in which there are qualified staff to high schools in which there are too few qualified students to justify hiring a teacher;
- Teach advanced placement courses from a university directly to several high schools simultaneously;
- Deliver courses taught from a local science museum or library and broadcast directly into several elementary schools;
- Transmit courses from anywhere via satellite (particularly to rural areas where it is often difficult to offer a wide array of more advanced courses).

The third way to use technology is to tap into a vast knowledge base. The information that students will need in the future is too vast and rapidly-changing to be committed to memory or even to access in a library by browsing through books. In the years since the invention of the printing press the amount of information available to us has been growing at a more rapid rate that we can assimilate and remember it. It has been estimated that a single copy of the *Wall Street Journal* contains more information than the Renaissance man had available to him in his entire lifetime. The use of a wide range of technologies opens up a vast new world for education. The ability to expose learners to an exciting array of information presented in stimulating and thought-provoking ways will undoubtedly stretch the potential of our children more than can be done by the teacher alone. The appropriate use of technology employing videodiscs, videotapes, CD-ROMs, and computers in the classroom will help contribute to maximizing that potential. Utilizing computers and modems, students can now access information from databases, publications, research organizations, or from other students thousands of miles away.

We now turn to three technological applications that administrators will be considering during the next decade: instructional computing, teacher work stations, and interactive television. *The descriptions are not designed to make the reader an expert on instructional technology. Rather, they are designed to acquaint administrators with the kinds of potential these technological applications have and the issues administrators must explore as they consider the purchase of these or other technologies.*

The first two examples describe the use of computers for instruction and teacher work stations and are provided in the framework of request for proposals (RFP's). It is in the RFP that the school system signals its needs to technology vendors. The discussions that follow are designed to ensure that administrators become sensitive to the kinds of issues that must be raised and the kinds of proposals that they must receive to allow them to make informed selection decisions. (The following examples of RFP's are abbreviated. Although they do provide descriptions of many of the parameters considered by administrators as they procure technology, they do not represent all of the issues or complete RFP's). The third example provides a brief description of an interactive television system including its purposes, design, and effectiveness.

XXI. Instructional Computing

Recent advances in hardware and software, combined with the need to increase direct instructional time for all students, require that school systems have appropriate and sufficient computer technology to help teachers ensure that all of its students maximize their learning potential. This technology ranges from networked classroom computers to stand-alone computer laboratories, from interactive data systems allowing teachers, principals, and central office administrators to query and relate student/school level data, to electronic media centers. The likely first step into the technology arena that most administrators will take will be the purchase of computers to enhance instruction. Although administrators need not become technology experts, they should have clear and compelling reasons for purchasing these instructional computer systems.

The clearest finding in the research concerning the use of instructional computers is that, properly used, they represent a cost-effective instructional delivery system that can supplement an existing instructional program in grades K–12. Experience teaches us that these systems are also effective in supporting other instructional objectives for specific student populations including those who require remedial help, gifted education, and special education, and other special students.

One of the earliest decisions administrators will have to make relates to the configuration of computers in the classroom. Until recently most computers have been configured in separate stand-alone or limited networked laboratories. These laboratories most typically contain about 25 computers and are staffed by computer aides. More recent thinking is causing administrators to make changes in this traditional pattern for elementary schools. Many now believe that while stand-alone laboratories in elementary schools may be effective for teaching computer literacy and a few basic skills, they do not meaningfully involve the classroom teacher in their use and, therefore, do not represent the very best use of the technology. The emphasis should now be on placing computers directly in classrooms and making the classroom teacher responsible for *integrating them into the daily instructional program.*

At the high school level subject-area-dedicated laboratories represent the configuration of choice. These laboratories, preferably one for each subject matter department, provide an opportunity for students to use computers for special projects, research, and general word processing purposes. There is also a sense that placing several computers in each science laboratory as an aid to experimentation and simulations would be helpful, particularly used in concert with various probes and other external devices.

Given these configurations, administrators may want to develop requests for proposals (RFP's) that give vendors an opportunity to bid on providing the desired systems. *The RFP's should make the instructional purposes of the desired system transparently clear and specify its desired characteristics.* Following is an example of the elements that could be considered to be part of an RFP for an elementary/middle school instructional computing system.

I. The Purpose

The overall objectives of the instructional computing system includes:

1. Installing five work stations in each elementary and middle school classroom, expandable to ten in each classroom.
2. Making the classroom's instructional delivery system more effective and efficient through the use of a computer-assisted instructional management system that supplements the existing instructional program in reading, language arts, writing, mathematics and science. These computers must have the capacity to deliver integrated curriculum modules for reading, language arts, writing, mathematics, and science. Problem solving should represent a focus within each content area to accommodate the needs of all students. Content coverage in all areas should extend through the 9th grade level. Mathematics lessons should include extensive courseware in algebra and geometry. Science lessons should include extensive courseware in life science, physical science, and earth science.
3. Using computer technology as a means of improving classroom management practices.
4. Improving student achievement by increasing student time-on-task.

II. Issues to be Addressed in the Request for Proposal

A. System Issues

1. Proposals must include a completely configured system. Software manufacturers *must* configure a system which includes hardware.
2. Vendors should be prepared to enter a conditional sales or lease-purchase agreement with the school system for the purchase of this system.
3. Vendors must provide evidence that every component in the proposed system will not become outdated in the near future.

Vendors must also describe the potential expansion capabilities of the system, particularly in the case of computer and networking hardware. Computer hardware should support high resolution color graphics and have sufficient random access memory.

4. Vendors should provide a detailed justification for the networking scheme they recommend. Ethernet or token ring are the preferred topologies.
5. Vendors should propose the type of wiring/cabling that they will use. Twisted pair is preferred over coaxial cabling. The systems should be capable of accommodating a fiber optic backbone if it is desired in the future. The networking topology and cabling scheme must have the capacity to support the proposed system *and* a wider range of multimedia interfaces and devices that are likely to become prominent in the next several years.
6. The successful bidder must provide a minimum of one on-site manager, one systems engineer, and sufficient full-time consultants to support the project for a period of at least five years.

B. Software Issues

The software must:

1. Be consistent with existing instructional objectives for reading, language arts, writing, mathematics and science,
2. Be favorably evaluated by teachers, principals, and curriculum specialists,
3. Allow for the instructional needs of all students, grades K-8, including remedial, talented and gifted, special needs, and second language students,
4. Be highly correlated with the state's curriculum requirements, the school system's standards and instructional objectives, and the major textbooks currently utilized by the school system in each content area,
5. Allow for continual update of objectives, prescriptions, and test items,
6. Be user-friendly, and
7. Be cost-effective.

C. Host Computer Issues

The host computer must:

1. Have sufficient memory for each grade's objectives in reading, language arts, writing, mathematics, and science and can accommodate all necessary recordkeeping and management functions,
2. Have the capacity to track each student throughout the grades, providing hard-copies of student progress at the request of school personnel,
3. Be interfaced with a printer(s) of 'near letter quality' or better and offer both friction and tractor feeding,
4. Be able to print all reports and student documents to any system printer, and
5. Include a real-time clock and battery back-up.

D. Student Station Issues

The student stations must:

1. Be networked to the host and operated as a stand-alone computer,
2. Support high resolution color graphics,
3. Contain a fast microprocessor and have sufficient random access memory,
4. Have at least one 3.5" high density floppy disc drive,
5. Have speech capabilities (high quality digitized), and
6. Be capable of uploading and downloading software via the network if student stations are microcomputers.

E. Productivity, Integrated Software, and Utility Issues

The system must:

1. Provide a basic integrated software package that includes word processing, database, and spreadsheet capacity,
2. Provide teacher utility software to enable teachers to generate graphics, banners, certificates, and crossword puzzles; and

3. Provide an easy-to-use teacher's gradebook and test generation software.

F. Local School and District Level Training Issues

Proposals must provide:

1. Training for teachers which includes hardware orientation and operation, curriculum content and classroom integration, classroom usage recommendations, reading and interpreting student reports, using accompanying support materials, and utilizing student reports for regular classroom instruction,
2. A one-half day overview for school board members, superintendents, principals, administrative staff, and other groups determined by the school system,
3. Consultants for the school system who will make frequent regularly scheduled visits to the sites and are available for phone consultation on an as needed basis, and
4. Training six school system employees who will be able to train new teachers as they enter the school system each year.

G. Management System Issues

The management system must include:

1. Adaptive placement testing through which students can automatically be placed into appropriate mathematics and reading lessons,
2. Individualized instruction and detailed student achievement reports upon teacher request. Management-system-based unit tests that assess student achievement after a fixed instructional sequence of lessons are mandatory. Teachers must be able to use these data to place students at a lower or higher instructional level if the student's performance warrants. The curriculum management system must also provide reports that show:
   - Adaptive test placement information for the mathematics and reading programs;

- The time students have spent on lessons and unit tests over a specified time interval as well as the completion date for lessons and unit tests;
- Average lesson and unit test results for a class over a specified time interval;
- An individual student's lesson and unit test results over a specified time interval with comments alerting teachers to low scores on unit tests;
- A more in-depth analysis of each unit test a student has completed over a specific time interval. Information should be available concerning student performance on objectives/concepts measured by the test as well as on items requiring higher order thinking skills. Suggested review lessons should be provided if a student has had difficulty with an objective/concept contained in the unit test;
- Lesson results for individual students over a specified time interval. This report should list all lessons completed with a minimum of percentage correct reported;
- Student progress towards mastery of objectives/concepts measured by unit tests. Information will be available to identify students mastering/not mastering specific objectives/concepts on any unit test. This report is intended for grouping purposes;
- Achievement results for individual students, for teachers' classes, for grade levels, for special instructional groups, and for the entire school;
- Aggregate time spent on the system for individual student or class groupings.

3. Immediate feedback to students;
4. The capacity to re-teach skills when necessary;
5. Student access to the curriculum management system and lessons from any student station. Teachers must be allowed to simultaneously access the curriculum management system from any student station or host station at will;
6. Operating system software and management system software for record keeping, student achievement reporting, and the operation of the curricula software;

7. Detailed documentation procedures for inputting student information; inputting teacher information, assigning instructional groupings of students, assigning software/courseware to students, generating and printing instructional summary reports; and uploading student performance data to external computer systems;
8. Branching that is transparent to the user in order to provide an even flow of material;
9. The capacity to operate and deliver multiple lessons and curricula simultaneously.

H. Software Issues

The software for the content areas must meet the following requirements:

1. Reading/Language Arts

- All instructional courseware must be closely correlated with the leading basal textbook series, the school system's curriculum objectives, and the State's required curriculum. *(A chart illustrating these correlations must be submitted as part of the proposal.)*
- Lessons must be sequentially chained, interactively managed by the management system, individually assigned to each student and each student's performance must be recorded by the management system for each lesson or test, and highly motivational to students. Individualized student instruction is essential. Each student must be able to proceed at their own instructional pace;
- All lessons must be delivered to each student learning station in high resolution color. Graphics must be unique to each lesson;
- Instructional courseware must be able to run on current model microcomputers;
- The courseware must promote higher-order thinking and problem-solving skills throughout the curriculum. *Unit tests should also require students to use this same level of higher-*

order thinking skills and student performance on items requiring higher-order thinking skills should be reported separately. Higher-order thinking skills can be categorized as those skills requiring students to obtain an answer to a problem or question that is not immediately evident from the information given and requiring students to use evaluative thinking and/or their ability to make generalizations;
- Sufficient numbers of curriculum lessons and unit tests must be provided to ensure an intensive and complete range of instruction from kindergarten through ninth grade;
- Lessons must provide immediate feedback to students. Lessons should allow several tries for a student to obtain a correct answer to a question or problem;
- Multiple modality of inputs should be available, such as keyboard, mouse, and speech;
- Evidence of regular and frequent updates to courseware, unit tests, and management system should be present;
- Rigorous research and development components directed at new product development should be evident;
- All curricula must include continuous review, evaluation, and updates. Bidders must provide a schedule identifying the frequency of their courseware/management system updates and new product releases over the past three years. Bidders must also ensure that courseware/management system updates are installed in a timely manner on the system, at no additional charge, for a period of five years;
- Reading curriculum must include word analysis, vocabulary, comprehension, and study skills;
- Language arts curriculum must include an age-relevant word processor for student use. The word processor must be capable of exporting ASCII files to third party publishing software such as The Children's Writing and Publishing Center or The Writing Center;
- Language arts curriculum must include instruction and student activities in pre-writing, drafting, revising, editing, and publishing. Writing revision files should be available for access by all students as co-operative learning or individual lessons;

- The courseware/curriculum must co-ordinate reading and writing activities;
- Keyboarding lessons must be included as an integral part of the language arts courseware/management system;
- Lessons should be designed so that a teacher can access them for a group presentation using an LCD device or large-screen TV monitor.

2. Mathematics

- All instructional courseware must be closely correlated with the leading basal textbook series, the standards recommended by the National Council of Teachers of Mathematics, the school system's curriculum objectives, and the State's required curriculum; *(A chart illustrating these correlations must be submitted as part of the proposal.)*
- Courseware should provide extensive numbers of lessons in algebra and geometry;
- Courseware should provide opportunities for students to use manipulatives and conduct wide ranging simulations;
- Courseware should provide for the integration of a four function calculator in grades 1–6 and a scientific calculator for grades 7–8;
- Courseware must provide opportunities for students to investigate/explore mathematical concepts;
- Problem solving requiring higher-level thinking skills should be integrated throughout the lessons and should be readily apparent;
- When appropriate, multiple strategies for solving problems should be presented.

3. Science

All instructional courseware must be closely correlated with the leading textbook series, the school system's curriculum objectives, and the state's required curriculum. *(A chart illustrat-*

ing these correlations must be submitted as part of the proposal.)

- Courseware should provide extensive numbers of lessons supporting life science, physical science, and earth science;
- Courseware should provide opportunities for students to conduct wide-ranging simulations;
- Courseware must provide opportunities for students to investigate/explore scientific concepts;
- Problem solving requiring higher-level thinking skills should be integrated throughout the lessons and should be readily apparent;
- When appropriate, multiple strategies for solving problems should be presented;
- Hardware must be capable of accepting scientific probeware to make real-time measurements of temperature, voltage, resistance, pH, and other pertinent experiment variables.

I. The System's Hardware and Peripherals

This RFP requests all pertinent information, including but not limited to: product performance, system cost, support services, special discounts, and access to parts and manuals. The number and types of products and services purchased will depend on the quality of the proposals, need and the availability of funds.

All equipment bids must be:

- Supported by the curriculum software publisher/manufacturer;
- Submitted as prescribed in the curriculum software manufacturer's approved system configurations;
- Approved by Novell for use with Novell Netware in DOS based applications or a network management system in non-DOS based applications recommended by the bidder and approved by the school system.

The bidders' offered hardware must support a state-of-the-art integrated learning system and be composed of microcomputers and peripheral equipment designed and manufactured using the latest industry technology for stand-alone operation and configu-

> ration into local area networked environments. Each delivery system shall consist of a file server and networked student learning stations. Networking hardware and topology must be capable of accommodating a high rate of data transmission (10 megabits per second) to allow for the potential future use of the computer hardware in multimedia networks utilizing Digital Video Interactive (DVI) technology.

XXII. Teacher Work Stations

The classroom of the future will be equipped to allow teachers to use a wide variety of technologies to access, analyze, and display data to entire classrooms of students. The configuration of these technologies can be installed in a teacher work station, a section of the classroom dedicated as a control center for instruction. An integrated technology-based teacher work station can consist of a computer, videodisc player, and a liquid crystal display or very large monitor. The work station can be used for classroom presentations, lesson development and presentation, student presentations, classroom preparation, and management purposes.

A teacher work station can make use of a variety of instructional videodisc materials which are widely available. In fact, some school systems are using some of these videodisc materials as approved textbooks. Utilizing a work station, a teacher can instantly access an instructional lesson or demonstration from a videodisc, and easily program daily or weekly video-based lesson plans. The work station can also be used for classroom-wide software demonstration purposes, as an electronic chalkboard and as a utility for teacher grading and analyses.

As school systems consider the purchase of teacher work stations, a number of key issues will be considered. Here is a brief listing and description of the issues that should be included in the school system's request for proposals (RFP). The example focuses on the purchase of work stations for kindergarten through eighth grade, for the teaching of science and health. The issues, however, are appropriate for all subjects and for high schools as well.

CHAPTER 4 Transforming the Content and Delivery of Curriculum

Teacher Multimedia Work Stations

I. Background and General Information

The primary objective of this section is to provide for the acquisition of computer hardware, software and peripherals, videodisc hardware, software and peripherals, a large group presentation/display system, and all needed furniture, for a teacher multimedia/computer work station. Teacher work stations are to be designed as a station for teachers to prepare and deliver technology-based presentations, including videodisc based lessons, software demonstrations, large and small group demonstrations, multimedia presentations, software based simulations and 'electronic blackboard' uses. All students in a typical classroom should be able to view the computer or video information simultaneously as a group.

The videodisc component is an integral part of this system. Consideration should be given to developing a package that will make most effective use of videodisc materials currently available in the areas of science, social studies, and health education. Vendors should submit a plan to provide similar hardware systems for all classrooms. Sufficient sets of videodiscs, manuals, curriculum guides, and accompanying software must be provided for each school.

It is expected that the videodisc vendor will correlate their science, social studies and health discs with school system and state curriculum requirements. The vendors should provide the school system with this correlation document in their proposals.

Teachers should be able to use this work station as a tool for preparing classroom print materials, recording grades, developing tests and graphics, and maintaining records in a database. In addition, teachers should be able to use the work station to access student records, and run lessons on the networked classroom computers. If needed, this work station should be able to double as a student station.

This RFP will collect all pertinent information including, but not limited to: product performance, system cost, support services, special discounts, and access to parts and manuals.

Vendors should propose a configuration of work-station presentation systems that includes a computer and video disc workstation that uses a 25" to 27" video monitor/receiver and an LCD, or a video board for the computer, for classroom presentations. (There should be an option to this plan which makes use of existing television receivers in many of the classrooms.)

(*NOTE:* This is expected to be a turnkey system. All software should be loaded by the vendor. All equipment should be mounted, wired, and tested by the vendor. All cables and peripherals should also be included.)

II. Issues for the Request for Proposal

1. Instructional videodiscs and software included with the teacher work stations should be consistent with the school system's instructional objectives, the state's standard course of study and leading textbook series. All applicable software must be loaded onto each computer. Manuals for all software and videodiscs must be provided for each work station. Grade appropriate videodiscs and curriculum manuals for the kindergarten through eighth grade curriculum covering the following topics should be supplied: life science, earth science, physical science, social studies, space exploration, geology, ecology, oceanography and drug education;

2. Teacher support software should be purchased, licensed, and loaded onto each teacher computer to enable them to maintain gradebooks, generate their own test generation software program, produce graphic materials, and generate word processing, data base, and spreadsheet products. It is also preferable that teachers have access to software that will allow them to customize videodisc lessons for their classroom;

3. The teacher work stations for all K–8 classrooms must:

    - Consist of a fast microprocessor and have sufficient random access memory;

CHAPTER 4 Transforming the Content and Delivery of Curriculum

- Be capable of being interfaced with the classroom computer network and printer and contains all peripherals and software necessary for such a connection;
- Have a hard disc drive that contains sufficient storage for software applications and teachers files;
- Be interfaced with a videodisc player, and either an external video monitor or an LCD;
- Be capable of effectively running all software as part of this RFP, and have the capacity of running other applicable instructional software provided by the school system for classroom inclusion and/or presentation;
- Include a videodisc player capable of interactive multimedia instruction and running the videodiscs, and related software, chosen for this system, with the following peripherals:
  - bar code reader (designed specifically for the selected videodisc player)
  - wireless remote (designed specifically for the selected videodisc player)
- And either
  - an LCD with all applicable cables and a television monitor/receiver, with two or more inputs and a wireless remote, sized between 25" and 27"

                    OR

  - a television/monitor receiver and a video board for the computer. (Note: An option should be provided to make use of existing television receivers requiring appropriate RF connectors to be provided and installed by the vendor.)

4. The vendor will be responsible for all on-site training. Topics should include, but not be limited to: operating videodisc software packages, videodisc hardware and peripheral operation, and integration of computers with videodiscs. In-service training sessions should be a minimum of three half-days in

> length (or full day equivalents), to be held at each elementary and middle school. Vendors should provide an in-service plan with their response to this RFP with an indication of the number and types of relevant in-service training programs they have previously conducted. If available, evaluation compilations and reports from prior in-service sessions should be included with this response.

XXIII. Interactive Television

School systems throughout the nation are learning about the uses of television as a means of delivering instruction to students and staff development to teachers. Most interest focuses on the use of pre-recorded videotapes or tuning in to a program on broadcast or cable television channels. Although this practice is expanding, the more significant potential of television is in its capacity to link several classrooms or schools with one another and with the source of teaching, whether it be a master teacher, a scientist, museum curator, or linguist. This potential is most commonly referred to as distance learning. When educators typically think about distance learning they envision a system which delivers courses to students via satellite or other technologies (such as full motion and compressed video), on a one-way video, two-way audio basis. Such delivery networks beam courses to students nationwide, statewide, and/or regionally, and can usually accommodate very large class sizes. These networks can be somewhat successful at addressing general, universal needs that many school systems share in common.

However, the limitations of one-way video make it difficult to involve kindergarten through twelfth-grade students most meaningfully in instruction. If K–12 distance learning programs are to be successful, they must offer students in various sites the opportunity to communicate with each other and with the instructor. Here is a brief description of a full two-way audio and two-way video system which other school systems may want to consider. The system that is described consists of six high schools, a school system central office building, and a community college. The interactive television system was designed to serve the following purposes:

CHAPTER 4 Transforming the Content and Delivery of Curriculum

- To reduce the inequity of course offerings between small high schools and large high schools;
- To provide advanced courses to students in a school where there were too few students to justify hiring a teacher;
- To compensate for the fact that there are relatively few teachers qualified to teach the more advanced level courses;
- To provide staff development to teachers who ordinarily would have to travel long distances for staff development courses offered after school;
- To deliver college courses on a concurrent enrollment basis to students while they remain in high school in remote parts of the county.

The system that was developed to fulfill these purposes had the following features:

- Full two-way audio communication;
- Full two-way video communication;
- Full two-way computer communication;
- Availability of videodisc, videocassette, and other audiovisual devices;
- Ability to transmit to students homes via local cable television channels;
- Availability for use before, during, and after school hours for a variety of purposes.

CASE STUDY

Interactive Television: A Case Study

1. Transmission

The primary mode of transmission was via cable television. As is the case with most cable television systems, channel and spectrum space availabilities were somewhat limited. Only two cable channels were available for this project. Maximum use of the two channels was made by using one of them in a quadrangular split format and the second in a traditional full screen format. Thus, five classrooms were viewed at any given time. Signals from the classrooms were sent to the cable company on existing cables. To preserve the integrity of the video signals, approximately 20 miles of fiber optic cable were installed within the main infrastructure of the cable system.

2. Classroom Design and Equipment

When designing this interactive television network attention was paid to developing a setting for students that was conducive to learning, non-threatening, and technically and financially possible to implement. Since the interactive television system was being designed initially to provide advanced placement courses where there were none, classrooms were selected which could accommodate 12 to 15 students. Classrooms were arranged in a seminar style layout with conference tables positioned together in a 'U' shape. This allowed for one camera to see all of the students at one time while, at the same time, being able to zoom in on a particular student. The television equipment used in the classroom includes 50-inch monitor/receivers, a high-quality TV camera, desktop mounted microphones, a videocassette recorder, a laser videodisc player and an audio mixer.

Desktop microphones were attached to the tables, and two 50-inch television sets were located in the front of the room. Fifty-inch television sets were needed because one of the channels was in a quadrangular split format which resulted in the equivalent of four 25-inch pictures. Students can easily view the television sets to see their teacher and fellow classmates in other schools. The interaction which occurs is similar to traditional classes; students raise their hands to be called upon, speak freely, and discuss and debate naturally.

Teachers were also provided with new versions of their old tools; chalk, blackboards, and overhead projectors. The new version was an electronic chalkboard on which, through the use of a special writing tablet and pen, teachers were enabled to write things which were viewed instantaneously in each of the sites. As the teacher uses prepared materials, pictures, maps, or other printed items, a scanner quickly scans and transmits this information to each site where it is then printed.

3. Instructional Aide

To provide adult supervision in the classroom (as required by many state codes) an instructional aide was hired for each of the classrooms. These aides are responsible for classroom management, supervising students, operating all of the equipment in the interactive television classroom, and distributing and transmitting testing materials. Although some distance learning systems have attempted to forgo hiring this type of person, experience teaches that the instructional aides are invaluable.

The training for the instructional aides takes approximately five full days in which they are taught how to operate all of the equipment in the interactive television classroom, how to work with the computer software, classroom management techniques and equipment trouble shooting. Specific school rules on classroom management issues and disciplinary actions are dealt with at each of the schools.

4. Uses of the Interactive Television System

The primary intent of the interactive television network was to provide advanced courses where there were previously none. During the first year of the project courses were offered in AP Calculus, AP Modern European History, AP Art History, AP American Government, AP Comparative Government, Spanish 4, and French 3.

Other uses of this interactive television system included staff development courses provided after working hours simultaneously at several convenient locations, mock trial competitions, SAT preparation courses, community college courses, parent outreach programs, teleconferences, and inter-school conferences and meetings.

5. Teacher Training

One of the most important steps in implementing this distance learning project is the training of the teachers. If the teachers are not comfortable with teaching on television, or if there is a lack of understanding for how the technology works, then the true potential of distance learning will not be met. Teacher training took approximately three weeks. The format included lectures, discussions, hands-on time with the equipment, preparation time, and practice lessons. The topics covered during this training process included:

- Distance learning concepts and practices;
- Introduction to the technology;
- Teaching over television (addressing the camera, inclusion of the audience, use of visuals, and so forth);
- Identifying learning styles;
- Adjusting teaching styles;
- Adapting the curriculum to the technology;
- Co-operative learning over distances;
- Humanizing the medium;
- Utilization of the computer hardware and software.

6. The Costs

Although the upfront costs of $300,000 to equip seven classrooms is significant, after three years the costs are recoverable as indicated in the table below.

	Annual Interactive Delivery Costs	Annual Traditional System Delivery Costs
Teachers	$ 35,000 (1 teacher)	$240,000 (7 teachers)
Aides	$ 90,000 (7 aides)	0
Maintenance	$ 10,000	0
	$135,000	$240,000

The annual cost savings are $105,000.

7. Program Effectiveness

The major findings of the evaluations of the interactive television system were:

1. Generally speaking, the responses from students indicate they adjusted very well to the television classroom. There was some initial 'camera shyness' and apprehension regarding the

equipment, but after an orientation and a few class sessions, students remarked that they felt very comfortable in the 'technical' classroom. Students respond that in most instances teachers put forth additional efforts to assure that students from all sites interact and get to know each other. They view this acquisition of new classmates and friends as a significant asset of the program.

Other favorable aspects of the interactive television program mentioned by students include the opportunity to take advanced placement classes, the use of the videotaped lessons for missed classes, the exposure to new technologies, and the opportunity to take classes taught by teachers from other schools.

2. Teachers indicated that although there are occasional technical difficulties, class 'down time' was minimal. The most favorable aspects of the program include the challenge of working with innovative technology, the creativity the program allows, the opportunity to teach students from several high schools, the benefits afforded students, the advantages offered by the possibility of reviewing classes on videotape, the training and in-service sessions, and the sharing of ideas among interactive television colleagues.

3. Analysis of the first-year data reveals that neither statistical nor practical differences exist in the grade-point averages or advanced placement test scores of students in classrooms with the teacher present compared to students in the remote sites with the teacher available only via television.

In this era of hard-to-find teaching expertise for higher-level courses in science, mathematics, and foreign languages, the interactive television approach can be used to train teachers to be more proficient in these fields. Teachers in need of training could supervise the classroom (instead of the aides described above). While providing the supervision, the teacher receives expert guidance from the person teaching to all the classrooms. Here the cost savings from using aides are not realized, but the long-range impact of training a broader cohort of teachers results in increased teaching expertise.

XXIV. Restructuring and School Dropouts

The issue of school dropouts has plagued educators for generations. *The typical response to this problem has been to develop strategies to help these students succeed in the very educational environment in which they have already failed.* Thus tutoring programs and special classes for at-risk students were designed to bring them back into the mainstream. It was never recognized that the mainstream had already let these students down, and that what they needed was a change in kind and not in degree.

Administrators at all levels can address the dropout problem effectively by implementing a three-phased program. *First,* the early identification of those students who are likely to drop out. *Second,* the implementation of practices by principals and teachers a. to minimize the chances that at-risk students will drop out and b. to create an atmosphere of concern and caring in the school. *Third,* the creation of programs to recover those who have already left the school system.

Early Identification

Research indicates that several indicators serve as predictors of dropping out. They include:

- Chronically poor grades;
- Being held back in school more than once;
- Having undiagnosed learning disabilities;
- Being involved in truancy or other delinquent behavior;
- Using alcohol or other drugs.

Administrators and teachers must continually identify children to determine whether one or more of these indicators are impacting their lives. Once identified, it is their responsibility to develop a plan for minimizing the chances for later impact. The following section describes strategies that administrators and teachers can use to minimize school dropouts.

Procedures for Minimizing School Dropouts and Creating a Caring Environment

Preventing school dropouts requires that superintendents, other central office administrators, principals and teachers work hard to create an environment in which students can succeed. The environment must be humane and considerate of the personal circumstances of the students. To accomplish this goal administrators and teachers must ensure the following:

- Daily monitoring of attendance and grades, with follow-up phone calls or home visits to parents;
- Smaller class sizes, or organizational changes which result in a situation where students can relate to each other and their teachers;
- Adequate and appropriate testing to identify possible learning disabilities;
- Remedial and cross-grade tutoring for high-risk students and dropouts;
- Flexible schedules planned around students' work hours;
- Before- and after- school classes to make up credit requirements;
- Alternative ways to earn credit, such as credit for work or real-life experiences;
- Special guidance and counseling, such as peer-mentor programs and family counseling;
- Job skills training and volunteer or paid work experience programs;
- Special training for teachers to help them increase their understanding of certain student behaviors;
- Increased contact between teachers and students' families;
- Curriculum content for all students that prevent them from being bored and/or increases relevance to the real world;
- Maintenance of easily available information on student achievement and attendance;
- Consistent emphasis on dropout prevention as a goal beginning in elementary schools.

A special and growing population in need of dropout prevention services is teenage mothers. The number of such young girls is growing at an alarming rate. Schools cannot stand by and watch these girls leave school and begin the process of raising children who themselves are likely to drop out of school. School systems must acknowledge that there is a problem and must take ownership of the problem by providing these girls with constructive alternatives.

One way that school systems are addressing this problem is by establishing programs in the regular school. The first step is to survey young mothers who dropped out of high school to determine their reasons for dropping out. Common reasons include inadequate day care, insufficient money to pay for day care, and inconvenience of day care locations. Typically, prior to leaving school these students have a daily attendance rate of 50 percent. Approximately 70 percent of them intend to drop out of school prior to graduation.

Such analyses along with other data can then lead to the development of a plan to keep these girls in school. The heart of the program is an on-site child care center, usually designed to accommodate about twelve infants and toddlers daily, from early morning to late afternoon. Each teen parent is required to spend a single class period in the center and is taught positive parenting techniques, infant stimulation, assessment, and monitoring of developmental and health concerns. While the infants receive expert care, mothers are being taught parenting skills and are given special counseling and academic support.

Dropout Recovery

Many students drop out of school because of their inability to cope in a regular school environment. Whether it is inability to follow rules, a sense of futility at being enrolled in lower-level courses, a failure to see the connection between school and later life chances, or even plain boredom, they just cannot cope. Dropping out does not mean that the administrators' responsibilities for these students ends. Consideration should be given to recovery programs designed to bring students back to school to earn their diplomas.

> **KEY POINT:** *Although recovery programs are important, we need to underscore the point that bringing dropouts back to the kind of institution that failed them in the first place is not likely to work.*

The primary goal of recovery programs is to provide opportunities to students to have a second chance to earn their diploma. These programs should be highly personalized with flexible schedules and small classes. Students must be actively recruited through churches, community organizations, and visits to local shopping centers and other places where young people congregate. The programs should embody two major goals. For those students for whom it is feasible, they should be helped to make the transition back into a regular high school. Those students who cannot cope in regular high schools should be given the opportunity to earn their degree in the more flexible environment.

One flexible recovery program operates in a storefront location donated by a local business. The program is open to any 16–21-year-old residents of the county who left high school before receiving their diplomas. Up to 75 students are enrolled at a time. The students receive their education in small classes (8–10 students) which generally meet for two hours twice a week. Teachers are selected for their content and skills knowledge and for their ability to work effectively with adolescents. What is particularly exciting and effective is the wide variety of learning options, including computer-assisted instruction, community-based education programs, and independent study courses, that can be employed in this setting.

There are three other components of the program which affect the success rate of the students: *advocacy services, employment assistance,* and *transition planning.*

Advocacy services. Program staff should develop links with counseling, health, housing, child support, day care, transportation, and social-service agencies throughout the area, and, through a case management approach, broker for and with students to make sure that needed services are received. It is expected that this approach will remove barriers to success and/or enable students to cope effectively with impediments to success.

Employment services. Through contacts with local employment services and through job development activities, students who want jobs are helped to get them, and those with jobs who want to change to more meaningful or more lucrative employment are assisted.

Transition planning. Prior to graduation, through counseling sessions, students should be encouraged to develop short- and long-range goals, and make plans for attaining those goals. Every effort is made to ensure that students are already engaged in the next phase of their education, training, or employment before graduation day arrives.

Students in recovery programs are generally defined as at risk. It is important that services provided to them not end with graduation. Students must be encouraged to contact the program for additional services after graduation. Additionally, 6-, 12-, and 18-month follow-up contacts should be initiated by school staff to ensure a smooth, successful transition.

Discipline

Although we believe that most discipline problems have their roots in inappropriate classroom instruction in the early grades, the reality is that secondary schools are faced with many students who cannot or will not adapt to a regular school setting. School systems should take a strong position and let it be known that behavior which disrupts education for the majority will not be tolerated. We advocate high academic standards, but those standards are unattainable without high discipline standards. The traditional response to chronically disruptive students has been to expel them, but this merely transfers the problem from the schoolhouse to the streets and does nothing to help the student. As much trouble as these students may be, we should not abandon them. For those students for whom counseling and other strategies do not work, strategies similar to those used in the dropout recovery programs should be considered.

XXV. Restructuring and Choice

Educational choice has been viewed by many as an important component of educational reform. The more orthodox adherents of choice argue that if marketplace dynamics were allowed to operate, bad schools would go out of business and good schools would thrive. Although early proposals envisioned private and public schools competing for the same students, recent versions have focused on public-school-system-*only* choice programs, manifested most typically by magnet schools. As the focus shifted to public schools, the concept of schools going out of business changed. The public school model assumes that if a public school is not doing well and parents do not support it by enrolling their children, the school would adopt a new program and if necessary, be restaffed. The threat of losing enrollment is the incentive to develop and maintain high-quality programs.

CHAPTER 4   Transforming the Content and Delivery of Curriculum   **183**

> **KEY POINT:** *Principals of schools of choice must ensure that their programs live up to their billing. If the program description claims to provide an enriched experience in foreign languages, then such experiences must be provided. Principals must have flexibility to staff their schools as they deem appropriate. They must hire teachers who are excited by the opportunity and have the requisite skills to perform effectively. And perhaps most importantly, principals must understand that in choice programs, parents and students will vote with their feet. If they do not believe that the program is working or is as advertised, they will change schools.*

Choice programs are justified on two grounds. First, they encourage equity for poor and minority students. In choice programs these students have the same options as anyone else to attend any school in the system. In theory, this means that no child will be forced to attend a school that actually has or is perceived to have an ineffective educational program.

The second justification for choice programs lies in the belief that they result in better education for all. Such programs improve student learning through increased program diversity and quality, improving student achievement and motivation, and enhancing parent involvement and satisfaction. Others argue that the creation of new program options will also revitalize the teaching staff by enabling them to do things differently. Further, the theory argues that no school will want to lose enrollment and, therefore, staff will work harder to succeed.

Principals of schools of choice must ensure that their program lives up to its billing. If the program description claims to provide an enriched experience in foreign languages, then such experiences must be provided. Principals must have flexibility to staff their schools as they deem appropriate. They must hire teachers who are excited by the opportunity and have the requisite skills to perform effectively. And perhaps most importantly, principals must understand that in choice programs, parents and students will vote with their feet. If they do not believe that the program is working or is as advertised, they will change schools.

The mark of a quality administrator is one who can take problems and turn them into opportunities. Desegregation is one of those problems that if handled properly can provide an opportunity for enhancing education for all students. Choice not only provides the vehicle for the voluntary integration for schools, it can also be the vehicle to drive incremental change in the districts entire delivery system. Although most districts' taxpayers will frown upon a total revolution, appropriately planned and implemented choice programs can be the vehicle that will drive the transformation. By investing in a reasonable number of choice schools, the administrator can prove that the additional costs associated with this delivery system will result in dramatically improved student performance and parental satisfaction.

Choice programs are a viable alternative to forced busing. They allow administrators to put money into education and not transportation. In addition to the obvious equity considerations associated with choice programs, superintendents should consider the implementation of these programs as a strategy for bringing about school improvement throughout their systems. Experience has shown that once a number of choice schools are established in the system—with extra resources and public attention—pressures begin to build from others who want their children to attend these special schools or who want to upgrade the quality of their assigned schools to match that of the choice schools.

Properly cultivated, the success of choice schools can be used to convince others that all schools must be brought up to the same standards. It will be the keen superintendent who will be able to use these demands to build wider support in the political community for improving all of the schools. As the choice programs prove to be successful, dissatisfaction will grow among those attending traditional programs. This dissatisfaction cannot be allowed to threaten the investment in the choice programs, but instead should be the driving force to invest the same additional resources to reform all schools.

Chapter 4: Further Reading

Adams, Marilyn Jager. 1990. *Beginning to Read: Thinking and Learning About Print.* Cambridge, Ma: MIT Press.

Adler, Mortimer J. 1984. *The Paideia Program: An Educational Syllabus.* New York: Macmillan.

American Association for the Advancement of Science. 1989. *Science for all Americans: Project 2061.* Washington, D.C.: A.A.A.S.

Bennett, William J. 1987. *James Madison High School: A Curriculum for American Students.* Washington, D.C.: United States Department of Education.

Boyer, Ernest, L. 1983. *High School: A Report on Secondary Education in America.* New York: Harper and Row.

Bradley Commission. 1988. *Building a History Curriculum: Guidelines for Teaching History in Schools.* Washington, D.C.: Educational Excellence Network.

Carnegie Commission on Science, Technology and Government. 1991. *The Federal Government and the Reform of K-12 Math and Science Education.* New York: Carnegie Commission.

Conley, David T. 1991. *Restructuring Schools: Educators Adapt to a Changing World (Trends and Issues).* Eugene, Oregon: ERIC Clearinghouse on Educational Management.

Langer, Judith A. et. al. 1990. *Learning to Read in Our Nation's Schools.* Princeton, N.J.: Educational Testing Service.

Lezotte, Lawrence, and Barbara C. Jocoby. 1990. *A Guide to the School Improvement Process Based on Effective Schools Research.* Okemos, Mi: Michigan Institute for Educational Management.

Liberman, Myron. 1990. *Public School Choice: Current Issues/Future Prospects.* Lancaster, Pa: Technomic.

Mathematical Sciences Education Board, National Research Council. 1990. *Reshaping School Mathematics: A Philosophy and Framework for Curriculum.* Washington, D.C.: National Academy Press.

National Research Council. 1989. *Everybody Counts: A Report to the Nation on the Future of Mathematics Education.* Washington, D.C.: National Academy Press.

National Academy of Education. 1985. *Becoming a Nation of Readers.* Washington, D.C.: National Institute of Education.

National Commission on Excellence in Education. 1983. *A Nation at Risk: The Imperative for School Reform.* Washington, D.C.: U.S. Department of Education.

National Council of Social Studies. 1989. *Charting a Course.* Washington, D.C.: National Commission on Social Studies in the Schools.

National Council of Teachers of Mathematics. 1988. *Curriculum and Evaluation Standards for School Mathematics.* Reston, Va: NCTM.

National Council of Teachers of Mathematics. 1989. *Professional Standards for Teaching Mathematics.* Reston, Va: NCTM.

Office of Technology Assessment. 1990. *Linking With Learning*. Washington, D.C.: Government Printing Office.

Peterson, A.D.C. 1986. *Schools Across Frontiers: The Story of the International Baccalaureate and the United World Colleges*. La Salle: Open Court.

Schiller, Scott. 1991. Educational Applications of Instructional Television and Cable Programming, *Media and Methods*, March/April.

Schiller, Scott and Barbara Noll. 1991. Utilizing Distance Learning in a Larger Urban School System. *Tech Trends*, Volume 36, Number 1.

Sizer, Theodore, R. 1984. *Horace's Compromise: The Dilemma of the American High School*. Boston, Ma: Houghton Mifflin.

U.S. Department of Education. 1989. *Becoming a Nation of Readers: What Principals Can Do*. Washington, D.C.: U.S. Department of Education.

U.S. Department of Labor. 1991. The Secretary's Commission on Achieving Necessary Skills. *What Work Requires of Schools: A SCANS Report for America 2000*. Washington, D.C.: U.S. Department of Labor.

Walberg, Herbert J. 1984. Improving the Productivity of America's Schools. *Educational Leadership*, May.

Weisen, Mark. 1991. The Computer for the 21st Century. *Scientific American*, September.

CHAPTER FIVE

TOOLS FOR DIAGNOSIS, PRESCRIPTION, AND ACCOUNTABILITY

Do not put your faith in what statistics say until you have carefully considered what they do not say.

William W. Watt

ISSUES

Tests and their appropriate use
Disaggregating data
School audits
School report cards

The recent attention to school improvement has included new emphases on the roles that test and other data can play as part of public accountability programs and efforts to improve instruction. The contemporary administrator has to understand the implications of a wide range of data and to ask the right questions of school staff. In addition, staff at every level of the school system are going to require access to student performance data that will enable them to evaluate current programs and make necessary modifications.

I. Tests and Their Appropriate Uses

The innovative administrator must be prepared to address one of the key controversies in contemporary public education: the role of assessment and the claim that testing frustrates the instructional process. To many, testing has distorted all reasonable attempts to improve education. These critics point to the fact that the content of standardized tests has driven our curriculum, and many teachers are doing little more than teaching to tests. To many others, testing represents the salvation of our educational system, the process that will bring it out of mediocrity. Both positions contain elements of the truth. If we have failed to get one message out to the members of the education profession, it is that testing cannot play a positive role in improving education unless educators understand the purposes of each major type of test and use tests that are appropriate for the kind of decision they need to make.

Adminstrators face two sorts of questions that test results can help answer. The first is, how do we stack up? Are our schools as effective as they used to be? At what grade levels does the curriculum appear to be strong or weak? How do we compare to other districts throughout the state or nation? The answers to these questions are useful for reporting progress to the community and for identifying broad areas of improvement, decline, or stagnation. The tests used to answer these questions are known as standardized norm-referenced tests. Even though these tests can answer these important questions, they should not be used to make decisions about individual children. These tests do not tell you how much of what a child has been taught he or she actually knows. Rather, such tests tell you the relative position of a student compared to the average performance of students who were part of the test's norming sample. Furthermore, these tests do not usually reflect precisely what is being taught, and when it is taught, in any given school system.

In recent years there have been efforts to improve our capacity to make statements about the comparative performance of groups of students. The National Assessment of Educational Progress is having a major impact in this area by breaking ground in the development of new kinds of test items and through reporting results by proficiency levels. At the same time, individual states are abandoning the traditional standardized norm-referenced tests and are piloting alternatives. However, these new tests are not yet ready, so administrators must rely on the old stand-bys to answer questions concerned with public accountability and with examining the progress of their district or groups of students within their district.

If administrators clearly understand that the standardized norm-referenced tests should not be used to make decisions about individual students, they can save themselves much effort and staff time *by not administering these tests to all children.* Instead, the tests can be given to a scientifically selected, relatively small sample of students, allowing conclusions to be drawn about the progress of the system and large groups of students in that system. Ceasing to give these tests to all students will also relieve the pressure on teachers to distort or otherwise narrow their curriculum to match the objectives on the usually narrowly construed norm-referenced tests.

Although testing to provide information to the public and educators concerning overall progress in the school system is a key ingredient of any effective school reform program, it will not provide the kind of information that will improve instruction. And this leads to the second kind of question that administrators must ask for each and every child in the system, school, and classroom. How much does the child know and not know? This category of question can best be answered by specially designed diagnostic tests—tests that tell the teacher precisely what individual students do and do not know. Tests used for this purpose are typically called criterion-referenced tests. These tests are designed to measure how much of what is being taught or will be taught is known by the student. If a criterion testing program is successful, it will weaken the sharp distinction between testing and teaching and will be perceived by teachers as a useful diagnostic tool. Teachers are expected to use the results of these tests to adjust instruction for each of their students. Principals are expected to monitor the extent to which such adjustments are made. These tests, administered several times during a school year, will soon become an integral and essential part of all new curriculum and will be used for:

- Assessing individual student mastery of skills or knowledge;
- Making grouping decisions about students;
- Diagnosing students' strengths and weaknesses;
- Modifying instruction during the school year;
- Enabling teachers and principals to develop a sense of various strengths and weaknesses in the curriculum;
- Communicating student progress to parents.

Criterion-referenced tests should reflect what a school system expects every student to know and be able to do, grade by grade and subject by subject. Properly developed, with appropriate teacher involvement, these tests typically generate support from teachers, principals, administrators, parents, and the community at large. However, even these tests 'walk the line' between accountability and instructional improvement and administrators must be aware of that 'line.' For example, a mathematics test which identifies what each second-grade student knows in mathematics in a given classroom is very useful to teachers in that they can individualize their instruction to best meet the needs of each student. To retain this positive characteristic of the test, however, the results cannot be used to make individual decisions about the future employment of that teacher. If this is done, the 'curriculum narrowing' and 'teaching to the test' that we have seen with norm-referenced tests will occur with criterion-referenced tests. Administrators should consider using other information—secure year-end tests, principal's observations documenting the presence or absence of effective classroom teaching practices, and parent and student surveys—to make employment decisions about individual teachers.

It will be a surprise to many administrators that another series of tests they can use for instructional purposes is the PSAT's, SAT's, and ACT's. Careful item analyses of the results for all of those who take these tests will reveal patterned weaknesses that can be addressed through curriculum revisions, staff development for teachers, or ensuring higher enrollment in courses that embody richer curriculum and higher standards. It is ironic that these tests—given their importance to the future of our children—are not 'owned' by many principals and teachers. They do not see it as their responsibility even to expose students to the knowledge required for performing well on these tests. This makes sense only if they believe that the courses offered in their schools should not expose students to the content assessed on the tests. This is ludicrous. Administrators must assume the responsibility for ensuring that as many students as possible are enrolled in courses that expose them to the type and level of curriculum reflected in these important tests. Even the most casual review of the tests reveals that an extensive knowledge of language, literature, algebra, and geometry is necessary to perform well. If the schools do not provide these opportunities, who should?

We now briefly describe each major type of test that administrators are required to use. These descriptions focus on the most appropriate uses of each test and the pitfalls of test use.

II. The Standardized Norm-Referenced Test

Until recently norm-referenced standardized achievement tests were the primary means of assessing the effectiveness of most educational programs. Although these tests do provide some useful information, their use is limited and those limitations ought to be understood by educators. A norm-referenced standardized test is designed to provide a uniform measure of student performance that allows comparisons to be made *among groups of students*. All students take the same test, based on the same directions, according to the same rules. The group of students with whom a student's performance is compared is called a norm group. The norm group consists of students of the same age, the same grade, who took the same test when it was first developed. It must also be understood that standardized norm-referenced achievement tests are not designed to assess the extent to which students have mastered the school system's curricula. Rather, they are designed to assess the extent to which students master what the test publishers deemed to be important.

Standardized tests provide information about how students in a given class, school, group, or school system are doing in relation to other students; not about how much they have learned.

The two most common ways of describing results are by percentile rank and by grade equivalent. The percentile rank reveals how a student is ranked in relation to the performance of other students who took the test. It indicates the percentage of the students in the group being tested who did worse than the students in the norm group. A percentile rank of 70 means that a student scored better than 70 percent of all children who took the test. (It does not mean that the student answered 70 percent of the questions correctly!)

Grade equivalent scores show *only* whether the child's performance is above, below, or the same as other students in the grade. They do not tell you what level of work a child should be given. A grade equivalent score of 8.0 for a fourth grader does not mean that the child knows as much as eighth graders or is ready to do 8th-grade work. If you want to know whether or not a 4th grader can do 8th-grade work, you have to give him/her an 8th-grade test. If a 4th-grade child is at a grade equivalent of 2.0, it does not mean that the child belongs in the 2nd grade. He/she may only need extra help. This fact has important implications for what should and should not be told to parents about their child's performance.

The biggest problems with standardized tests are not built-in limitations. Rather, they involve the misuse of scores. The most common misuse is making these tests the primary basis for classifying, labeling, or placing students in a fixed track or special class. Standardized test scores should not be used alone, or even in significant part, to label a student as incapable of learning, place a student in a grade, give a student a report-card grade, identify the specific skills a student needs to learn, or place a student in a track in gifted, remedial, or special education classes.

These tests cannot be used for these purposes for two reasons. The first is the relatively narrow range of skills measured by the test. Second, there is a certain amount of inaccuracy in every student's score. If a student had to take the test again with no additional instruction, his/her score would probably not be the same. The student's score would fall somewhere within a specified range of scores. This specified range or band of scores is called the standard error of measurement. Because of this range, it is difficult if not inappropriate to use standardized test scores *to make decisions about individual students*. On the other hand, group scores, such as class or grade-level scores, are much more stable than scores for individual students.

> **KEY POINT:** *Standardized tests provide information about how students in a given class, school, group, or school system are doing in relation to other students; not about how much they have learned.*

No discussion of norm-referenced standardized achievement testing is complete without addressing the issues of norms. Recently, 48 of the 50 states reported that their students were above average in performance on their norm-referenced standardized achievement tests! When considering this finding, it is important to realize that if the test was normed

CHAPTER 5 Tools for Diagnosis, Prescription, and Accountability **193**

in 1980, then what is really being said is that the school system is 'above average' when compared to the performance of the students in the norming sample of 1980.

With All of Their Limitations, What Are the Legitimate Uses of Standardized Achievement Test Scores?

It is important to understand the form and nature of the test data in question. If only a total score for all fifth graders is available, only three questions can be answered: How did fifth graders compare to the national norm group? How did fifth graders compare to the prior year's fifth graders? and, How did fifth graders in this school compare to fifth graders system-wide? At best the information provides some general knowledge as to how things were going in the fifth grade. It does not identify which groups of students or teachers need the most help. To provide information that would help identify specific areas of group strengths or weaknesses, the data must be disaggregated.

Disaggregating data means that the data are analyzed separately for students with different personal and learning characteristics; for example, for girls or boys, or blacks or whites, or high or low achievers. *The purpose of using disaggregated data from norm-referenced achievement tests is to find the groups in your school who are not benefitting from instruction.*

Data from norm-referenced achievement tests can play a useful role in creating a snapshot of how things are going, particularly over a period of time if the results are disaggregated on a few key variables, such as race, gender, or socio-economic status. The problem is to use the data most effectively for improving student achievement. The nature of your use will be a function of the kinds of decisions you have to make. The table which follows outlines the reasons that staff in different places in the school system may want to conduct disaggregated analyses with norm-referenced test data.

Using Norm-Referenced Standardized Achievement Test Information

The Users	The Reason for the Analysis
Principals and Teachers	1. To evaluate performance throughout an entire grade level at a given point in time. These analyses should be conducted by race, sex and socio-economic status for each subject area to determine the extent to which all students are benefiting from the instructional program. 2. To determine how students of different races, socio-economic groups, and gender are benefiting from the school's programs over time. 3. To determine the effectiveness of specific school programs that impact groups of students. **The intent of these analyses is to enable school staff to gain a very general understanding of strengths and weaknesses by grade and subject, and to sensitize them as to the unmet needs of any group of students.**
Central Office Staff	1. To monitor the system-wide effectiveness of instruction, by grade, race, gender and socio-economic status to determine if the program benefits some students more than others. 2. To determine the overall effectiveness of instruction in different schools. 3. To identify weak spots in the curriculum. **The intent of these analyses is to identify grades, schools, or curriculum areas to which resources should be directed.**
Superintendent	1. To determine the system-wide effectiveness of instruction, by grade, socio-economic status, race, and gender; particularly as a measure of progress over time. 2. To compare and contrast the effectiveness of different school programs and principals. 3. To determine the effectiveness of instuctional programs. **The intent of these analyses is to allow the superintendent to:** • **Make judgments concerning the extent to which the system's goals are being met;**

The Users	The Reason for the Analysis
	- Identify schools, grades, or subjects which seem particularly strong or weak;
- Identify those groups of students, by race or gender, who are not benefiting from the system's programs;
- Track the progress of the system and schools over a period of time;
- Target resources where they are most needed.

III. The Criterion-Referenced Test

As the standardized norm-referenced achievement tests are designed to provide comparative information about large groups of students, criterion-referenced tests generate information about specific skills or knowledge areas that individual or small groups of students master. *First and foremost, criterion-referenced tests should be designed to reflect the school's curricula.* The tests provide information about the extent to which individual students are learning the curriculum that they are being taught or already know the material that would normally be taught. The primary purpose of using criterion-referenced tests is to obtain information useful for making informed adjustments in the instructional process. Classroom decisions about grouping, regrouping, re-teaching, and reporting student performance to parents are enhanced by the results of a criterion-referenced test. Additionally, criterion-referenced test results may be used to enhance classroom-level decisions related to reducing or extending time allocated to a unit, adjusting instructional strategies, arranging for needed teacher in-services, and modifying instructional materials.

Results can also be used to monitor the extent to which students are learning or schools are teaching the school system's approved curricula. Given that criterion-referenced tests reflect a school system's curricula, the tests will vary somewhat from school district to school district. However, many instructional objectives are similar from district to district and, therefore, sharing test items with others should be encouraged.

Given that the primary purpose of criterion-referenced tests is to provide teachers and principals with information for adjusting instruction, it is important that these tests at least be administered at the beginning and at the middle of the school year. Year-end administration of the test is also recommended as a means of assessing how much a student or group of students has learned, and to enable administrators to determine how well a school or group of schools performed.

The strength and weakness of a criterion-referenced test is that it can be used for the dual goals of improving instruction and for accountability. However, it is important to understand that it is difficult for teachers to use the test for instructional purposes if they believe that evaluative judgements will be made about them or their schools based on the test. Perversions in test administration, teaching to the test, and overzealous coaching can occur. Ideally, if there is a desire to use a criterion-referenced test for accountability purposes, then it would be best to use a secure and different form of the test at the end of the year, and to sample students rather than test them all.

As the array of available tests becomes larger and more sophisticated, administrators should improve their understanding of the proper uses of each. They have to develop an understanding of the appropriate applications of various test results and be wary of being led astray by those who are not sensitive to the differences. Armed with such information, administrators can be in a position to make informed judgments about the effectiveness of their programs, schools, and, in some cases, personnel. A major step in this process is to understand the basic differences between norm-referenced and criterion-referenced tests. The following table provides examples of cases where each type of test may be used most appropriately.

Appropriate Uses of Norm-Referenced (NRT) and Criterion-Referenced Tests (CRT)

Purpose	Test	Examples	Primary Users
To compare achievement of local students to achievement of students in the nation, state, or other districts.	NRT	A comparison of achievement of local schools' 3rd-graders to achievement of 3rd-graders in the nation, state, or other districts.	Central office (including school boards), parents.

CHAPTER 5 Tools for Diagnosis, Prescription, and Accountability

Purpose	Test	Examples	Primary Users
To compare achievement of subgroups of local students to achievement of similar subgroups in the nation, state, or other districts.	NRT	A comparison of achievement of local black students to the achievement of black students throughout the nation, state, or other districts.	Central office staff.
To compare achievement of one local school's student subgroup to achievement of another such subgroup to determine the equity of educational outcomes.	NRT	A comparison of achievement of black and white students in local schools to determine and monitor any gap in achievement.	Central office staff, principals.
To assess the extent to which students in a single grade-level (at the district, building, or classroom level) have mastered the essential objectives of the school system's curriculum.	CRT	A comparison of differences between results of September and May criterion-referenced tests to determine the extent to which 3rd-graders at a given school attained 3rd-grade objectives in reading.	Teachers principals, central office staff.
To assess the extent to which a given student is learning the essential objectives of the school system's curriculum and, subsequently, to adjust instruction for that student.	CRT	The use of the results from the September and January criterion-referenced tests as one indicator to help determine if a student is properly placed in an instructional group.	Teachers principals, parents.
To track achievement of a cohort of students through the system or area to determine the extent to which they are mastering the system's curriculum.	CRT	An comparison of the progress of all 3rd-graders in a system, administrative area, or school from one year to the next.	Central office staff, principals.

Purpose	Test	Examples	Primary Users
To track achievement of a cohort of students in a given school to determine the extent to which they learn essential objectives of school system's curriculum as they go from grade to grade.	CRT	The use of May criterion-referenced tests (or perhaps gains from September to May), to follow the progress of children over time to determine the extent to which they learned the curriculum from one year to another.	Principals, teachers.

IV. The Cognitive Ability Test

Although there are those who strongly believe that cognitive ability tests (COG's) serve a useful purpose in assessing students' potential and group placement, there are some who hold that more than any one factor these tests hinder rather than accelerate student learning. In theory COG's are designed to measure students' ability and potential to learn. (However, the instructions to many of these tests imply that the tests will give a student the chance to show what he/she knows and what he/she thinks). The answer to the question concerning the usefulness of the COG is based on the extent to which you are a believer in the capacity of any test administered to a young child to accurately identify or predict the capacity of that child to learn.

For a test to be used as a real measure of ability—of potential—it must generate scores which are in some way consistently related to achievement. To test whether or not such a positive relationship between cognitive ability scores and achievement scores exists, the table below presents results from a testing program in a large urban school system. The testing program employed a reputable cognitive ability test and an equally reputable standardized norm-referenced achievement test. The results in these tables provide an answer to an extremely important question: Is performance on COG's an accurate indicator of how students will perform on achievement tests? If the answer to the question is no, then serious consideration should be given to dropping these tests from the system's testing programs. If the answer is yes, then why not just give the achievement test?

Grade 3

School	Cognitive Ability Test	Reading	Language	Mathematics
A	40	58	62	65
B	40	75	87	80
C	40	60	79	82
D	40	50	65	66
E	40	44	50	58
F	40	63	77	78

Grade 8

School	Cognitive Ability Test	Reading	Language	Mathematics
A	81	65	77	66
B	57	81	88	81

Even the most cursory review of these tables reveals that the relationship between COG scores and achievement test scores is contrary to folklore that is prevalent in much of the education profession. Such folklore is based on the belief that cognitive ability tests are true measures of potential and, as such, predict how students will perform on achievement tests. These data reveal that the relationship between the two tests is relatively independent. Unfortunately, however, too many teachers and principals believe that if a student's cognitive ability score is low, then that student should be placed in a low-achievement group; this decision, typically made in the early grades, condemns many of our students to an inadequate education and guaranteed placement in lower-level groups.

As a means of explaining how a student with a low COG score scores high on an achievement test, many educators employ the mystical concept of overachiever: a student who should not have achieved so much in light of their COG score. The aforementioned tables debunk the folklore. The data reveal that students with low or high cognitive-ability scores can score high or low on achievement tests. If for some reason these data are not compelling, consider two points. First, apply a commonsense standard. Do you really believe that a paper and pencil test can predict the learning *potential* of a seven-year-old student? And second, we know that if children are in low-achievement groups in the early grades they are likely to remain in low groups for the balance of their school careers. So why not give these students the benefit of the doubt and at least try to help them succeed at a higher level? If they fail at the higher level, they will be no worse for trying.

A further response to those who truly believe that COG scores measure student performance is found in the nature of many of the COG test items; particularly those administered in the early elementary school grades. Typically these questions test children on issues related to shapes, sizes, and relationships among objects. The COG adherents would lead you to believe that such questions measure things that are innate to a child; neither learnable nor teachable. However, once again applying a commonsense standard, we know that children from middle-class backgrounds and/or those who had meaningful day-care experiences prior to entering school score higher than those who do not have such experiences. Are the implications of this that:

- The middle class and day care students have higher potential than those who are not in these groups?

or

- These students were taught such things as shapes, sizes, and relationships before they entered school?

If you answer affirmatively to the first of the two questions, the implications for schools are that they are but caretakers for many of our students, and it is important to isolate them from more normal students for fear that they will somehow dilute the quality of instruction for the normal students. If you answer affirmatively to the second question there is hope that all children will receive whatever services they require for success at a high level. As a matter of fact, it is likely that instructional goals for low-performing children must even be higher than those for children who are already performing at high levels. If not, the gap between our 'haves' and 'have-nots' will never be eliminated.

V. Performance Assessment: An Emerging Methodology

Although multiple-choice criterion-referenced tests do provide useful information about the extent to which students are learning the curriculum that is taught, they cannot reflect the rich diversity of student performance found in most classrooms. In addition to the norm- and criterion-referenced instruments discussed above, a creative and, some claim, potentially more productive form of assessment has emerged recently: performance assessments. Through the use of such options as portfolios, manuscripts, exhibits, demonstrations, and community-based learning options, students can demonstrate their mastery of key learning outcomes in what might be called more real-world settings.

Performance-based assessment is the more holistic means of assessment, and it will certainly establish itself as the best and broadest assessment form. The object is to align curriculum and assessment directly and completely so that the assessment measures exactly what the desired outcomes of the curriculum goals are expected to achieve. Examples of such measures include portfolio assessments, written compositions, science experiments in essay form, performance-based mathematical problems showing how students arrived at their answers, musical performance, examples of art work and communicating orally in a foreign language.

At the heart of this model is the concept that paper and pencil multiple-choice instruments frequently fail to encourage critical thinking, decision-making, and problem-solving at anything but the most basic, micro-skill level. Performance assessment instruments allow students to demonstrate mastery of a whole battery of skills manifested in a holistic, synthesized context, rather than a decontextualized one. Through the use of process folios, for example, students can reflect all facets of and interactions involved with the thinking and product-generation process involved in a science, math, or language arts experience, from initial start-up documents and products to culminating ones.

The effective administrator must work with staff in the use of performance assessments to ensure that they are scored using clearly identified criteria. Moreover, training must be provided to ensure consistency of staff understanding and sensitivity to the issues implicit in the process. A variety of performance assessment measures should comprise a part of any effective teacher's repertoire. Such measures might include:

- **Writing Portfolios,** including options for students to demonstrate their mastery of content and concepts through essays rather than multiple-choice tests;
- **Experiential Learning Options,** including the use of manipulatives and laboratory experiences in the fields of science and mathematics. Students might be asked to design and solve their own scientific or mathematical puzzle or problem and present as their final project a detailed overview of the problem-solution process they employed;
- **Open-Ended Questioning,** with students asked to deal with learning experiences and questions that allow for more than a single right answer. Students are expected to demonstrate their individual solutions as well as the steps they employed to arrive at it;
- **Experience-Based Culminating Activities,** including panel presentations and open forums in which students present and discuss their work within a given discipline or subject area.

> **KEY POINT:** *The creative and innovative educational leader must assist his/her staff to ensure that all facets of student learning are both encouraged and measured. They should require that a mix of assessment strategies be used to measure intuitive or holistic understanding, factual material, and applications of knowledge to problem solving situations. This requirement should be supported with training at the school in teacher-designed curriculum-embedded performance assessments. Additionally, central office personnel spearheading efforts in testing and evaluation should incorporate performance assessment wherever possible as a major component of system level assessment and accountability efforts.*

VI. Diagnosing Problems through the Disaggregation of Data

Even with the best of intentions, many well-designed educational initiatives and programs are hard to find in practice within months of their implementation. It is even difficult to collect information about the implementation and effectiveness of a school system's most basic programs. Given the preoccupation of teachers and principals with delivering basic educational services on a daily basis, it is understandable that the implementation of new programs and the documentation of what is happening tends to be swallowed up by normal day to day activities. However, unless the superintendent—as well as all other staff—have a sense of what is working and what is not, it is impossible to bring about meaningful school improvement.

> **KEY POINT:** *It is the responsibility of the superintendent to convince staff that the collection of data is not an unnecessary burden. The superintendent must make it clear that appropriate data will improve the capacity of all staff to do their jobs more effectively. Such information will enable (a) principals and teachers to understand who is and is not benefitting from their efforts; (b) principals to understand the breadth and depth of performance in their school; and (c) central office staff to understand the extent to which various curricular strategies are having an impact and school system goals are being met. It is hard to think of any professionals, other than educators, who perform their jobs in the absence of sophisticated information about their clientele. It must also be noted that school system staff cannot be expected to understand the collection and use of extensive information without special training provided by the system.*

If only one lesson has been learned about implementing effective school improvement programs, it is that staff throughout the school system must have more information—information about who is benefiting from programs and who is not; information about the nature of the instructional process that students are experiencing; and information describing whether or not programs are meeting or failing to meet reasonable expectations. Equally as important as collecting information is the use to which the information is put. The expectation should be that all staff, classroom and resource teachers, principals, and those in the central office do something positive with the information. They must be taught to use information to answer questions about program effectiveness and participation; to identify students, teachers, and principals who are doing well and those who require additional special assistance.

Although the information required to maintain meaningful school improvement will vary somewhat from system to system, there is a common core of data that all systems will find useful. The required information can be grouped into the following four categories:

Category 1: Descriptive and demographic information including the number of students, students' race, gender, age, and socio-economic status (for example, eligibility for free and reduced lunch or parent educational level). This information should be collected and available at the classroom, school, regional area (if appropriate), and school system levels.

Category 2: Achievement and outcome information including the number of children achieving at or above grade-level in reading and mathematics, test scores in a range of subjects, the number of elementary school students who advance from one reading or mathematics group to a higher-level group, enrollment in higher and lower level classes, SAT or ACT scores, and numbers of students going on to colleges and universities. This information should be presented by classroom, school, regional area, and school system. The information should also be categorized by relevant demographic factors, such as race and gender.

Category 3: Program participation information including student and teacher attendance, suspensions and expulsions, the number of awards given to students, the number of students enrolled in AP classes and successfully passing the examination, the number of students taking the PSAT, ACT, and SAT, the number of students who drop out of school, and the number of students in extracurricular activities. Once again, this information should be presented by classroom, school, regional area, and school system. The information should also be categorized by relevant demographic factors, such as race, gender, and socio-economic status.

Category 4: Information collected from students and their parents concerning their perceptions of what is happening in the schools can serve a useful purpose to central office and school-based personnel. It is often the case that school staff have a sense that things are going well while, at the same time, the school's major clients do not share those beliefs.

(Appendix B provides examples of data collection forms that could be used as a guide for assembling information to serve the needs of both central office and school-based staff. The information generated by these forms will be useful for designing school improvement programs, assessing the extent of their implementation, and guiding the day-to-day activities of principals and teachers).

The issue of using data in schools is not new. For years schools have pointed to their average test scores as indicators of how well they were doing. Local newspapers publish the results of testing programs and rank schools in their jurisdiction from high to low. The federal government and many states disseminate information about high-performing schools based on test scores and, in many cases, declared schools as exemplary based on those test scores. In recent years, however, as dissatisfaction with the academic performance of American students grew, the demand for improving schools has intensified. Those demands created a burden on education administrators to figure out what was wrong and fix it. What was ignored was the fact that many administrators had neither the experience nor the know-how to fix what was wrong. The major ingredient that was missing was the capacity to identify a system's, a school's, or a student's problems and then accurately determine the causes of those problems.

> **KEY POINT:** *The local school's ability to use data effectively is wholly dependent on the system's ability to provide the necessary data in usable formats, in a timely manner. These requirements may very well require a change in the organization, function, or philosophy associated with the system's data collection efforts.*

Traditionally, diagnoses of educational problems were made on the basis of personal judgments and best guesses. Sometimes they were right and sometimes they were wrong. As the nature of our student body became more heterogeneous—more complex in terms of learning needs—the personal judgment method became less useful. It is almost like a patient going to a doctor complaining about a stomach ache after eating a meal of hot chilli peppers. The doctor does not need a lot more information to make his diagnosis of severe indigestion. On the other hand, if the patient goes to the doctor and complains of general stomach pains and does not provide further clues, the doctor must conduct many more tests to determine the problem. Fortunately for doctors (and, of course, for patients), much of their formal training was based on learning how to determine the causes of various problems.

They were trained to ask the right questions, to order the appropriate tests, and to analyze a wide variety of data. Educators, on the other hand, are rarely exposed to the kind of coursework that could help them develop such diagnostic skills.

The ability to identify problems and diagnose causes is dependent upon one's ability to use information—to use data. The bad news is that many educators are going to have to overcome the anxiety that they feel when they deal with numbers. The good news is that they will not have to become sophisticated statisticians to develop the needed skills. The following case studies are designed to provide administrators with a sense of how to ask the right questions and how to examine data to yield the best possible answers to those questions. The information illustrates the kind of logic that goes into the use of data for diagnostic and decision-making purposes. In using data to understand what is happening in schools, it is important to note that there will be many cases in which the clues are not self-evident. Educators are going to have to examine the data and, based on that examination, continually ask questions until they believe that they have enough information and insight to understand the causes of the problem.

CASE STUDY 1

Using Test Results to Identify Problems

Step 1

The most typical example of using data relates to norm-referenced achievement testing. We are most familiar with the annual announcement from the Hypothetical School System (HSS) that they scored at the 75th percentile in the total test battery at the fifth grade. Usually such an announcement is reason for joy. After all the national average is at the 50th percentile and the 75th percentile far exceeds that figure. Nevertheless, the announcement fails to mention that the 75th percentile score of HSS students is being compared to the performance of students who were in the norming sample *ten years ago.*

CHAPTER 5 Tools for Diagnosis, Prescription, and Accountability   **207**

CASE STUDY 1   *continued*

Putting aside the issue of the norming sample, what does the 75th percentile mean? When asked this question many people reply that it means that these students accurately answered 75 percent of the questions. WRONG! Once again, it means that on the average the students scored better than 75 percent of the students who took the test as part of the norming sample. As a matter of fact, many students could have answered fewer than 75 percent of the items correctly. Perhaps 70 percent; 65 percent; 60 percent. You can't tell from a percentile figure. The main point here is that the average scores on a standardized norm-referenced achievement test do not provide information about how much knowledge or how much of a curriculum a student masters.

Although the use of norm-referenced test data is limited, it does provide some useful comparative information. Over a period of time you can track the overall progress of groups of students. So, if last year the 5th-grade students in the HSS scored at the 70th percentile and this year were at the 75th percentile, then there is some reason for optimism. However, the data do not tell you if those improvements occurred at just one or two schools or were system-wide. They do not tell you if the improvement was for white students while the scores of black students remained stable or even declined. They do little to help you understand why the scores are the way they are. It is important to note that if your only interest is reporting test scores to the public or holding school employees accountable for student performance, these overall average scores may be sufficient.

Step 2

Assume that your interest is in school improvement, and you want to understand what the 75th percentile score in the fifth grade really means. The first thing that you would do is disaggregate the data on some key elements. The first element should be *the two subject area tests* that constitute the total battery; reading and mathematics. When we examine the results in this manner we find the following:

CASE STUDY 1 *continued*

	This Year (in percentiles)	Last Year
Total test battery score	75	70
Total reading score	70	67
Total mathematics score	84	74

These findings provide an interesting perspective. The overall test battery score indicates improvement; the reading scores improve slightly while the mathematics scores show a dramatic improvement. Although it seems that it is time to celebrate, caution should prevail. It is important to note that using these data over time has its limitations. This year's 5th-grade students in HSS may or may not have the same characteristics as last year's 5th-grade students. What if there were 20 percent more youngsters from low-income families last year than this year? Or, what if there was a large-scale housing development opened in the district last year accounting for significant increases in overall enrollment? Is it not possible that these differences in student populations from one year to the next could influence the average test scores? Of course it is!

When presenting scores from one year to the next it is important to determine the extent to which each year's student populations are similar to that of prior years. These populations should be compared on the basis of such factors as racial composition, gender, years of attendance in the school system, eligibility for free and reduced lunch, and any other socio-economic factors that may be available.

(For the purposes of this case study assume that the populations were similar in each of the two years.)

Step 3

Although the data illustrate that things seem to be all right, there is still not enough information to guide school improvement activities. The next step is to discover whether or not there are any cases in which students did particularly well or particularly poorly. Therefore, you may want to disaggregate

CASE STUDY 1 *continued*

the data for fifth grade students by school building. Assume that HSS consists of six elementary schools. Here is the test information for each of the six schools:

	School (5th Grade)					
	A	B	C	D	E	F
Reading	74	**60**	80	73	77	73
Mathematics	79	77	81	72	**84**	82

Step 4

The data reveal that school B has unusually low reading scores, while school E appears to be doing exceptionally well in mathematics. You then have to discover what accounts for that variance. To accomplish this goal, you need to be aggressive in asking questions of the data. For example, do the scores differ by the race of the student? By gender? By classroom? Or, is everyone more or less high? Or low? For purposes of illustration, *for reading in school B,* the fifth grade scores were next disaggregated by race and then by classroom and, *for mathematics in school E,* by race and gender.

Reading

School B (reading percentile scores)

Race	
White	75
Black	55

These reading data provide a powerful clue as to where problems may exist. The white students are scoring above the

CASE STUDY 1 *continued*

average level of performance for fifth grade students in HSS while the black students are performing lower. The next question: Is the relative poor performance of black students the same throughout the grade or are there examples of their successful performance? To answer this question, data should be further disaggregated by classroom.

School B (reading percentile scores)

Race	Classrooms		
	1	2	3
White	81	55	88
Black	64	50	82

Although further analyses of these scores should be done for each of the classrooms, for purposes of this case study, focus will be placed on classrooms 2 and 3. The distribution of scores in those classrooms deviate significantly from the average.

From this point on in the analyses, do not use the standardized test results. As noted earlier, they are only reliable for making judgements about groups of students. As we begin to examine what is happening in classrooms, we need to look at different indicators. In addition, we do not need any further information to indicate that something different may be happening in these classrooms. The question now is—what is causing these differences?

To better understand what is happening with respect to reading in classrooms 2 and 3, *reading instruction in those classrooms must be observed. Principals must determine what accounts for the high or low scores and the extent to which effective grouping, time management, and instructional practices are used.* The following hypothetical observations are patterned after actual observations that have been conducted in a number of elementary school classrooms.

CASE STUDY 1 *continued*

Classroom 2

In this classroom both black and white students are significantly below the school average and the school system average. For reading and language arts, 90 minutes per day are available. The teacher divides the students into three equally-sized groups for reading instruction; a slow group, a medium-paced group, and a fast group. Each group gets a maximum of only 30 minutes of direct instruction per day. During the non-direct instructional time, the students complete worksheets, copy from the board, or get a head start on their homework. An examination of the grouping reveals that almost every child is in the same group toward the end of the year as he or she was in the beginning of the school year.

Classroom 3

In this classroom, both black and white students are above the school average and the school system average. The same 90 minutes are available for reading instruction. However, the teacher uses one hour of the time providing direct instruction to all students using a variety of techniques including co-operative learning and several computers that are in the classroom. For the remaining 30 minutes, the teacher organizes the students into small skill groupings and moves from one group to another helping students as needed. In this classroom, students receive at least one hour and ten minutes a day for direct instruction.

The results of these observations make it abundantly clear that the major reason accounting for the differences in standardized achievement test scores may be the way teachers organize time and deliver instruction. School administrators are reminded that the test scores alone have limited use. *In this case, the test scores indicated a need to observe the instruction taking place in the classroom.* These findings are consistent with the findings from educational research which indicate that student achievement is most likely to be high where the time spent on direct instruction is also high.

CASE STUDY 1 *continued*

Mathematics

The total mathematics score was 84 for school E. However, it is important to determine if all students are benefiting from the program or if the high scores of some students are masking the fact that others are not doing well. Accordingly, the following analyses were performed:

School E (mathematics percentile scores)

Total Test Score Grade 5	Race/Total Test Score
84	White 90
	Black 80

These data indicate good news. Although there is a gap between the scores of black and white students, both groups are scoring very high. As the search for clues continues, however, the following is revealed when the data are examined by gender.

School E (mathematics percentile scores)

Total Test Score Grade Five	Race	Gender/Total Test Score Male	Female
84	White	97	83
	Black	87	73

The earlier good news is now tempered with the finding that there is a gap, that should be addressed immediately, between black females and all other groups. At this point, the use of standardized test scores to identify further causes of the problems diminishes. Administrators must now examine teach-

CHAPTER 5 Tools for Diagnosis, Prescription, and Accountability

CASE STUDY 1 *continued*

ing practices, classroom organization strategies, teacher expectations, and curriculum similar to the inquiry conducted with respect to reading.

CASE STUDY 2

Using Data to Identify the Causes of Suspensions

The only high school in the HSS district reported that its student suspension rate began to increase three years ago and is now at an all-time high. When administrators first discovered the problem, they trained all of their staff in behavioral management techniques and established an in-school suspension program. Unfortunately, even in the presence of these interventions the rates increased. Using a variety of data sources, HSS administrators attempted to discover the causes of the high rates of suspension.

Step 1

Last year's suspension data must be examined.

HSS High School: 30 percent of students suspended

Race	Percent of Students Suspended
White	15
Black	40

At this point, the apparent conclusion is that the problem is disproportionately affecting the black students. However, prior to taking any action some additional analysis is required.

CASE STUDY 2 *continued*

It is important to see if there are any significant differences by both race and gender.

Step 2

HSS High School (percentage of students suspended by race and gender)

Race	Male	Female
White	90	10
Black	90	10

These findings verify that the problem is predominantly a male problem. It now appears that any intervention must be directed toward improving the behavior of males, not black males as indicated in Step 1. However, once again, before making any final decisions, proceed to the next step.

Step 3

Before making any final decision about how to fix the suspension problem, determine if that problem is equally distributed throughout the school. This is done by examining the data in terms of who is actually referring the students for suspension. The following table illustrates this point. (Assume that there are only ten teachers in HSS).

CASE STUDY 2 *continued*

Teacher	Percentage of suspensions resulting from each teacher's referrals
1	5
2	5
3	5
4	20
5	5
6	5
7	30
8	20
9	0
10	5

The data from this table turns earlier suppositions upside down. Rather than concluding that the suspension is somehow related to the behavior of black students, and rather than fixing the problem by training all teachers and establishing in-school suspension programs, it now appears that 70 percent of all suspensions can be accounted for by the referral behavior of three teachers. Building principals must determine why these few teachers are suspending black youngsters with great frequency. Is it a matter of low expectations? Or is it that these teachers don't understand cultural differences that relate to behavior?

KEY POINT: *Whatever the specific explanation for the results in each study, it is not what it first appeared to be in step 1.*

VII. School-Based Auditing: A Means of Identifying Problems and Determining the Extent of Program Implementation

Although many questions that the superintendent and senior administrators ask can be answered by examining a variety of outcome data and observing instructional strategies, some situations require that a team be sent into a school to conduct focused interviews and observe what is happening. This audit team—usually consisting of teachers, guidance counselors, principals, subject matter specialists, and central office administrators—can be used to conduct audits of two types. The first type of audit responds to or explores the possibility that problems exist in a school, identifies those problems, and suggests corrective actions. The second type of audit determines the extent to which a specific program (such as school-based management, shared decision-making, or co-operative learning) is actually and appropriately being implemented in a given school. There are some circumstances in which the audits can simultaneously address both purposes.

The audits provide superintendents and others with rapid feedback, allowing them to respond quickly to a wide range of problems. The members of the audit team must be selected with as little notice as possible so that the staff at the audited school cannot formally prepare their responses. Prior to the audit, superintendents should meet with audit team members to express their concerns about the school and to clarify their expectations for the kinds of information that would be most useful. Given these concerns and expectations, audit team members then generate a list of the categories of people that they need to interview, including teachers, administrators, specialists, students, and parents. Finally, the team develops the questions and lines of inquiry it wants to pursue during its visit. Most audits can be completed in a single day and the team's report submitted to the superintendent within a few days of the visit. The school to be audited should be notified by the superintendent of the audit and its purpose.

We now look at an audit report submitted to the superintendent of the HSS. The audit was conducted at the Hypothetical Middle School in response to a series of concerns expressed to the superintendent by a few of the school's teachers, several parents, and the school system's supervisor of reading and language arts. Their concerns focused on a lack of consistency in policy implementation, poor communication, and an inadequate educational focus. Similar concerns had been raised in the past and attempts were made to remedy them but continuing complaints indicated that earlier corrective actions may not have worked.

The seven audit team members met to prepare their questions and develop their schedule. The questions were designed to elicit concerns about and suggestions for improving the program at the school. Interviewees were given every opportunity to state that the school was functioning well and concerns were at a minimum. For a concern to be considered for inclusion in the report to the superintendent, it had to be reported by several interviewees to more than one interviewer. Provisions were also made to debrief the principal at the end of the day by briefly summarizing the major concerns that were identified, and to elicit the principal's explanations for the presence of the problems.

The superintendent notified the principal in the morning that the audit team would be there within the hour. The principal was told the purpose of the audit and was asked to make staff and others available to the audit team. As soon as the team arrived, they gave the principal a list of those that they wanted to interview and set about the task of gathering information. Some interviews were with individuals while others were with groups. In addition to the interviews, team members observed classrooms, hallways, and the cafeteria.

> **KEY POINT:** *It is important that the staff at the school being audited understand that the purpose of the audit is to make things better for them, to improve their professional environment, and to effectively use whatever resources the school and school system can provide to alleviate any problems.*

Here is a copy of the audit report that was submitted to the superintendent by the audit team a few days after the completion of the audit.

Hypothetical School System

Memorandum

To: The Superintendent
From: Members of the Hypothetical Middle School Audit Team

Subject: Results of the audit

Per your request we conducted a site-based audit of the Hypothetical Middle School on December 7th. The primary purposes of the audit were to assess the extent to which problems that were reported to you actually existed, their seriousness and causes, and suggestions for remediation. We would like to take this opportunity to thank you for the chance to conduct the audit. Without exception we have gained new insights and believe that the process can be used in a way to support our staff and further our school improvement programs. Based on your input we focused on an examination of official and unofficial school policies, communication structures and processes, curriculum and instruction, and student behavior, discipline, and management. Attached to this summary are copies of the verbatim notes that each audit team member developed during the interview sessions and observations. For obvious reasons, the specific identities of those who were interviewed are not revealed. As we discussed, anonymity was promised to all concerned. And finally, as you suggested, we told the school's principal and staff that you will meet with them to discuss the audit team findings, give them a chance to respond to the findings, and to discuss any corrective actions that you require. Our report is organized around each of the general concerns that you had.

Concern 1: A need for coherent written policies and procedures

Specific concerns expressed by interviewees and verified by team members

- There is a lack of coherent, consistent written policies and procedures addressing such areas as teacher and administrator

CHAPTER 5 Tools for Diagnosis, Prescription, and Accountability

duties and responsibilities, student discipline, student attendance, and student activities;
- The school calendar does not reflect the events of the month and day; there are frequent impositions upon instructional time by unexpected announcements or unannounced events;
- Teachers and other staff are not involved in the development of those policies and procedures which define the structure and content of their school day.

Recommendations

- A team of teachers, resource personnel, and administrators should be created to develop policies and procedures concerning teacher and administrator duties and responsibilities, student discipline and management procedures, attendance, and after-school activities;
- A procedure should be instituted to ensure that the school calendar reflects all school activities in a timely manner. Except in cases of emergency, no activities should be scheduled in violation of the agreed upon calendar;
- A system should be instituted to identify (on a daily basis) all after-school activities, participants, and appropriate supervision. Activities and sponsors of those activities should be posted in a public setting.

Concern 2. Quality and consistency of communication within the building

Specific concerns expressed by interviewees and verified by team members

- Communication between the administrative team and the rest of the staff reflects a lack of consistency in information shared and in interpretation of policies and procedures;
- Inter- and intra-grade level communication needs to be improved to ensure consistency in planning and student management throughout the building.
- There is a lack of communication between the guidance department and most teachers.

Recommendations

- An agenda for each teacher, team, and administrative meeting should be posted and filed for future reference;
- All specialists including the reading, mathematics and media specialists should attend teacher grade level and team meetings. These specialists should also be encouraged to call their own meetings with both teaching and administrative staffs;
- Total staff meetings should be held at least once a month with every staff member having an opportunity to influence the agenda. These meetings should be designed for sharing of ideas and suggestions for improving the instructional program. If the principal feels the need to berate the staff, such action should not be taken at these regular meetings;
- Teachers should be encouraged to explore opportunities for co-operative learning arrangements across grades and across classrooms within a grade;
- All specialists, including the guidance counselor, should publish a monthly newsletter containing suggestions that would be of use to teachers and summaries of recent literature on effective practices in their specialized areas of interest;
- An effort should be made by the administration to schedule events which are social in nature.

Concern 3: A lack of consistency and effectiveness of school-wide discipline procedures

Specific concerns expressed by interviewees and verified by team members

- There is a backlog of discipline referrals resulting in a lack of timely response and inadequate feedback to teachers;
- Expectations for student behavior varies from teacher to teacher; moreover, there is no process in place to resolve the problems resulting from this variation;
- The in-school suspension center is frequently closed because of the use of the co-ordinator as an emergency substitute;
- Teachers have not been provided help in developing ways of handling classroom discipline problems.

Recommendations

- A clearly defined system of discipline should be implemented consistently by teachers and administrators. This system should be the result of the work of a committee comprised of teachers and administrators who solicit input from the entire staff as to priorities and expectations;
- The in-school suspension room must be kept open at all times; even if it means the short-term re-assignment of administrators to supervise the activity;
- Feedback on discipline referrals should be given to teachers within 48 hours;
- There must be an initiative to enforce discipline problems uniformly by all staff. Enforcement of these policies should not be limited to students for whom a teacher is immediately responsible;
- The principal must assume responsibility for providing, or having others provide, relevant training to all staff in effective school and classroom management strategies.

Concern 4: A lack of a cohesive program of curriculum and instruction in grades 6–8

Specific concerns expressed by interviewees and verified by team members

- The 6th-grade team has received no feedback concerning its proposed curriculum restructuring plan;
- The 7th-grade mathematics teachers are not allowed to accelerate student learning past the approved curriculum for that grade level;
- The computer laboratory is not functioning. A consistent schedule is not followed. Assistance is not provided to teachers in securing appropriate software and training them in how to integrate that software into their lessons;
- The library is inaccessible after 3:15 PM.

Recommendations

- The 6th-grade teachers should be allowed to implement their proposed schedule with the stipulation that mathematics and

> reading will be carefully monitored and evaluated in terms of student achievement;
> - The 7th-grade teachers should be encouraged to advance students in the mathematics curriculum as quickly as possible. If central office supervisory staff objects, then the principal should appeal to the superintendent;
> - Qualified supervision must be available for the computer laboratory and a schedule for its full time use developed. Teacher training must be provided to build staff awareness and competence to use the computers;
> - Equitable use of the library for all grades should become a priority and ways must be found to keep the library open longer for student use.
>
> The information described above represents a summary of the highlights of the audit. We stand ready to provide you with more detail and documentation on any of the points that were raised. Thank you once again for the opportunity to participate in this process.

The summary audit described above was reviewed by the superintendent and within two weeks of receiving it, he met with the principal of Hypothetical Middle School. The principal essentially agreed with the audit's findings and agreed to develop, jointly with his staff, a plan to correct the problems. In addition, it was made clear to the principal that his future annual evaluations would, in part, be based on the progress made in accomplishing the objectives of the plan.

VIII. School-Level Report Cards

As a means of informing their communities of school progress, and as a strategy for ensuring that school staff focus on student outcomes, administrators should require the issuance of report cards documenting the nature and extent of student progress that is made in each of the system's schools. These report cards should present and track progress on key student outcomes. The data should be intended for use by the following four audiences:

CHAPTER 5   Tools for Diagnosis, Prescription, and Accountability

- Parents who will be able to judge the progress of their child's school as compared to other schools in the system;
- Community members who are owed an accounting of the outcomes of the investment that they are making in local education;
- Individual school staffs who can quickly assess the nature of learning and participation at their schools and, where weaknesses are identified, can take appropriate remedial actions;
- School-system central office staff who will use the information to identify system strengths and weaknesses and then allocate resources and special help accordingly.

Although the report cards will provide very useful information to a wide range of audiences, several notes of caution are warranted:

- First, while some of our schools are characterized by low achievement and have quite a bit of room to improve on any one of the measures used on the report card, other schools are already performing well and, for them, maintenance of their positive results may be a reasonable standard;
- Second, in almost all cases, the measures used to track student progress over time do not assess the same students. For example, this year's 3rd-grade student population may not represent a mirror image of last year's population. They may differ somewhat in average achievement level, race, or nature of pre-school experiences. Although these differences are usually slight, they can account for small variations in average scores;
- Third, in tracking the progress of an individual school, care must be taken to determine whether or not there were any boundary or programmatic changes which altered the nature of the student population from year to year.

It is equally important to understand that while each element represented on the report card implies a specific goal, school staff are not being asked to automatically make things better by inflating grades, teaching to the tests, or refusing to discipline children. To the contrary, efforts should be intensified to ensure that the highest professional standards are maintained in every school and classroom.

As new measures of student performance are adopted, the range of report card elements should expand accordingly. Appendix C provides examples of elements that could be included as part of an annual report card system.

Chapter Five: Further Reading

ERIC Clearinghouse on Tests, Measurements, and Evaluation. 1989. *Understanding Achievement Tests: A Guide for School Administrators.* Washington, D.C.: American Institutes for Research.

Hynes, Donald L. 1991. *The Changing Face of Testing and Assessment: Problems and Solutions.* Washington, D.C.: American Association of School Administrators

Mitchell, Ruth. 1992. *Testing for Learning: How New Approaches to Evaluation Can Improve American Schools.* New York: Macmillan.

Mitchell, R. 1989. A Sample of Authentic Assessment. *Beyond the Bubble.* Long Beach, Ca: Curriculum/Assessment Alignment Conferences.

National Commission on Testing and Public Policy. 1990. *From Gatekeeper to Gateway: Transforming Testing in America.* Chestnut Hill, Ma: National Commission on Testing and Public Policy.

Office of Technology Assessment, Congress of the United States. 1992. *Testing in American Schools: Asking the Right Questions.* Washington, D.C.: Government Printing Office.

Report of the Study Groups. 1985. *The Nation's Report Card: Improving the Assessment of Student Achievement.* Washington, D.C.: National Academy of Education.

Wiggins, Grant. 1989. A True Test: Toward More Authentic and Equitable Assessment. *Phi Delta Kappan,* 70: 703–713

Wolf, Dennie, Janet Bixby, John Glenn III, and Howard Gardner. 1991. To Use Their Minds Well: Investigating New Forms of Student Assessment, in Gerald Grant, editor, *Review of Research in Education.* Washington, D.C.: American Education Research Association.

CHAPTER SIX

REWARDING EXCELLENCE: EVALUATING STAFF AND RECOGNIZING EXEMPLARY PERFORMANCE

It is not enough to be busy . . . the question is: what are we busy about?

Henry David Thoreau

ISSUES

Evaluating staff   Recognizing exemplary performance

High expectations for student performance must be coupled with equally high expectations for staff performance. We cannot give staff rave reviews in their annual evaluations while the students in their charge are failing. An effective school system is one in which there is a clear relationship between what is taught and what is learned. The evaluations of all staff should focus on this relationship. If not, schools and school systems will become a refuge for adults who put in their time but do not produce results.

I. Evaluating Staff Performance

Staff evaluation systems should be based on two equally important factors. First, they must address the issue of the extent to which the actions of each employee contribute to an agreed-upon set of school system, school, or classroom goals. And second, they must document the extent to which each employee utilizes effective management and educational practices. Both goals should be part of every personnel evaluation system. For example, it is not reasonable to hold principals and teachers solely accountable for improved student outcomes. This exclusive focus could tend to narrow the curriculum and, in the worst cases, lead to teaching to the test. In addition to the focus on outcomes, every teacher should be expected to use instructional strategies that maximize the learning of the students in their classrooms without regard to predetermined low expectations for those students.

Working toward specific goals and using effective instructional practices is also pertinent for central office and area administrators. Although they too should be judged on how much children are learning, they are first and foremost responsible for creating the best possible teaching and learning conditions for principals, teachers, and students. The degree to which they create these conditions is a vital component of their annual evaluation.

Specific rating elements in an evaluation process should reflect the nature of the problems that a school system is facing at any point in time. This is particularly true for central and area office personnel who are responsible for achieving the goals established by the board and the superintendent. For example, if increasing the number of students who successfully enroll in and complete higher-level mathematics is a school system's goal, this factor should be an important element in the evaluation goals for senior central office staff. Specifically, they may be held responsible for creating policies that provide increased student access to the courses, they may develop teacher training programs to upgrade the skills of the mathematics teachers, or they may devise a set of criterion-referenced tests to help teachers teach mathematics more effectively.

All effective staff evaluation systems should incorporate:

- Linkages to a clear, specific, and focused school system mission statement;
- Performance objectives or goals for every staff member at every level of the organization;
- Critical feedback to all employees on a regular basis;

- A process to allow subordinates to evaluate the performance of their supervisors;
- A process to allow clients (parents and students) the opportunity to evaluate school staff.

> **KEY POINT:** *Personnel evaluations should be closely aligned with identified system and building-level objectives. The performance elements should encourage the practice of those educational strategies believed most likely to reinforce or otherwise improve student learning.*

II. Evaluating Senior Central Office Administrators

Central office senior administrators are responsible for implementing the goals and policies established by boards of education and superintendents. Their activities should be defined and guided through an annual agreement with the superintendent which clearly specifies the goals for which they are responsible. The goals should be realistic but, at the same time, cause administrators to reach to achieve them. For example, assuming that the system's objectives are to increase the number of students who can read at advanced levels, infuse curriculum with appropriate multicultural elements, and reduce the number of high school suspensions, the goals for those central office staff who are responsible for these functions can include:

- Training all teachers in a variety of techniques that increase student engaged learning time, including co-operative learning, creative grouping strategies, and the use of computers and other technologies;
- Developing criterion-referenced reading tests to be administered regularly during the school year;
- Training all principals by the end of the school year to improve their capacity to analyze student performance and participation data as a means of identifying poorly-served or underserved populations;
- Reviewing all subject matter curricula to ensure that they reflect the contributions made by a wide variety of cultural groups and, wherever appropriate, expose children to the rich heritage of all peoples;
- Training all high school guidance counselors in the newest mediation and behavioral techniques to reduce the number of student suspensions;

- Frequently evaluating the performance of new teachers and providing them and their principals with meaningful feedback in a timely manner. Such feedback should focus on the extent to which the teachers are using practices considered to be effective and appropriate for the mix of students in that teacher's classroom;
- Creating data-reporting formats which make the analysis of data by school-level staff easier and more relevant to their needs;
- Evaluating the performance of tenured teachers in a way that ensures that optimum performance is encouraged, outstanding performances are recognized, and remediation or improvement needs are documented.

Once the major staff evaluation goals are established, they should be supplemented by goals designed to improve specific skill weaknesses in individual staff members. For example, if a staff member has difficulty in communicating to groups of citizens, that staff member should be required to strengthen their skills in this area. Or, if a staff member has difficulty in being appropriately critical in staff evaluations, improvement in this area should be made an explicit part of their evaluation for the coming year.

At the end of the school year, the superintendent should provide all senior staff members with a written evaluation of their performance based on the goals that were agreed upon earlier. Staff members should be given the opportunity to provide the superintendent with any evidence that they may have documenting their progress toward achieving the goals. The written evaluation should be complete and focus on both strengths and weaknesses, and include suggestions for improvement. Following is an example of an annual evaluation for a senior central office administrator responsible for curriculum and instruction.

Hypothetical School System

Memorandum

To: Assistant Superintendent for Curriculum and Instruction
From: The Superintendent
Subject: Annual Performance Evaluation

Following is my written evaluation of your job performance for the past school year.

I firmly believe that personnel evaluations are a valuable tool for assessing organizational progress, for pointing out strengths and weaknesses, and for charting new directions for the future. The evaluation process is also a means for allowing an exchange of perceptions between me and senior staff. If you have any questions or concerns concerning my evaluation of your performance, do not hesitate to bring it up to me in the meeting that I will schedule in the near future. As I developed this evaluation, I used several sources of information, including the list of accomplishments that you submitted to me, my observations of your performance, and my assessment of your office's accomplishments.

Here is a brief summary of the conclusions that I reached based on my analyses. Rather than provide an exhaustive document, I have limited my comments to those areas that warrant commendation or improvement. I hope that you find this evaluation useful and can use it as a focal point for moving ahead in the coming school year.

This past year has been marked by some very significant changes in your program. The progress that has been made relative to the new technology policy, co-operative learning policy, and criterion-referenced test development and use, has been nothing short of remarkable. Your work to develop and integrate the effective schools and school-based management programs will undoubtedly pay us dividends in the near future. I appreciate your initiative in these and other areas.

Once again your positive and 'can do' attitude is a great asset for your office, as well as for the entire system. Your ability to provide follow-up to all assignments has been a real plus for all of us. Your willingness to address the problems in a timely and effective manner has been appreciated. I also value your loyalty to me and, once policies are developed, your willingness to embrace them and to represent those policies as your own.

I have been particularly impressed with the development and progress of the problem-solving initiative, and the continued almost flawless installation and accelerated use of the computerized assisted instructional program. You and your staff are to be commended. It is important, however, that this year be marked by serious efforts to continue the implementation of these programs and to create new and more effective ways of ensuring that all school-based staff share our knowledge of these efforts and those procedures that they can use to implement the programs at their sites.

Although on balance you have had a successful and in some ways ground-breaking year, I am concerned about a few issues. For example, the issue of staff evaluations is a perplexing one. As you know, I am a firm believer that performance evaluations should discriminate among those employees who make greater and lesser contributions to the organization. You also know that we are trying to develop an organization in which all employees are accountable for the performance of students. Yet, a review of your evaluations of your senior staff, and a review of their evaluations of their staffs, reveals that everyone is rated as at least "satisfactory." I think that we both know that the quality of the work produced by your senior staff varies considerably. The impression is that they are all doing as much as possible and you know that that is not the case. Given the overall laudatory nature of the evaluations, it is hard to imagine how they can be used as a tool for improving behavior in the future. Next year, I expect the evaluations to be more analytical, to suggest areas for improvement, and to reflect a rating scale which discriminates among various levels of performance.

A second point is related to staffing in your office. Although I am aware of your activities relative to streamlining the staffing pattern in your office, I am just not satisfied that we are moving quickly enough. Last year we activated a group of itinerant school-based instructional specialists which should have allowed you to reduce the total number of your central office staff. What happened? When will this new initiative affect your current staffing configuration?

You should take great pride in the progress that you have made this year with the criterion-referenced tests. The coming year, however, should be marked by more aggressive efforts to help our principals and teachers learn how to use the tests to adjust instruction on a regular basis.

> Finally, I want to make two important general points. First, I ask you to make sure that I am made aware of any major problems that are brewing in the school system. I would rather be inundated with too much information than be surprised as often as I was this past year. And second, you and your staff must be more willing to take appropriate actions against those staff who are not effective or do not reflect our policies and practices.
>
> Based on my review of your goals, your interaction with the management team, your creative solutions to many of our problems, and my faith that you can effectively address the problems noted above, I am rating you above average. However, if the problems noted above are addressed effectively, next year's rating should be one of excellent.
>
> Thank you for a very productive year and your ongoing participation on my management team. Within five days of receipt of this letter, please forward to me a copy of the specific goals, including the ones noted above, that you will undertake in the coming school year. I will integrate those personal goals with those noted above and those that the board has established into a new performance agreement. Once again, thank you for a good year, your loyalty, advice and counsel.

III. Evaluating Regional or Area Administrators Responsible for Monitoring Progress in a Cluster of Schools

Many large school systems assign responsibilities for managing and monitoring the progress of a cluster of schools to a regional or area superintendent. Sometimes these staff are responsible for a cluster of elementary, middle, and high schools, while other times they are responsible for all elementary, all middle, or all high schools. In all cases they serve as the superintendent's representatives in the field and, as such, should be judged on the extent to which they and their schools make progress on those goals that are most important to the superintendent. The more effective regional superintendents will be those who are pro-active in *making things happen* as opposed to those who view their jobs as monitoring and reporting the progress of schools.

Following are examples of instructionally related goals for which regional or area staff could be held accountable and which represent their assuming a pro-active stance:

- *The placement of elementary school students in reading and mathematics groups will be based on the regular and appropriate use of criterion-referenced or other diagnostic tests.* Adjustments in instructional groupings during the year will be frequent and long-term membership in low-level groups will not be tolerated;
- *The percentage of elementary school students who master at least 75 percent of the objectives on an end-of-year test in reading and mathematics will increase by at least five percent when compared to last year;*
- *The gap in performance on all measures for economically advantaged and disadvantaged students—or majority and minority students—will decrease by ten percent when compared to last year;*
- *The performance on the norm-referenced test will increase by ten percentile points in reading and mathematics and the gap between advantaged and disadvantaged students will decrease by ten percent;*
- *The amount of time spent in elementary school on direct instructional activities will increase by ten percent when compared to last year;*
- *The percentage of students who complete the 6th grade and are appropriately recommended for and prepared to enter pre-algebra in the 7th grade will increase by twenty percent;*
- *The percentage of students suspended, by school, will decrease by five percent as compared to the prior year and any gap by race will decrease by ten percent.* This will be accomplished while maintaining the district's standards for having a positive school climate;
- *The enrollment in middle and high school lower-level courses will decrease by ten percent;*
- *Evaluations of principals will accurately reflect the strengths and weaknesses of a school; including but not limited to student outcomes, staff morale, willingness to seek innovative solutions and take risks, and appropriate uses of tests and other diagnostic procedures for adjusting instruction.* In those cases where disciplinary or other action needs to be taken, appropriate documentation is

to be provided to the Superintendent in a timely manner which would allow such action to occur;
- *Appropriate technical assistance concerning data analysis and interpretation will be provided to principals by appropriate central office staff;*
- *A careful and on-going review of all new placements in special education must be conducted to ensure that children with behavioral and/or language problems that are unrelated to serious emotional or physical disabilities are not classified as special education students.* If required, special training should be provided to principals and teachers of regular education classes on how to deal with these students in a regular or mainstream classroom setting.

Merely establishing clear outcome goals does not in and of itself constitute an effective personnel evaluation system. At year's end a focused evaluation of the performance of the area or regional administrator must be conducted. Here is a hypothetical year-end evaluation of an assistant regional superintendent. This evaluation is based primarily on a set of goals that were agreed upon by both parties during the prior year.

Hypothetical School System

Memorandum

To: Regional Assistant Superintendent
From: The Superintendent

Subject: Annual performance evaluation

Following is my written evaluation of your job performance for the past school year.

As you know, this evaluation is based on agreements that you and I developed prior to the past school year. Much of what follows represents my assessment of the extent to which you met the terms of those agreements. The evaluation process itself is also a means for allowing an exchange of perceptions between the two of us. If you have any questions concerning my evaluation of your performance, do not hesitate to raise them in the meeting that I will schedule in the near future. As I developed this evaluation, I used several sources of information, including the list of accomplishments that you submitted to me, my observations of your performance, the nature of educational outcomes in your area as compared to other areas and the system's average, and my own assessment of your office's accomplishments. Following is a brief summary of the conclusions that I reached. Rather than provide an exhaustive document, I limited my comments to those areas that warrant commendation or improvement. I hope that you find this evaluation useful and can use it as a focal point for moving ahead in the coming school year.

Performance Outcomes

A review of the outcome data reveals both positive and negative news. On the positive side, the schools that you are responsible for showed impressive growth on criterion-referenced reading tests. The middle schools showed good progress in addressing the pre-algebra/algebra initiative. More students than ever are enrolled in pre-algebra and algebra courses. And finally, I was glad to see that your high schools enrolled relatively few students in lower-level courses. However, the one exception to this is Hypothetical High School where I would expect to see significant improvement this coming school year.

On the more troublesome side, I am concerned about the relatively low performance of your elementary schools in mathematics on both the criterion-referenced test and the norm-referenced standardized achievement test. Only 30 percent of the grades achieved their math growth goals. A second area of concern is related to the suspension rates of your middle schools. Two of your middle schools registered actual increases in the suspension rates while also showing a widening of the gap between black and white student suspensions. And finally, only one of your four high schools met its suspension rate reduction goals. I fully expect you to develop, in concert with the appropriate principals, a concrete plan for correcting these problems. The plans should be developed within the next few weeks, submitted to me for review, and implemented very early in the school year.

The recently announced dismal performance of our students on the SAT mathematics achievement tests is also reason for very serious concern. Several years ago we required all high schools to develop plans for improving those achievement test scores. Your job was to approve those plans, to help schools implement them, and to monitor progress in achieving the plan's objectives. Since I have not heard from you about any difficulties relating to these plans, I assumed that things were going well. However, our continual slide in these tests indicates that all was not well. We can no longer say that most of the students who take the test did not take appropriate level prerequisite courses; about 90 percent of last year's test-takers had taken the required prerequisite courses. The only viable explanation is that our demands for academic excellence are too soft, and the quality of much of the teaching and learning in our classrooms is inadequate. And, as you know, you must bear a significant responsibility for these inadequacies.

Style of Management and Principal Evaluations

I want you to know that I recognize that you work hard and long in your job, and many of your outcome measures attest to the effectiveness of much of that work. However, I continue to be fearful that your supervisory style is exacting a price. In your zeal to get your work done, I sense that you often become rigid and over-demanding in your interactions with many principals, particularly elementary school principals. Perhaps if you worked on improving your interpersonal relationships, your contributions to the school system would be more positive than they are now.

I am concerned that you are not using the principal evaluation process as an improvement tool and/or for taking appropriate action. This past year, of 150 possible ratings (25 principals multiplied by 6 rating elements) you neither gave any needs to improve nor rated any principal as unsatisfactory on any element. If I converted these evaluations to a more traditional grading scale, most of your principals received **A's** and none less than a **C**. I can only attribute this pattern of responses to one of three things. First, the outcomes from every one of your schools met or exceeded your expectations. Second, the outcomes are not as high as they ought to be, but you are hesitant to confront principals with this fact on their formal evaluation. Third, you do not have a clear idea of what is actually happening in the schools and therefore have difficulty documenting anythingless than a satisfactory. An examination of your schools' outcomes reveals that the first explanation does not apply.

As a means of reflecting the importance of relating staff evaluation more closely to actual staff performance, I will be including the quality, timeliness, and appropriateness of principal evaluations as a new goal for the coming school year, ensuring that next year's principals' evaluations more accurately reflect their performance. Related to the issue of principal evaluations are the evaluations your principals gave to their vice-principals and guidance counselors. I am continually hearing from principals and from my senior administrators about serious problems related to the performance of vice-principals and guidance counselors. Yet, not a single vice-principal or guidance counselor received a 'needs to improve' in your schools during this past year. We cannot have it both ways. On the one hand, we cannot complain about low student outcomes and staff performance while, on the other hand, we evaluate our staff at least as satisfactory. If you disagree with this belief, I want to know about it.

Conclusion

Finally, I want to make two important general points. First, I ask you to make sure that I am made aware of any problems that are brewing in your schools. I would rather be inundated with too much information than be surprised as often as I was this past year. Secondly, we must all be willing to take corrective action against those staff who are not effective or do not reflect our policies and practices. It is hard to argue that we are all here for the children and still allow ineffective staff to remain in their positions. Based on my analysis of your performance, your final evaluation for this year is borderline 'average'. If I do not detect marked progress in the next year, I will be forced to re-assign you to a position more in line with your style of management.

Within five days of receipt of this letter, please send me a copy of the specific goals noted above and those that you personally would

> like to undertake in the coming school year. I will add the system-wide goals for which you will be responsible. By no later than the end of September, we will be meeting to agree on a format that will we can use to record and transmit the progress that you make on each of the goals during the coming school year.

IV. Evaluating Principals

Appropriate evaluation of principals is vital for school improvement. Superintendents should make it clear that evaluation provides meaningful feedback to principals, and that whenever that feedback doesn't result in improvement, it will constitute the documentation required for dismissal. Principals cannot hide behind tenure laws. *Even the most stringent tenure laws allow for dismissal because of incompetence.* The superintendent should ensure that the annual evaluation system accurately reflects the quality of leadership provided by the principal. Those doing an excellent job should be rewarded. Those who need to grow should be provided with a specific growth plan. Those who cannot perform should be removed. This requires a measure of courage and willingness to stand up to vested interest groups.

The issue of establishing annual evaluation goals for principals is complicated. On the one hand, it is easy to say that if a superintendent establishes goals for the school system, then those goals should be transmitted directly to principals. Accordingly, if the superintendent sets a school system goal of increasing reading test scores by ten percent, a variation of this goal can be included in every principal's evaluation. However, merely passing on this goal can be counterproductive and may force the principal to focus narrowly on the goal and distort both the curricula and teaching process. Such phenomena as teaching to the test and focusing too intensively on the basics are likely to result. This is not to imply that the principal should not be held accountable for specific quantifiable results.

Principal evaluations should consist of criteria that encourage them to employ and elicit those educational practices most likely to generate positive results. Following are examples of the kinds of goals that can be incorporated into the evaluation of building principals that could lead to improved student performance:

- Performance on the norm-referenced achievement test will increase by ten percentile points and the gap between economically advantaged and disadvantaged students will decrease by ten percent;
- The number of students who display mastery of reading and mathematics objectives on criterion-referenced tests at the end of the school year must increase by ten percent when compared to last year;
- Significant numbers of students will be moved from one achievement-level grouping to a higher one during the academic year;
- Teachers will be given freedom to use a variety of instructional techniques to meet the needs of the students in their classes;
- Principals will teach teachers how to use a wide range of assessment techniques to be used for monitoring and adjusting instruction;
- Principals will be responsible for ensuring that the school environment is orderly and conducive to learning;
- Principals will carefully document both effective and ineffective performance of teachers and, in the latter cases, take appropriate remedial actions;
- Parents will be given extensive opportunities to become involved in the school improvement process through participation in decision-making and problem-solving groups and programs, including School Planning and Management Teams and Parent Teacher Student Associations;
- Staff development programs at the school level will involve peer coaching as a primary vehicle for fostering instructional modifications and improvement.

We now give an example of a hypothetical evaluation of a school principal based on criteria that were agreed upon during the prior year.

Hypothetical School System

Memorandum

To: Elementary School Principal
From: Superintendent
Subject: Annual Performance Evaluation

This is my written evaluation of your performance during the 1991–92 school year.

I believe that personnel evaluations are an integral part of any school improvement plan. It is through the evaluation process that we establish our goals relative to instructional improvement and determine the extent to which we achieve those goals. It is critical that we have a common understanding of your strengths and the areas requiring improvement. The following is a brief, and I hope helpful, summary of your performance based on my observations and analysis. I hope that you will use it as a focal point for moving ahead in the coming school year.

On the positive side, I am pleased about the high staff morale present in your school. From direct observation, parental involvement and comment, and analyses conducted by my assistant superintendents, it is clear that you have successfully engaged staff in the school improvement process. As the low absenteeism and suspension rates indicate, the positive morale extends to the students in your charge.

On the other hand, I have a real concern that you are not using the teacher evaluation process as a tool for improving teacher performance or for taking appropriate action. Your evaluation of staff was uniformly glowing in the absence of any documentation that they made a real difference in the education of children. In fact, you neither gave any 'needs to improve' nor rated any teacher unsatisfactory on any element, despite the relatively poor performance of your school on standardized and criterion-referenced tests and several other key student indicators including student retentions and readiness to enter higher grades. If I converted these evaluations to a more traditional grading scale most of your teachers received A's and none less than a B. I cannot see any relationship between staff evaluations and student performance. I can only attribute this pattern of responses to one of the following:

1. The circumstances in and outcomes from every one of your classrooms met or exceeded your expectations or;
2. You are hesitant to confront teachers with the fact that outcomes are not as high as they ought to be on their formal evaluations or;

> 3. You do not have a clear idea about what is actually happening in the classrooms and, therefore, have difficulty documenting anything less than a 'satisfactory'.
>
> We cannot accept low student outcomes, complain about staff, still rate all staff satisfactory or better, and claim we have accountability in our school system. As a means of reflecting the importance of relating staff evaluation more closely to actual performance, I will be including the quality, timeliness, thoroughness, and appropriateness of teacher evaluations as a new goal for you in the coming school year. You need to make it your business to ensure that the necessary documentation is collected throughout the year to support your determinations. I expect you to set improvement goals in conjunction with your staff. Then, if a teacher is having trouble meeting those goals, I expect you to give him/her constructive criticism and appropriate technical assistance. After a reasonable period of time, if there is no improvement, I expect you to take the necessary action, which might include a recommendation for dismissal.
>
> Within five days of the date of this letter, please forward to me a copy of the specific goals you will undertake in the coming year. I ask that you include the goals outlined above as well as any other goals you personally think ought to be included.

V. Evaluating Teachers

The evaluation of teachers is one of the more complex issues that administrators must address. As school systems embrace accountability as a way of life, they must wrestle with the issue of how their teachers are evaluated. The checklist mentality that has guided these evaluations must give way to procedures that encourage teachers to use those instructional strategies in their classrooms that are most likely to produce desired student outcomes. In the future, the use of portfolios which characterize the content and richness of teacher performance will be an integral part of any well-rounded teacher evaluation system. However, at this time the technology for such portfolio assessments is not sufficiently developed.

An effective system for evaluating the performance of teachers serves two major purposes. The first is to provide teachers with meaningful feedback about their performance to enable them to become more effective in their jobs. The second purpose is to enable principals and others to assess the extent to which their teachers are competent and are effectively implementing the system's teaching and learning program. A question raised by many is whether or not any single system can play both roles; one which focuses on accountability and has ramifications for pay and advancement, and the other designed to help employees become more effective. Administrators may decide to separate the two functions. For instance, teachers' peers or staff development experts can observe the performance of teachers to provide them with frequent feedback on their teaching practices and work with them to make them more effective, and principals can conduct the year-end evaluations to determine if the appropriate instructional goals were achieved.

On the other hand, it is possible that properly trained school principals can serve both roles. The choice of combining the two purposes into a single procedure or separating them lies with the superintendent. The examples described below can be tailored to each approach. In either case, teachers should be involved in the development, testing, and monitoring of any teacher evaluation process.

Most current teacher evaluation systems are not designed to yield information concerning either of the two purposes. They do not detect markedly deficient or exemplary performance and are not likely to produce the information required to promote effective teaching. To meet these needs the evaluation systems must be redesigned. At the very least the new systems should be supported by the following actions:

- The school system's expectations for student and teacher performance must be clear and widely disseminated;
- Teachers must have been involved in the development of those student and teacher expectations;
- Staff development time must be made available to ensure that teachers understand the criteria by which they are to be evaluated;
- Procedures must be put into place to objectively assess learning outcomes;
- Provisions must be made to provide teachers with meaningful feedback on their teaching performance *on every communication they receive and in meetings with the principal;*
- Opportunities must be made available for teachers to acquire needed skills.

No matter who actually collects information about teacher performance, or provides teachers with feedback on their performance, principals should understand that they cannot improve poor teachers only by giving positive strokes. The more the evidence builds that teachers are not effective, the more prescriptive principals must become. If this direct assistance doesn't result in improved teacher performance, then principals need to initiate termination proceedings. Teachers who remain ineffective, after all good-faith efforts to help them improve have failed, cannot be allowed to stay in the classrooms. To make terminations a reality, principals must document the teacher's performance, efforts to improve that performance, and the teacher's continued inability to respond.

The actions noted above are necessary but insufficient components of an effective teacher evaluation system. The building principal must have the capability to conduct meaningful teacher observations. Teaching is a complex process and any attempt to define it must recognize that its complexity necessitates the consideration of many factors rather than the isolation of a small number of criteria. The principal who is a careful observer, who focuses on searching for the presence of those instructional elements which are known to make a difference, and who provides meaningful feedback to teachers based on those elements, can make a real difference in classroom teaching. The issue of meaningful feedback cannot be minimized. Merely handing a checklist to teachers requesting their signatures is not likely to result in changed behaviors. To be effective evaluators, principals and others must:

- Be aware of effective instructional strategies;
- Be able to define and enforce teaching standards for the school;
- Provide feedback in a constructive manner;
- Suggest ideas and modifications in instructional delivery, content, and/or classroom management strategies;
- Establish, with the teacher's involvement, goals or checkpoints during which periodic reviews of progress toward improving deficiencies can be discussed;
- Require formal coursework or staff development that will help the teacher correct any deficiencies;
- Provide feedback to teachers on their attempts to improve instructional effectiveness.

> **KEY POINT**: *An effective teacher evaluation system is one that is fair, appropriate, and discriminates between effective and ineffective teaching. The elements included in the system must reflect what we know constitutes effective teaching. The observation of those elements should not be reduced to trivial behaviors that are easy to observe. For example, research tells us that the effective teacher brings closure to every lesson. Closure is meant to include a review of the lesson's objective and a summary of key points that were made. In a recent series of teacher observations the observer noted that the teacher failed to bring closure to the lesson because she ended by asking if the children had any questions. This questioning was interpreted as opening up and not closing the lesson. The folklore in this school now dictates that whenever teachers are observed, they must not ask students if they have any questions. This kind of mindless application of sound research findings must stop so that teachers and others can develop confidence in the evaluation process.*

The following evaluation form is an example which reflects what has been learned about effective teaching and learning, and can be used as a guide for tailoring teacher evaluation systems more closely to the needs of a school system. It can be used as a tool for initiating discussions between teachers and administrators concerning what is important in the teaching process. The form consists of two sections that relate directly to instruction. The first represents a checklist of elements that really make a difference in instruction, while the second incorporates specific outcome goals for which teachers will be held accountable.

Each of the rating elements in the first section was selected on the basis of research which indicates that it is an important and documented component of effective teaching. Although the elements represent meaningful teacher behaviors, *it is vital that observers observe teachers for sustained periods of time, over time, to detect the presence or absence of effective practices implied by each element.*

The second section of the form, entitled "achievement outcomes", requires that the teacher and principal negotiate some form of student outcome as a component of the overall evaluation. These outcomes can include such things as performance on year-end tests, percentage of curriculum objectives mastered by students at the end of the year, percentage of students prepared at the end of the year to proceed on or above grade-level in the next grade, and percentage of students who moved during the year from one level of instruction to another. It is important that these goals be non-trivial, student-outcome-oriented and, if all of the teachers' goals in a school are met, enable that school to have met the goals established for it by the superintendent.

Directions for the Proper Use of This Teacher Evaluation Form

Rating Options

An evaluation system can be fair and effective only when there is common agreement and understanding between the principal and the teacher as to the criteria for each of the rating options. The following descriptive explanation of each of the rating options is provided to ensure a common understanding of each:

Outstanding: A rating of outstanding is reserved for those teachers whose performance in a given rating element **consistently far exceeds** normal objectives, and/or those teachers who initiate a special project related to the rating element in an extraordinary manner, with far-reaching consequences to students or the school.

Satisfactory: A rating of satisfactory means that performance is consistently adequate and acceptable. A satisfactory rating indicates that the teacher has effectively executed the tasks referenced in the rating element.

Needs to Improve: A rating of needs to improve means that performance is sometimes inadequate and unacceptable. Additional assistance and supervision may be required.

Unsatisfactory: A rating of unsatisfactory means that performance is inadequate and the teacher has failed to respond to assistance. Weaknesses or deficiencies are of such a serious nature that meaningful student learning has not or will not likely occur.

Note: Principals are to place a check in the most appropriate box for each rating element.

Achievement Outcomes

At the beginning of the school year, the principal and teacher must agree on a reasonable set of outcomes for the students to achieve. The outcomes could include performance on the CRT's, performance assessments, or any other outcomes that the principal and teacher believe are reasonable. During the last three weeks of school, the principal will review the agreed-upon outcomes and the actual achievement of each. Those agreed-upon goals should be included as an attachment to this evaluation form.

Comments

The "Comments" section may be used to record any information the principal determines to be appropriate to the evaluation. It *must* be used to explain the basis for an outstanding rating. It may also be used to list extra duty contributions.

Hypothetical County Public School System

Teacher Evaluation Form

Teacher's Name _____

Social Security Number _____

Name of School _____

School Year _____

(Note: After each rating factor, space should be provided for a *required statement* from the principal, citing the reasons supporting the selection of one of the four options.)

Section I: Elements of Effective Teaching

1. Effective Teaching Practices

A. Planning and Preparation

Implements lessons which provide for instruction of students at appropriate achievement levels, reflect an appropriate sequencing of instruction, and are based on approved curricular objectives.

Outstanding ___ Satisfactory ___ Needs to Improve ___ Unsatisfactory ___

B. Learning Climate

1. Creates a classroom climate that is warm and inviting. Promotes the development of positive self concept for all students.

Outstanding ___ Satisfactory ___ Needs to Improve ___ Unsatisfactory ___

2. Involves students at all instructional levels in each lesson and encourages and receives inquiries, ideas and opinions that relate to those lessons from the students involved.

Outstanding ___ Satisfactory ___ Needs to Improve ___ Unsatisfactory ___

3. Presents lessons in such a way as to encourage students to employ higher-order thinking skills.

Outstanding ___ Satisfactory ___ Needs to Improve ___ Unsatisfactory ___

4. Demonstrates fairness and consistency in the handling of student discipline.

Outstanding ___ Satisfactory ___ Needs to Improve ___ Unsatisfactory ___

C. Instruction

1. Demonstrates knowledge of subject matter and transmits that knowledge in an interesting manner using a variety of techniques and/or materials to accomplish the objectives of instruction.

Outstanding ___ Satisfactory ___ Needs to Improve ___ Unsatisfactory ___

2. Maximizes the use of time for instructional purposes, with all students being involved in meaningful learning activities.

Outstanding ___ Satisfactory ___ Needs to Improve ___ Unsatisfactory ___

3. Uses a wide range of assessment information (including but not limited to observations by the teacher, CRT results, etc.) to regularly adjust student instruction.

Outstanding ___ Satisfactory ___ Needs to Improve ___ Unsatisfactory ___

4. Makes clear the purpose and/or practical importance of the lesson and how the content of the homework assignment relates to that lesson.

Outstanding ___ Satisfactory ___ Needs to Improve ___ Unsatisfactory ___

5. Provides prompt and appropriate feedback on work completed by students.

Outstanding ___ Satisfactory ___ Needs to Improve ___ Unsatisfactory ___

6. Demonstrates a keen understanding of the needs, concerns, abilities and interests of each student in such a manner that leads to the delivery of needed instructional or other resources.

Outstanding ___ Satisfactory ___ Needs to Improve ___ Unsatisfactory ___

7. Performs so that there is observable satisfactory growth in children.

Outstanding ___ Satisfactory ___ Needs to Improve ___ Unsatisfactory ___

2. Professionalism

8. Uses current curricular and instruction practices which relate to effective education.

Outstanding ___ Satisfactory ___ Needs to Improve ___ Unsatisfactory ___

9. Actively participates in program improvement activities.

Outstanding ___ Satisfactory ___ Needs to Improve ___ Unsatisfactory ___

10. Works co-operatively as a team member to achieve school goals and objectives.

Outstanding ___ Satisfactory ___ Needs to Improve ___ Unsatisfactory ___

11. Demonstrates accuracy in record keeping and promptness in meeting deadlines.

Outstanding ___ Satisfactory ___ Needs to Improve ___ Unsatisfactory ___

12. Follows established school policies and procedures.

Outstanding ___ Satisfactory ___ Needs to Improve ___ Unsatisfactory ___

13. Demonstrates effective oral and written communication skills.

Outstanding ___ Satisfactory ___ Needs to Improve ___ Unsatisfactory ___

14. Relates without difficulty to staff members and parents.

Outstanding ___ Satisfactory ___ Needs to Improve ___ Unsatisfactory ___

Section II. Achievement Outcomes

(Items 1 and 2 are completed at the beginning of the school year)

1. The agreed upon goals for the school year are:

2. The criteria or measures that will be used to determine if the outcome goals were achieved are:

3. The actual achievement of the outcome goals was:

III. General Comments

IV. Overall Rating

Outstanding ___ Satisfactory ___ Needs to Improve ___ Unsatisfactory ___

V. Teacher's Response

_____
_____
_____
_____
_____
_____
_____
_____
_____
_____
_____
_____
_____
_____

VI. Determination

(Principal, check one)

Reassign ___   Place on Probation ___   Terminate ___

_____   _____
Principal's signature at the   Teacher's signature at the
beginning of the year   beginning of the year

_____   _____
Principal's signature at the   Teacher's signature at the
the end of the year   end of the year

VI. Recognizing Exemplary Performance

Recent achievement test results and other educational outcomes indicate that under the right conditions, teachers can teach and children can learn. A decade of educational research indicates that although resources are important, the single most influential condition that leads to success is the provision of freedom and flexibility to talented principals and teachers.

School systems which are committed to creating the necessary degrees of freedom should consider adding an important missing ingredient: *special rewards for those schools which produce exemplary results.* We must balance the pressures that we place on our staff with public acknowledgement of a job well done. Accordingly, school systems should sponsor an annual recognition program to identify and reward their best schools. Depending on the philosophy of a system's leadership, as well as its fiscal conditions, awards can be of different types and made in different ways. For example, awards can be:

- Given to all teachers and others as bonuses;
- Given to teachers and others for such things as buying school equipment and supplies, purchasing software or computers, attending conferences, starting new programs, paying for substitutes or consultants, or whatever else the staff believes is important. It should be noted that the staff rather than the administration should decide how to spend the award money;
- Given to all or selected school staff in the form of public recognition;

KEY POINT: *What a School Recognition Plan Should Be*

- *The plan should be designed to reward those staffs which work together to achieve a common goal.*
- *The plan should not coerce teachers to teach to tests or to focus on a narrow range of curriculum areas. Although test performance does count in the overall assessment, the major emphasis should be placed on rewarding good teaching practices and special activities.*

The Nature of the School Recognition System

The purpose of a school recognition program is to reward those schools which are highly successful in achieving the goals of the school and school system. The program should recognize school staffs for superior performance reflected by student outcomes and good teaching practices. It could focus on providing rewards to school staff for accomplishing predetermined goals, or it could focus on recognizing schools or staff that employ unusually effective practices. The plan could be crafted in many ways. Following is an example of one which consists of two levels: one, the *Student Outcomes Level* (based on test scores and other indicators), which rewards the achievement of student outcomes, and the other, the *Educational Practices Level* (based on those practices known to result in improved student outcomes), which rewards the presence of exemplary practices. Each level carries its own award.

The Student Outcomes Level is, in fact, the qualifying criterion for the Educational Practices award. To be eligible for the Educational Practices Level award, a school must first be successful at the Student Outcomes Level. The Student Outcomes award should be smaller than the Educational Practices award. Some schools may just get a Student Outcomes award, while others may get both the Student Outcomes and Educational Practices awards. Given that the Student Outcomes Level qualifies a school to compete for the larger Educational Practices award, schools cannot receive just an Educational Practices award. Thus, *the largest awards will be given to staffs that exhibit teaching practices known to promote high student achievement.*

Individual schools must have some flexibility and choice in how they can go about winning both the Student Outcomes and the Educational Practices awards. This provision of choice recognizes the differences between individual schools, their program emphases, and differences in the overall achievement levels of their students. Although schools may be required to submit applications for the awards, the program should not be designed to bog schools down in a lengthy application process; rather applications should be limited to two or three pages. It is expected that applications will be short, to the point, and directly related to the individual school's goals. While school staffs are likely to take a leadership role in developing the applications, students could also participate in the process.

We now give a description of each of the two levels of the recognition plan: the Student Outcomes Level and the Educational Practices Level.

Level 1: Student Outcomes Level

Two sets of criteria will be used for determining whether or not a school meets its Student Outcomes Level goals; the criteria must be objective and not subject to interpretation. The first set of criteria should be test results (these results can include criterion-referenced tests, norm-referenced tests or performance assessments). The second set of criteria will include a list of student performance indicators from which individual schools can choose.

A. Standardized Test Criteria

Elementary and Middle Schools. In elementary and middle schools, performance on criterion-reference tests (CRT's) or the norm-referenced tests (NRT's) can be used to determine whether or not a school has met or exceeded its goals. For example, a CRT/NRT index may be created so that the NRT constitutes 20 percent and the CRT 80 percent. This index recognizes that the NRT is limited in terms of content and grade levels, and underlines the importance of the CRT and the curriculum it reflects.

For the NRT portion of the index, a method to measure the extent to which *the entire distribution of scores moves upward* can be used. Using movement of the entire distribution of scores as the standardized test criterion for the Student Outcomes goal alleviates the problem of using mean score changes where the temptation may be to teach to the group with the greatest potential to improve. This method also addresses the issue of schools with very different achievement levels of students.

For the CRT portion of the index, performance can be based on either the size of gain achieved from the beginning to the end of the year (expressed in terms of the percentage of instructional objectives mastered). *The amount of growth and not the absolute level of performance will be most important. In this way, success is determined by the progress of the same students over the course of the school year.*

High Schools. The high school achievement goals could consist of performance on state mandated tests, the CRT's, end-of-year course tests, ACT's and the SAT achievement tests. An index combining performance on each of these tests can be developed with the greatest weight probably placed on the CRT's or end of year course tests. While the SAT/ACT tests are typically taken by those at the higher end of the distribution and not seen by some as the responsibility of the school, it is obvious that some middle and high school courses better prepare students for the SAT/ACT than do other courses. Therefore, it is not unreasonable to assume that performance on these tests are reflections of the courses in which students were enrolled as well as their performance in these courses.

> **KEY POINT:** *Functional tests should not be included as part of this index. These tests do little more than drive the curriculum in a downward direction.*

Schools whose population changes as a result of becoming a magnet or specialty school or experience a high mobility rate will have difficulty tracking changes over time. Separate methods for addressing this problem must be developed.

B. Student Performance Indicators

To allow for individual school differences and to encourage schools to focus on their particular problems, a set of student performance indicators chosen by each school should be included in the plan. For example, a school can be required to select three student performance indicators on which to focus. These indicators could include:

- Increases in enrollment in and successful completion of advanced placement courses;
- Evidence that an increased number of students take the PSAT, SAT, and/or ACT, and perform well;
- Increases in the number of students achieving at least a 2.0 grade point average;
- Decreases in the number of dropouts;
- Decreases in the number of student suspensions while maintaining high discipline standards;
- Increases in student attendance;
- Increases in the number of students on the honor roll;
- Increases in the number of students who go on to post-secondary education or find jobs;

- Increases in the number of student awards and scholarships in academic or vocational competitions (such as science fairs, essay contests, and industrial arts competitions);
- Increases in the number of students who attend and are successful in college.

Level 2: Educational Practices Level

Since the Educational Practices Level recognizes effective teaching practices that are known to result in high student achievement, this level could carry with it the greatest share of the award. Once again, however, schools and school staff cannot receive the Education Practices award unless they also qualify for the Student Outcomes award. Individual schools should have choices as to how they meet the criteria for this level of the program. They could select either two teaching activities, or one teaching activity and one special project. Both the teaching activities and the special projects must promote the conditions or practices which are correlated with high academic achievement. Possible activities for inclusion at the Educational Practices Level include, but are not limited to, the following:

Teaching Activities	**Special Projects**
1. Evidence that teachers make frequent adjustments in instruction and student grouping.	1. School-wide activities to address learning or discipline problems.
2. Evidence that the school uses extraordinary procedures for notifying parents of students' progress.	2. School-wide activities which demonstrate the more effective use of time for all students and teachers.
3. Evidence that teachers have real input in important decisions.	3. Comunity service projects.

As recognition plans are developed two points must be kept at the forefront. First, at least some part of the reward or recognition should be based on achieving significant and verifiable student outcomes. And second, teachers should be involved in the development, implementation, and monitoring of the plan.

Chapter Six: Further Reading

Andrews, Hans A. 1985. *Evaluating for Excellence.* Stillwater, Ok: New Forums Press.

Carnegie Forum on Education and the Economy. 1986. *A Nation Prepared: Teachers for the Twenty-First Century.* Report of the Task Force on Teaching as a Profession.

Frase, Larry (ed.). 1992. *Teacher Compensation and Motivation.* Lancaster, Pa: Technomic.

Langlois, Donald, and Richard McAdams. 1992. *Performance Appraisal of School Management.* Lancaster, Pa: Technomic.

National Board for Professional Teaching Standards. 1989. *Toward High and Rigorous Standards for the Teaching Profession.* Washington, D.C.: NBPTS.

Shanker, Albert. 1990. A Proposal for Using Incentives to Restructure our Public Schools. *Phi Delta Kappan,* January.

Shulman, Lee. 1987. Assessment for Teaching: An Initiative for the Profession. *Phi Delta Kappan.* September.

Strike, K., and B. Bull. 1981. Fairness and the Legal Context of Teacher Evaluation. In J. Millman (ed.), *Handbook of Teacher Evaluation. National Council on Measurement in Education.* Beverly Hills: Sage.

Wolfe, Kenneth. 1991. The School Teacher's Portfolio: Issues in Design, Implementation, and Evaluation. *Phi Delta Kappan.* October.

EPILOGUE

REVIEWING THE STEPS TOWARD TRANSFORMATION

Selling school improvement is not an easy task. Although many citizens decry the current condition of public schools and claim that they would like to see profound changes, there is likely to be opposition from many groups to any comprehensive improvement effort. Opposition is likely to come from:

- Those who believe that any new efforts would be expensive and likely to result in raising their taxes;
- Those who believe that the role of schools is to teach, and all of the social baggage that many students bring to the schools should not be treated by the schools;
- Those who believe that the best and the brightest will rise to the top and that vocational or other educational tracks should be available to all other students;
- Those who fear that school improvement activities will result in more heterogeneous classes thus allowing lower-ability-level youngsters to sit side by side with more able children and somehow taint them;
- Those school principals or teachers who understand that new school improvement activities are likely to require them to change their practices.

To counter these groups, and to gather momentum for new programs, it is important that superintendents develop a strong rationale for change and have in mind a series of steps that must be taken to give change a chance.

Superintendents must spend a great deal of time speaking to the public and to employees of the school system, explaining the new philosophy and building broad-based support. It is critical that the superintendent not be alone in this task. All school system staff should aggressively play the role of advocates for change and, to a major extent, their success in the organization should be based on their ability to be effective advocates.

As superintendents and others prepare to publicize their plans for change and school improvement, they should consider the following points:

1. Indicting the Status Quo

If all children do not have equal access to excellence, then the community must be made aware of the fact that the present system of schooling is failing; particularly for those children who come from minorities or from low socio-economic backgrounds. The social and economic costs of continual failures must be made public and be a serious topic of discussion within the community. The public must be made to understand that many children are failing because the schools themselves have not adjusted their organizational, teaching, and learning styles to the special needs of these children. *It must also be made clear that the issue is not one of lowering standards but, rather, of finding more effective means of exploiting the strengths of all students.*

2. The Willingness for a Quid pro Quo

The public is tired of long-term failures from schools in the face of rising costs of education. New initiatives for change, particularly those which require additional funding, must be coupled with a commitment from the school system to improve. This commitment, usually denoted by the term 'accountability,' must include recognition for those staff and schools that are successful, and mandated changes for those that are not.

> **KEY POINT**: *Superintendents must spend a great deal of time speaking to the public and to employees of the school system, explaining the new philosophy and building broad-based support. It is critical that the superintendent not be*

> *alone in this task. All school system staff should aggressively play the role of advocates for change and, to a major extent, their success in the organization should be based on their ability to be effective advocates.*

It is equally important that the public and the staff understand that accountability will work only if there is an awareness that the school administration must do whatever is necessary to provide appropriate teaching and learning environments for teachers and students. Bureaucratic barriers that stand in the way of teacher creativity must be removed and teachers must be given the freedom to experiment.

3. The Creation of a Context for Achieving Quality and Equity

School improvement cannot happen on a large scale unless all staff believe that achieving equity and quality of education for all students is the over-riding mission of the school system. They must understand why changes are required, and how each staff member can contribute to those changes. The effective schools research provides a framework for guiding staff development activities toward achieving school improvement. This research identifies specific school-based, organizational characteristics that can be used effectively to establish a foundation on which schools can create a vision, develop a mission, and define goals and objectives for school improvement.

4. The Need to be Honest, Forthright and to Demand Accountability

The superintendent must be willing to expose the system to the closest scrutiny and judgement by the school community and the public. All data concerning a wide range of student outcomes must be made available and open to debate and discussion.

5. Unyielding Support for Strategies or Interventions that Make a Difference in Teaching and Learning

'High yield' intervention strategies should be selected after reviewing relevant research literature. For example, if a priority is to 'maximize engaged learning time', the 'time on task' literature should be reviewed to identify which interventions are most likely to yield desired results.

6. The Organization and Empowerment of Staff to Bring About Change

Given that the school improvement process focuses on the local school as the unit of change, local school staff must be empowered to bring about needed change. If the school improvement process is to work, teachers must be actively involved and have direct and ongoing input in the functioning of the school. This involvement includes a broad range of activities such as needs identification, selection of strategies and activities, and evaluating school effectiveness.

7. Allowing School-based Control over how Resources Allocated to the School are to be Used

The final ingredient to include in the school improvement process is providing school-based control over those resources required to implement the improvement plan developed by the school, with the understanding that with control comes responsibility for results.

8. The Redefinition of the Roles of School System Staff

As a system undergoes restructuring, more focus, energy, and resources will move to the building level. The responsibilities and duties of central office positions must be redesigned to support individual school initiatives.

9. The Creation of Training Programs for Principals and Those Who Aspire to be Principals

Training programs must focus on key leadership skills as well as contemporary issues in administration, supervision, and instruction.

Internships, mentoring and shadowing opportunities should be available to building-level staff who aspire to leadership positions.

10. The Provision of Meaningful Staff Development to Teachers

Training in new methodologies to achieve system- and building-level goals is critical. Emphasis should be placed on long-term peer coaching programs, not one-shot training sessions.

11. (For superintendents only) *Have your bags packed and be ready to move*

If you were a successful change agent, you have probably made many people uncomfortable about their personal, professional, or political goals. You must remember that you are first and foremost an advocate for children and your example will hopefully inspire others to champion the cause. The needs of children must direct your every action. You cannot compromise system quality for personal security.

> **KEY POINT:** *A sufficient number of courageous leaders will need to sacrifice personal comfort to accomplish real school improvement. Hopefully as our communities reflect on those contributions they will also recognize the concomitant need to elect responsible, caring, committed citizens to serve in those public offices that impact the future of this society. The personal interests of some of our elected officials and their desires to be popular with their constituents should not be allowed to derail us as we move toward excellence.*

APPENDIX A

GROUPING STRATEGIES FOR READING INSTRUCTION

There follows a list of strategies that make available 60 minutes of direct instruction per day. Each strategy assumes that there is a daily, 90-minute block of time available for reading and language arts and that at no time are there more than two formal instructional groups. Not indicated in the charts are those grouping strategies which incorporate the use of several classroom computers. In these cases, computer use can be substituted for any one of the smaller group activities. These strategies do not represent an exhaustive list. They are provided to stimulate ideas as to how direct instructional time can be increased in a classroom without significantly more resources.

Strategy 1

Whole Class Instruction (30 Minutes) Focusing on a Single Literature Section	
Group 1 (60 Minutes)	**Group 2 (60 Minutes)**
• Direct instruction	• Independent reading of literature selection
• Independent reading of literature selection	• Direct Instruction

Strategy 2

Whole Class Instruction (30 Minutes)
Research Skill Lesson
(60 Minutes)
▪ Co-operative learning group
▪ Research Project

Strategy 3

Whole Class Instruction (30 Minutes)	
Research Skill Lesson	
(60 Minutes)	(60 Minutes)
▪ Teacher guidance with co-operative learning groups on the research project	▪ Co-operative learning groups working independently on the research project
▪ Independent work by groups on the project	▪ Teacher meets with groups

Strategy 4

Whole Class Instruction (30 Minutes)	
Whole Group Predictions of Stories From Illustrations	
Group 1 (60 Minutes)	Group 2 (60 Minutes)
▪ Paired reading and project development	▪ Teacher-directed guided reading

Strategy 5

Whole Class Instruction (30 Minutes)	
Creative Writing Based on Assigned Idea (e.g., humor, fun, excitement) From Personal Experience	
Group 1 (60 Minutes)	Group 2 (60 Minutes)
▪ Teacher-assisted reading of related story	▪ Group shared reading of related story
▪ Teacher-led discussion of comparison, sequence and comprehension	▪ Comparison of personal and read stories

Strategy 6

Group 1 (45 Minutes)	Group 2 (45 Minutes)
▪ Teacher-directed skill group	▪ Independent reading/writing activity
▪ Independent practice of skill lesson	▪ Teacher-directed skill group
Whole Class (45 minutes)	
Teacher-directed functional reading lesson with co-operative learning group	

APPENDIX A Grouping Strategies for Reading Instruction

Strategy 7

Whole Class (15 Minutes Primary Level) Read-Aloud Story	
Whole Class (15 Minutes) Phonics Lesson	
Group 1 (60 Minutes)	**Group 2 (60 Minutes)**
▪ Teacher-directed basal reader lesson	▪ Independent reading/writing activity
▪ Independent reading/writing activity • Computer activities	▪ Teacher-directed basal reader lesson • Computer activities

Strategy 8

Whole Class Instruction (30 Minutes) Read-Aloud Story with Graphic Organizer	
Group 1 (60 Minutes)	**Group 2 (60 Minutes)**
▪ Teacher-directed lesson applying graphic organizers to basal story	▪ Journal activity and/or computer activities
▪ Journal activity responding to basal story/literature selection and/or computer activities	▪ Teacher-directed lesson applying graphic organizers to basal stories

Strategy 9

Whole Class Instruction (30 Minutes) Study Skills Lesson	
Group 1 (40 Minutes)	**Group 2 (40 Minutes)**
▪ Teacher-directed guided practice applying study skills to appropriate material	▪ Independent application of study skills to appropriate materials
▪ Independent application of study skills to appropriate materials	▪ Teacher meets with individuals or pairs of students
Whole Class (20 minutes) Vocabulary game	

Strategy 10

Whole Class Instruction (30 Minutes) Content Reading Lesson	
Group 1 (40 Minutes)	**Group 2 (40 Minutes)**
▪ Teacher-directed application of skills to content material	▪ Independent reading of content material
▪ Independent reading of content material	▪ Teacher-directed application of skills to content material
Whole Class (20 minutes) Discussion of Content Material	

Strategy 11

Whole Class Instruction (30 Minutes)	
▪ Regroup grade level students by interest for book clubs ▪ Use literature sections to build prior knowledge and vocabulary	
Group 1 (60 Minutes)	**Group 2 (60 Minutes)**
▪ Paired reading and project development	▪ Teacher-directed guided reading

Strategy 12

Whole Class Instruction (30 Minutes Primary Level)	
Reading Beyond the Basal Activities with Read-Aloud Section	
Group 1 (60 Minutes)	**Group 2 (60 Minutes)**
▪ Teacher-directed lesson using basal reader	▪ Extension activity from reading beyond the basal
▪ Extension activity from reading beyond the basal	▪ Teacher-directed lesson using basal reader

Strategy 13

Whole Class Instruction (30 Minutes)	
Thematic Introduction for Literature Unit	
Group 1 (60 Minutes)	**Group 2 (60 Minutes)**
▪ Teacher-directed lesson using basal story that supports selected theme	▪ Self-selection of literature book to accompany reading/project based on theme
▪ Self-selection of literature book to accompany reading/project based on theme	▪ Teacher-directed lesson using basal story that supports selected theme

Strategy 14

Whole Class Instruction (30 Minutes)	
Introduce Metacognitive, Self-Monitoring, Reading Strategy	
Group 1 (60 Minutes)	**Group 2 (60 Minutes)**
▪ Teacher-directed guided practice of strategy	▪ Independent practice of strategy
▪ Independent practice of strategy	▪ Teacher-directed application of strategy to other material

APPENDIX A Grouping Strategies for Reading Instruction

Strategy 15

Whole Class (20 Minutes Primary Level) Phonics Lesson	
Group 1 (30 Minutes) • Teacher-directed vocabulary introduction/background building/purpose setting	**Group 2 (30 Minutes)** • Paired re-reading of basal story
• Silent reading of selection	• Teacher-directed discussion of reading selection
Whole Class (40 minutes) • Read-Aloud Story • Listening Activity	

APPENDIX B

MAINTAINING A REALITY CHECK: DATA COLLECTION FORMS FOR AUDITING PROGRESS AND IDENTIFYING PROBLEMS

Form 1: School Improvement Diagnostic Inventory

This form can be used to collect information for the entire school system, to help initially design a school improvement program, and then to monitor progress in implementation of the program (TO BE COMPLETED BY THE SUPERINTENDENT'S STAFF AT THE END OF EACH SCHOOL YEAR).

In this example, students are categorized by race. If other socio-economic measures are available, they may be substituted.

Name and title of person completing this form: _____

Date: _____

A. Demographics

1. What was the total student enrollment as of the past September 30? _____
2. What was the enrollment, by race, this year compared to past years?

	White students	Black students	Hispanic students	Other
a. present year	_____	_____	_____	____
b. prior year	_____	_____	_____	____
c. prior year	_____	_____	_____	____
d. prior year	_____	_____	_____	____
e. prior year	_____	_____	_____	____
f. prior year	_____	_____	_____	____

3. What were the average percentile scores on your norm-referenced test, by grade, by race, and by subject, for the past two years for the entire school system? (T = total students, B = black students, W = white students, H = Hispanic students, O = other students)

Present School Year

Grade	T	B	W	H	O	Grade	T	B	W	H	O

Prior School Year

Grade	T	B	W	H	O	Grade	T	B	W	H	O

APPENDIX B Maintaining a Reality Check

4. What was the distribution of percentile scores on the norm-referenced test, by grade, by race, and by subject for every school in the system in which the test was administered for each of the past three years?

   School Name _____

Grade	T	B	W	H	O	Grade	T	B	W	H	O

5. If your school system administers a criterion-referenced test or some other year-end test in reading and mathematics, complete the forms below for each school by entering the number and percentage of students who achieved at least 70 percent on the tests.

   Reading   School Name _____

Grade	T	B	W	H	O	Grade	T	B	W	H	O

Mathematics   School Name _____

Grade	T	B	W	H	O	Grade	T	B	W	H	O

6. What was the percentage of students (by race and gender) for every elementary school who in the prior year were moved from one reading or mathematics group level to a relatively higher group level during that year? (Relatively higher refers to moving from the lowest to middle, or middle to highest group. It does not mean progressing from one reading book to another if that book represents a group that is at the some relative level as the prior book.)

School Name _____
Number and Percent of All Students Moved to Higher Level Reading Groups

	Number White	Percent White	Number Black	Percent Black	Number Hispanic	Percent Hispanic
Male						
Female						

Number and Percent of Students Moved to Higher Level Mathematics Groups

	Number White	Percent White	Number Black	Percent Black	Number Hispanic	Percent Hispanic
Male						
Female						

7. What number and percentage of students, by race, in each elementary school, were categorized as follows?

School Name _____

	Number White	Percent White	Number Black	Percent Black	Number Hispanic	Percent Hispanic
Gifted and talented						
Special education						

8. What number and percentage of students, by race, in each middle school, were categorized as follows?

School Name _____

	Number White	Percent White	Number Black	Percent Black	Number Hispanic	Percent Hispanic
Gifted and talented						
Special education						
Enrolled in algebra						
Enrolled in pre-algebra						

9. What number and percentage of students, by race, in each high school, were categorized as follows?

School Name _____

	Number White	Percent White	Number Black	Percent Black	Number Hispanic	Percent Hispanic
Gifted and talented						
Special education						
Enrolled in algebra or higher-level mathematics						
Suspended at least once						
Dropped out of school						

10. What number and percentage of students, by race, for each high school, applied to at least one institution of higher education?

School Name _____

Number White	Percent White	Number Black	Percent Black	Number Hispanic	Percent Hispanic

Form 2: School Improvement Diagnostic Survey

This form can be used to collect school building information for the initial design of a school improvement program and then to monitor progress in the implementation of that program (TO BE COMPLETED BY THE PRINCIPAL AT THE END OF EACH SCHOOL YEAR).

In this example, students are categorized by race. If other socio-economic measures are available, they may be substituted or added.

Name of person completing this form: _____

APPENDIX B Maintaining a Reality Check 275

Circle whether an elementary, middle, or high school principal

Date: _____

Name of school: _____

A. All Principals

1. What was the total student enrollment in this school as of September 30? _____
2. What was the race and gender makeup, by number and percentage, of the student body?

	Number White	Percent White	Number Black	Percent Black	Number Hispanic	Percent Hispanic
Male						
Female						

3. What number and percentage of your student body, by race and gender, received special honors or awards?

	Number White	Percent White	Number Black	Percent Black	Number Hispanic	Percent Hispanic
Male						
Female						

4. What number and percentage of students, by race, in your school were categorized as follows?

School Name _____

	Number White	Percent White	Number Black	Percent Black	Number Hispanic	Percent Hispanic
Gifted and talented						
Special education						
Enrolled in algebra or higher-level mathematics						
Suspended at least once						
Dropped out of school						

5. What was the distribution of percentile scores on the norm referenced test, by grade, by race, and by subject for every school in the system for each of the past three years? (T = total students; B = black students; W = white students; H = hispanic students; O = other students.)

School Name _____

Grade	T	B	W	H	O	Grade	T	B	W	H	O

6. If your school administers a criterion-referenced test or some other year-end test in reading and mathematics, complete the forms below for each school by entering the number and percentage of students who achieved at least 70 percent on the tests.

Reading   School Name _____

Grade	T	B	W	H	O	Grade	T	B	W	H	O

Mathematics   School Name _____

Grade	T	B	W	H	O	Grade	T	B	W	H	O

7. How many discipline referrals, by race and gender, were submitted by teachers in your school during the past year?

___ number of referrals
___ number white   ___ percent white
___ number black   ___ percent black
___ number Hispanic   ___ percent Hispanic
___ number other   ___ percent other

8. List, for each teacher by race and gender of the students, the discipline referrals that each teacher sumitted during the past year.

    ___ number of   ___ number white   ___ percent white
          referrals   ___ number black   ___ percent black
                          ___ number Hispanic   ___ percent Hispanic
                          ___ number other   ___ percent other

B. Elementary School Principals Only

9. What was the percentage of students, by race and gender, for your elementary school, who were moved from one reading group level to a relatively higher group level during the year? (Relatively higher refers to moving from the lowest to middle, or middle to highest group. It does not mean progressing from one reading book to another if that book represents a group that is at the same relative level as the prior book.)

	Number White	Percent White	Number Black	Percent Black	Number Hispanic	Percent Hispanic
Male						
Female						

10. For every classroom teacher in your school, prepare the chart described in question 9.

C. Middle and High School Principals Only

11. What was the number and percentage of D's and E's, by race and gender, that were given to students at the end of the first semester on their report cards?

	Number White	Percent White	Number Black	Percent Black	Number Hispanic	Percent Hispanic
Male						
Female						

APPENDIX B Maintaining a Reality Check   279

12. What was the number of D's and E's, by race and gender, that were given to students on their final report cards?

	Number White	Percent White	Number Black	Percent Black	Number Hispanic	Percent Hispanic
Male						
Female						

13. What number and percentage of students in your school, by race and gender, applied to at least one institution of higher education?

	Number White	Percent White	Number Black	Percent Black	Number Hispanic	Percent Hispanic
Male						
Female						

Form 3: Elementary Classroom Teacher School Improvement Monitoring Form

This form can be used to collect classroom teacher level information for monitoring progress of a school improvement program (TO BE COMPLETED BY THE CLASSROOM TEACHER AT THE END OF THE END OF THE SCHOOL YEAR).

In this example, students are categorized by race. If other socio-economic measures are available, they may be substituted or added.

Name of classroom teacher completing this form:

_____

Date: _____

Name of School: _____

1. What grade(s) do you teach? _____
2. How many students are in your class? _____
3. What was the racial and gender makeup, by number and percentage, of your class?

	Number White	Percent White	Number Black	Percent Black	Number Hispanic	Percent Hispanic
Male						
Female						

4. By the end of the year, what was the number and percentage of students, by race and gender, for your elementary school classroom who were moved from one reading group level to a relatively higher group level during the year? (Relatively higher refers to moving from the lowest to middle, or middle to highest group. It does not mean progressing from one reading book to another if that book represents a group that is at the same relative level as the prior book.)

	Number White	Percent White	Number Black	Percent Black	Number Hispanic	Percent Hispanic
Male						
Female						

5. What was the average percentile scores on the norm-referenced test, by grade, by race, and by subject, for the past three years in your classroom? (T = total students; B = black students; W = white students; H = Hispanic students; O = other students.)

Grade	T	B	W	H	O	Grade	T	B	W	H	O

6. If your school system administers a criterion-referenced test or some other year-end test in reading and mathematics, complete the forms below for your class by entering the number and percentage of students who achieved at least 70 percent on the tests.

Reading

Grade	T	B	W	H	O	Grade	T	B	W	H	O

Mathematics

Grade	T	B	W	H	O	Grade	T	B	W	H	O

COMPLETE QUESTION 7 ONLY IF YOUR STUDENTS ARE GROUPED FOR READING

7. By the end of the year, what was the number and percentage of students, by race and gender, for your elementary school classroom, who were moved from one reading group level to a relatively higher group level during the year? (Relatively higher refers to moving from the lowest to middle, or middle to highest group. It does not mean progressing from one reading book to another if that book represents a group that is at the same relative level as the prior book.)

	Number White	Percent White	Number Black	Percent Black	Number Hispanic	Percent Hispanic
Male						
Female						

COMPLETE QUESTION 8 ONLY IF YOUR STUDENTS ARE GROUPED FOR MATHEMATICS

8. By the end of the year, what was the number and percentage of students, by race and gender, for your elementary school classroom, who were moved from one mathematics group level to a relatively higher group level during the year? (Relatively higher refers to moving from the lowest to middle, or middle to highest group. It does not mean progressing from one mathematics book to another if that book represents a group that is at the same relative level as the prior book.)

	Number White	Percent White	Number Black	Percent Black	Number Hispanic	Percent Hispanic
Male						
Female						

9. By the end of the school year, what percentage of all your students, by race and gender, received special honors or awards?

	Number White	Percent White	Number Black	Percent Black	Number Hispanic	Percent Hispanic
Male						
Female						

10. By the end of the school year, what number and percentage of discipline referrals, by race and gender, did you submit to the office?

	Number White	Percent White	Number Black	Percent Black	Number Hispanic	Percent Hispanic
Male						
Female						

Form 4: Middle and High School Teacher School Improvement Monitoring Form

This form can be used to collect classroom teacher level information for monitoring progress of a school improvement program (TO BE COMPLETED BY THE CLASSROOM TEACHERS AT THE END OF THE FIRST SEMESTER AND AT THE END OF THE SCHOOL YEAR).

In this example, students are categorized by race. If other socio-economic measures are available, they may be substituted or added.

Name of classroom teacher completing this form:

_____

Date: _____

Name of school: _____

1. What grade(s) do you teach?
2. What was the racial and gender makeup, by number and percentage, for each class that you taught?

Class One

	Number White	Percent White	Number Black	Percent Black	Number Hispanic	Percent Hispanic
Male						
Female						

Class Two

	Number White	Percent White	Number Black	Percent Black	Number Hispanic	Percent Hispanic
Male						
Female						

Class Three

	Number White	Percent White	Number Black	Percent Black	Number Hispanic	Percent Hispanic
Male						
Female						

Class Four

	Number White	Percent White	Number Black	Percent Black	Number Hispanic	Percent Hispanic
Male						
Female						

APPENDIX B Maintaining a Reality Check   285

Class Five

	Number White	Percent White	Number Black	Percent Black	Number Hispanic	Percent Hispanic
Male						
Female						

3. By the end of the school year, what percentage of all of your students, by race and gender, received special honors or awards?

	Number White	Percent White	Number Black	Percent Black	Number Hispanic	Percent Hispanic
Male						
Female						

4. FOR HOME-ROOM TEACHERS ONLY: What was the distribution of percentile scores on the norm-referenced test, by grade, by race, and by subject, for the past three years for the students in your home room?

Grade	T	B	W	H	O	Grade	T	B	W	H	O

5. If your school system administers a criterion-referenced test in a subject that you teach, complete the forms below for each class by entering the number and percentage of students who achieved at least 70 percent on the tests. (Complete a separate form for each subject tested.)

Subject _____

Grade	T	B	W	H	O	Grade	T	B	W	H	O

6. By the end of the school year, how many discipline referrals, by race and gender, did you submit to the office?

	Number White	Percent White	Number Black	Percent Black	Number Hispanic	Percent Hispanic
Male						
Female						

7. At the end of the second grading period, of all the D's and E's that you gave, what percentage went to students in the following categories?

	Number White	Percent White	Number Black	Percent Black	Number Hispanic	Percent Hispanic
Male						
Female						

8. By the end of the school year, of all the D's and E's that you gave, what percentage went to students in the following categories?

	Number White	Percent White	Number Black	Percent Black	Number Hispanic	Percent Hispanic
Male						
Female						

Form 5: School Improvement Survey to be Administered to Middle and High School Students

This form can be used to collect information for the initial design of a school improvement program and then to monitor progress in the implementation of that program.

1. My school has a written statement which describes its mission and major purposes.

   _____ yes   _____ no   _____ do not know

2. Teachers or other school staff have discussed the mission of the school with students.

   _____ yes   _____ no   _____ do not know

3. I find it easy to talk to teachers or others about a problem or concern.

   _____ yes   _____ no   _____ do not know

4. The principal in the school makes frequent classroom observations.

   _____ yes   _____ no   _____ do not know

5. Counselors are actively involved in the process of reviewing the progress of students.

   _____ yes   _____ no   _____ do not know

6. The administration of this school enforces school rules and the Code of Student Conduct.

   _____ yes   _____ no   _____ do not know

7. If students have problems with schoolwork, teachers take the time to re-teach the skills until the students learn.

   _____ yes   _____ no   _____ do not know

8. Teachers expect students to get good grades on assigned work and tests.

   _____ yes   _____ no   _____ do not know

9. All teachers in this school hold consistently high expectations for all students.

APPENDIX B Maintaining a Reality Check

_____ yes   _____ no   _____ do not know

10. When teachers communicate with parents, the communication gives equal time to the good things students do.

    _____ yes   _____ no   _____ do not know

11. Teachers talk about academic learning as being the most important part of school.

    _____ yes   _____ no   _____ do not know

12. Parent-school conferences result in specific plans for home-school co-operation aimed at improving student classroom achievement.

    _____ yes   _____ no   _____ do not know

13. Teachers send written messages home to parents.

    _____ yes   _____ no   _____ do not know

14. Teachers talk to parents either in person or by telephone.

    _____ yes   _____ no   _____ do not know

15. Parents regularly attend school activities such as open house, concerts and plays.

    _____ yes   _____ no   _____ do not know

16. This school is a safe and secure place to be.

    _____ yes   _____ no   _____ do not know

17. Students and staff are free from insults or other verbal abuse.

    _____ yes   _____ no   _____ do not know

18. When students are assigned seat work, teachers monitor it closely.

    _____ yes   _____ no   _____ do not know

19. The school building and grounds are neat, clean and comfortable.

   _____ yes   _____ no   _____ do not know

20. The students in this school are ready to start class promptly at the beginning of each period.

   _____ yes   _____ no   _____ do not know

21. Instruction begins upon the arrival of students to class.

   _____ yes   _____ no   _____ do not know

22. Students are given the opportunity to show responsibility.

   _____ yes   _____ no   _____ do not know

23. Classes are usually interrupted by outside sources.

   _____ yes   _____ no   _____ do not know

24. Instruction usually continues until dismissal from each of my classes.

   _____ yes   _____ no   _____ do not know

25. Student misbehavior disrupts classes.

   _____ yes   _____ no   _____ do not know

26. Students are recognized for their academic achievement.

   _____ yes   _____ no   _____ do not know

27. Teachers talk to students outside of class.

   _____ yes   _____ no   _____ do not know

28. Rules are clearly explained to students.

   _____ yes   _____ no   _____ do not know

APPENDIX B Maintaining a Reality Check

29. Teachers consistently communicate and apply the grading standards developed and approved for their classes.

    _____ yes   _____ no   _____ do not know

30. In my classes, students work independently on seat work for the majority of the allocated time.

    _____ yes   _____ no   _____ do not know

31. Grading standards are consistent in all of my classes.

    _____ yes   _____ no   _____ do not know

Form 6: School Improvement Survey to Be Administered to Students' Parents

This form can be used to collect information for the initial design of a school improvement program and then to monitor progress in the implementation of that program.

(Circle the correct response: SD=strongly disagree, D=disagree, N=neither agree nor disagree, A=agree, SA=strongly agree)

1. Parents generally feel welcome when they visit my child's school for scheduled parent-teacher meetings.

    SD   D   N   A   SA

2. My child's school encourages parents to visit if they have special concerns about their child.

    SD   D   N   A   SA

3. In my child's school, parents generally feel comfortable attending social events, like school plays or classroom parties.

    SD   D   N   A   SA

4. My child's school is sensitive to the special needs of children.

    SD   D   N   A   SA

5. My child's school is sensitive to the things that interest students.

   SD   D   N   A   SA

6. When parents are actively involved in their child's school, the teachers become more effective.

   SD   D   N   A   SA

7. My child's school is sensitive to the variety of backgrounds from which the students come.

   SD   D   N   A   SA

8. In my child's school the opinions of parents are *not* respected.

   SD   D   N   A   SA

9. At my child's school, it is easy for parents to get appointments to meet with the principals and teachers.

   SD   D   N   A   SA

10. My child's school is as safe and orderly place.

    SD   D   N   A   SA

11. At my child's school, the academic program is *not* very good.

    SD   D   N   A   SA

12. At my child's school, all the children are expected to do well in their work.

    SD   D   N   A   SA

13. At my child's school, the staff cares about students as individuals.

    SD   D   N   A   SA

APPENDIX B Maintaining a Reality Check

14. In my child's school, parents help make decisions about school activities and programs.

    SD   D   N   A   SA

15. In my child's school, parents do *not* generally support school activities.

    SD   D   N   A   SA

16. In my child's school, many parents don't care about their own children's education.

    SD   D   N   A   SA

17. In my child's school, the principal and teachers generally do *not* encourage children like they should.

    SD   D   N   A   SA

18. My child's school keeps in regular contact with parents.

    SD   D   N   A   SA

19. There is good discipline in my child's school.

    SD   D   N   A   SA

20. My child's school encourages parents to be involved in school activities on a daily basis.

    SD   D   N   A   SA

21. In my child's school, children generally feel that they belong.

    SD   D   N   A   SA

APPENDIX C

Examples of Information That Could be Included as Part of School-Level Report Cards

Elementary School Report Card

Section One: Student Participation
1. The percentage of students who were absent for 10 or more days, by race and gender, this year and compared to last year;
2. The percentage of students who were suspended at least once, by race and gender, this year and compared to last year;
3. The percentage of students who were retained, by race and gender, this year and compared to last year;
5. The percentage of students who were expelled, by race and gender, this year and compared to last year;
6. The percentage of students who were referred to special education, by race and gender, this year and compared to last year;
7. The percentage of students by grade, race and gender, who received less than a C as their final report card grade in mathematics, reading, science and/or social studies this year and compared to last year;
8. The percentage of students, by race and gender, completing the sixth grade with final grades of B or better in mathematics and reading, this year and compared to the prior year;
9. The percentage of sixth-grade students, by race and gender, who have been recommended to enroll in pre-algebra in the seventh grade, this year and compared to the prior year.

Section Two: Student Outcomes

1. Performance on the norm-referenced achievement test for reading, language, and mathematics for each grade tested. Performance will be measured by:
   - The absolute percentile ranking;
   - The gain achieved from the prior year with an examination of the number of students who moved from lower quartiles to higher quartiles;
   - The size of the gap between black and white students, and boys and girls.
2. The percentage of students, by race and gender, who at the end of the year mastered 70 percent or more of their grade level objectives in reading as measured by criterion-referenced tests.
3. The percentage of students, by race and gender, who at the end of the year mastered 70 percent or more of their grade level objectives in mathematics as measured by criterion-referenced tests.
4. Performance on the state writing tests. Performance will be measured for both mechanics and writing by:
   - The absolute score;
   - The gain achieved from the prior year with an examination of the number of students who moved from lower quartiles to higher quartiles;
   - The size of the gap between black and white students, and boys and girls.
5. Performance on the state criterion-referenced tests. Performance will be measured by:
   - The absolute score;
   - The gain achieved from the prior year with an examination of the number of students who moved from lower quartiles to higher quartiles;
   - The size of the gap between black and white students, and boys and girls.
6. The percentage of kindergarten students, by race and gender, recommended to begin first-grade instruction on level in reading and mathematics.
7. The percentage of first-grade students, by race and gender, recom-

mended to begin first-grade instruction in reading and mathematics.
8. The percentage of second-grade students, by race and gender, recommended to begin first-grade instruction in reading and mathematics.

Middle School Report Card

Section One: Student Participation

1. The percentage of students who were absent for 10 or more days, by race and gender, this year and compared to last year;
2. The percentage of students who were suspended at least once, by race and gender, this year and compared to last year;
3. The percentage of students who were retained, by race and gender, this year and compared to last year;
4. The percentage of students who dropped out, by race and gender, this year and compared to last year;
5. The percentage of students who were expelled, by race and gender, this year and compared to last year;
6. The percentage of students who were referred to special education, by race and gender, this year and compared to last year;
7. The percentage of students, by grade, race and gender, who received a D or less as their final report card grade in mathematics, science, social studies, English, and/or foreign language, this year and compared to last year;
8. The percentage of students, by race and gender, recommended for placement in at least one advanced placement course for the following school year and compared to the percent referred last year;
9. The percentage of students, by race and gender, completing the sixth grade with final grades of B or better in mathematics and reading, this year and compared to the prior year;
10. The percentage of 6th-grade students, by race and gender, who have been recommended to enroll in pre-algebra in the seventh grade, this year and compared to the prior year;
11. The percentage of students, by race and gender, completing the ninth grade and recommended for at least geometry in the tenth grade this year, and compared to the prior year;

12. The percentage of students, by race and gender, who are enrolled in foreign language courses, this year and compared to the prior year.

Section Two: Student Outcomes

1. Performance on the norm-referenced achievement test for reading, language, and mathematics. Performance will be measured by:
   - The absolute percentile ranking;
   - The gain achieved from the prior year with an examination of the number of students who moved from lower quartiles to higher quartiles;
   - The size of the gap between black and white students, and boys and girls.

2. Performance on the state writing test. Performance will be measured for both mechanics and writing by:
   - The absolute percentile ranking;
   - The gain achieved from the prior year with an examination of the number of students who moved from lower quartiles to higher quartiles;
   - The size of the gap between black and white students, and boys and girls.

3. Performance on the state criterion-referenced tests. Performance will be measured by:
   - The absolute percentile ranking;
   - The gain achieved from the prior year with an examination of the number of students who moved from lower quartiles to higher quartiles;
   - The size of the gap between black and white students, and boys and girls.

4. The percentage of students in the eighth grade, by race and gender, who at the end of the year mastered 70 percent of more of their grade level objectives in reading as measured by criterion-referenced tests.

5. The percentage of students in the eighth grade, by race and gender, who at the end of the year mastered 70 percent or more of their

grade level objectives in mathematics as measured by criterion-referenced tests.

High School Report Card

Section One: Student Participation

1. The percentage of students, by race and gender, who were absent for 10 or more days this year and compared to last year.
2. The percentage of students who were suspended at least once, by race and gender, this year and compared to last year.
3. The percentage of students who were retained, by race and gender, this year and compared to last year.
4. The percentage of students who dropped out, by race and gender, this year and compared to last year.
5. The percentage of students who were expelled, by race and gender, this year and compared to last year.
6. The percentage of students who were referred to special education, by race and gender, this year and compared to last year.
7. The percentage of students, by grade, race and gender, who received a D or less as their final report card grade in mathematics, science, social studies, English, and/or foreign language, this year and compared to last year.
8. The percentage of students, by race and gender, recommended for placement in at least one advanced placement course for the following school year and compared to the prior year.
9. The percentage of students, by race and gender, who will be attending an institution of higher education in the next school year, compared to the prior year.
10. The percentage of students, by race and gender, who are enrolled in foreign language courses, compared to the prior year.
11. The percentage of students who completed at least one advanced placement course and successfully passed the advanced placement examination as compared to the prior year.

Section Two: Student Outcomes

1. Performance on the norm-referenced achievement test for reading, language, and mathematics. Performance will be measured by:

- The absolute percentile ranking;
- The gain achieved from the prior year with an examination of the number of students who moved from lower quartiles to higher quartiles;
- The size of the gap between black and white students, and boys and girls.

2. Performance on the state writing tests. Performance will be measured for both mechanics and writing by:

   - The absolute score;
   - The gain achieved from the prior year with an examination of the number of students who moved from lower quartiles to higher quartiles;
   - The size of the gap between black and white students, and boys and girls.

3. Performance on the state criterion-referenced tests. Performance will be measured by:

   - The absolute score;
   - The gain achieved from the prior year with an examination of the number of students who moved from lower quartiles to higher quartiles;
   - The size of the gap between black and white students, and boys and girls.

4. Performance on the state competency tests. For each of the subject-matter tests, performance will be measured by:

   - The percentage of this year's tenth graders that passed the test;
   - The gain achieved from the prior year with an examination of the number of students who moved from lower quartiles to higher quartiles;
   - The size of the gap between black and white students, and boys and girls.

5. Performance on the scholastic aptitude test. For both the verbal and the mathematics tests, by race and gender, performance will be measured by:

   - The absolute score;
   - The gain achieved from the prior year;

APPENDIX C Information for School-Level Report Cards

- The size of the gap between black and white students, and boys and girls.

6. Performance on the PSAT in the tenth grade. For both the verbal and the mathematics tests, by race and gender, performance will be measured by:
   - The absolute score;
   - The gain achieved from the prior year;
   - The size of the gap between black and white students, and boys and girls.

7. Performance on the ETS achievement test scores. For each test, by race and gender, performance will be measured by:
   - The absolute score;
   - The gain achieved from the prior year;
   - The size of the gap between black and white students, and boys and girls.

8. Performance on advanced placement courses. For each test, by race and gender, performance will be measured by:
   - The abolute score;
   - The gain achieved from the prior year;
   - The size of the gap between black and white students, and boys and girls.

Index

Administrators, xi, 15–16, 93, 122–23, 132, 134–35, 158, 178, 179, 188, 226. *See also* Central Office staff; Principal; Superintendent
Arithmetic Teacher, The, 141

Becoming a Nation of Readers, 127
Boards of education, role of, 20–22
Boyer, Ernest, 34
Bradley Commission on History in Schools, 147
Business, role of, 34–35

Central Office staff, senior, 30–33, 71–74, 89–90, 101, 111, 114, 136, 194, 196, 197, 223, 227–30, 231–37, 269–74
Change
 need for, xi–xii, 1–7, 81–82, 228, 234–36, 239–40
 prerequisites for, 12–16, 108–11, 113–16, 257–61
 process of, 19–20, 36–37, 41–45, 60–61,82–90, 142, 179–82, 216–22
 case studies, 61–64, 65–70
Charting a Course: Social Studies for the 21st Century, 147–48
Children's Defense Fund, 5, 33
Choice. *See* Restructuring: and choice
Coalition for Essential Schools, 46
Comer, James, xi–xii, 35–36
Computers, 156, 157–68
Co-operative learning, 15, 128
Copernican model, 45
Criterion-referenced tests, 195–98. *See also* Norm-referenced tests; Tests
 compared to norm-referenced tests, 189, 190, 196–98
 in Reading, 126–27
 student outcomes in, 252, 271, 277, 281, 286

Curriculum. *See also* Mathematics; Reading; Technology
 Arts, 148–50
 change in, 57–58, 76, 88, 113–16, 116–17, 135–36, 155–56, 221–22
 International Baccalaureate, 151–53
 James Madison High School, 150–51
 outcome goals, 114–16, 118–19, 150–51, 152–53
 Paideia, 154–55
 restructuring, 155–56
 Science, 144–47
 Social Studies, 147–48

Data
 case studies, 206–13, 213–15
 collection forms for Central Office staff, 269–74
 collection forms for parents, 291–93
 collection forms for principal, 274–79
 collection forms for students, 287–91
 collection forms for teacher, 279–87
 diagnosis of, 76, 89–90, 202–6, 206–15
 for school report card, 295–301
Discipline, 73, 102–4, 182, 220–21, 277–78, 287, 287–91, 291–93
 and suspensions
 case study, 213–15
Dropouts, 178–82

Edelman, Marian Wright, 33
Educational Testing Service, 3, 6
Effective schools, 92–105
Expectations, 4–6, 7–11, 53–55, 57, 60, 72–73, 76–79, 88, 95–100, 108, 198–200, 269–287. *See also* Dropouts; Grouping
 case studies, 61–64, 65–70
 and standards, 3–4, 53–54, 232–33

303

Finn, Chester E., Jr., 4
Funding, 11–12

Government, role of, 33–34
Graham, Patricia, 34
Grouping, 8, 55–57, 70, 76–77, 88, 123–35, 263–67, 272–74, 276, 278, 280, 282. *See also* Expectations
case studies, 61–64, 65–70

Instruction. *See also* Curriculum; Mathematics; Reading
time on, 12, 43–44, 45–47, 55–57, 71–72, 98–101, 121–23, 135
Instructional television, 156, 172–173
case study, 173–77
International Assessment of Mathematics and Science, 2
International Baccalaureate, 151–53
International comparisons, 2–4, 11, 145

James Madison High School curriculum, 150–51

Language Arts, 116–19, 164–66. *See also* Reading

Mathematics. *See also* Grouping; Technology; Tests
change in curriculum, 133–35, 138–39, 151, 152
instruction, 137–44
outcomes, 135–36
case study, 212–13
technology for, 134, 166
tests, 134
Mission statements, 52–53, 83–84, 94–95
Monitoring achievement, 57, 125, 186–91, 222–23, 295–301

National Assessment of Educational Progress, 188
National Council on Social Studies in the School, 147–48
National Council of Teachers of Mathematics
guidelines for change, 134–35
regional conventions, 141
staff, 137, 139–40
standards, 133–35
National Research Council, 138, 145
National Science Teachers' Association, 145, 146

Norm-referenced tests, 191–95, 252, 270–71, 276, 281, 285. *See also* Criterion-referenced tests; Tests

Outcomes, 53, 57, 58, 67–68, 69–70, 72–73, 77, 84–86, 101–2, 135–36, 155, 252–54, 295–301. *See also* Data; Tests

Paideia, 154–55
Parents
role of, in schooling, 35–36, 59, 67, 104, 109, 142, 144, 196, 197, 223
survey for, 291–93
Performance assessments. *See* Tests
Policy
establishing, 66, 74–79, 83–84, 218–19
implementing, 74–80
manual, 51–60
reinforcing, 71–74
Practices, 60–70, 71–74, 74–80
Principal, 26–30, 68, 97–98
accountability of, 57, 194, 274–79
as administrative leader, 28, 105–107
as educational leader, 27, 54, 65, 87–88, 109, 110, 197, 198
evaluation of, 58–59, 237–240
Professional Standards for Teaching Mathematics, 139–40

Reading. *See also* Grouping; Technology; Tests
change in curriculum of, 116–19, 129–32, 151, 152–53
case study, 61–64
instruction, 119–23, 127–29
outcomes, 129–33
case study, 209–11
technology for, 164–66
tests, 116, 125–27
Ready to Learn, 34
Recognizing exemplary performance, 222–23, 249–54
Requests for proposals. *See* Technology: purchasing
Reshaping School Mathematics, 138
Restructuring, 82–90, 155–56, 178–82
case study, 65–70
and choice, 182–84
curriculum, 155
data driven, 89
and outcomes, 75–79, 114–15
and technology, 156–78

INDEX

SCANS Report, 115
Scheduling
  Copernican model of, 45–46
  elementary school, 42–45
  modified block, 46
  modular, 46
  secondary school, 45–47
School-based management, 86–87, 105–111
School improvement, 22–26, 258, 259, 261
  and business, 34–35
  and Central Office staff, 30–32
  diagnostic inventory for, 269–79
  and government, 33–34
  and parents, 36
  prerequisites for, 12–16
  and principals, 26–30
  and school boards, 20–22
  and superintendents, 22–26
School size, 46
Science, 144–47, 166
Sizer, Theodore, 46
Social Studies, 147–48
Staff development, 12, 36–47, 58, 75–79, 137–38, 139–42
  for principals, 37–41
  for teachers, 41, 109
Staffing, 110
Standardized Tests. *See* Tests
Standards, 3, 7–11. *See also* Expectations; Outcomes
Students. *See also* Discipline; Dropouts; Expectations; Grouping; Outcomes
  needs of, 4–6, 7–11, 53–55, 60, 78, 88, 95–96, 98–100, 129–131, 132, 135, 143, 144, 149
  participation of, 295–98, 299
  survey for, 287–91
Superintendent, role of, 22–26, 51–52, 68, 71–74, 74–79, 194, 216–22, 258, 259, 261
Surveys, diagnostic
  for classroom improvement, 274–301
  for school building improvement, 274–93
  for school system improvement, 269–74
Sustain Our Schools, 34

Teacher
  accountability of, 54, 57, 62, 64, 126, 132, 143–44, 194, 197, 198, 279–87
  change in role of, 41, 42–47, 68, 100–101, 120–21, 140, 141, 154–55, 168, 263–67
  evaluation of, 58–59, 240–50, 250–54
Teacher work stations. *See* Technology
Technology. *See also* Computers; Instructional Television
  instructional delivery, 156, 158, 164–67, 172–73, 175
  knowledge base, 156–157
  management systems, 162–64
  and Mathematics, 166
  purchasing, 157–58, 159–68, 169–72
  and Reading, 164–66
  and Science, 166–67
  teacher work stations, 168–72
Tests. *See also* Criterion-referenced tests; Norm-referenced tests; Outcomes
  instruction and, 58, 101–2, 189–90, 191, 195–98
  performance assessments, 201–2
  using results of, 187–91, 193–98, 198–200, 202–15, 298–99, 299–301
  case study, 206–13, 213–15
Textbooks, 57–58, 118, 120, 125, 128, 129, 141–42

Underclass, xi, 4–6